Central America

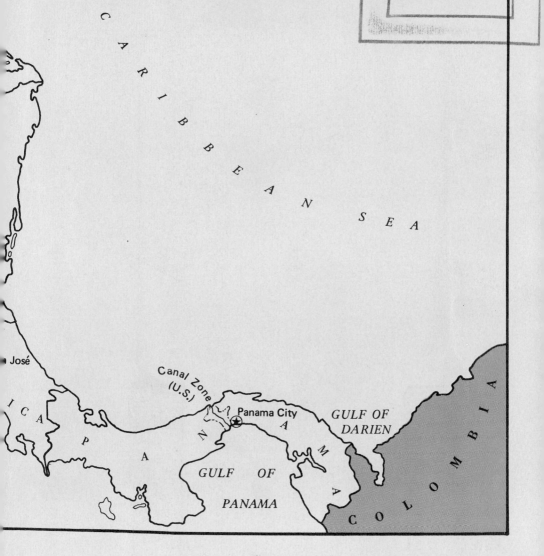

C A R I B B E A N   S E A

José

Canal Zone
(U.S.)

Panama City

GULF OF
DARIEN

P A N A M A

GULF OF

PANAMA

C O L O M B I A

Publications of the
CENTER FOR EDUCATION IN LATIN AMERICA
INSTITUTE OF INTERNATIONAL STUDIES
Teachers College, Columbia University

We Wish To Be Looked Upon

A Study of the Aspirations of Youth
in a Developing Society

VERA RUBIN and MARISA ZAVALLONI

Guidelines to Problems of Education in Brazil
A Review and Selected Bibliography

MALVINA ROSAT MCNEILL

Black Images

WILFRED G. CARTEY

THE
MIDDLE
BEAT

A Correspondent's View of
Mexico, Guatemala,
and El Salvador

by PAUL P. KENNEDY

edited by Stanley R. Ross

Teachers College Press
Teachers College, Columbia University

The maps in this book were prepared by Mr. James Weiler, under the supervision of Professor Robert Holz, of The University of Texas at Austin.

The Editor believes that this posthumous
book should be dedicated to

Diana

who shared the "middle beat" with Paul,
for that is how Paul would have wanted it.

Series Note

The Middle Beat is the fourth publication in a series sponsored by the Center for Education in Latin America. It is a posthumous work, issued here three years after the death of its author, Paul Kennedy, perceptive analyst of the Latin American scene and a distinguished foreign correspondent of *The New York Times.* Geographically, the book focuses on "Middle America," "a somewhat wedge-shaped area thining into an isthmus that descends from the northern border of Mexico to the northern border of Colombia," with particular care and attention given to the republics of Mexico, Guatemala, and El Salvador. By means of insightful commentary on critical events and leading personalties, Mr. Kennedy weaves a vivid picture of this often neglected and misunderstood region of the New World, concentrating on the period between 1954 and 1964. *The Middle Beat* should prove to be a valuable source for the scholarly evaluation of contemporary "Middle American" society as well as for the examination of its processes of development and change. The Center for Education in Latin America is honored to include *The Middle Beat* among its publications.

Professor Stanley Ross, Director of the Institute of Latin American Studies at the University of Texas at Austin, graciously consented to take editorial responsibility for the Kennedy manuscript as well as to supply its introduction, maps, and clarificatory appendices and footnotes. For these tasks, skillfully and elegantly accomplished, the Center is much indebted to him.

From a substantive point of view, the series of the Center for Education in Latin America attempts not only to illuminate the specifics of education, but also to provide, as in *The Middle Beat,* materials and analyses that place the educational process in meaningful context. It focuses on those political units, those nations, territories, and colonies, commonly referred to as Latin America and the Caribbean. Within this vast area, the constituent societies form a complex and heterogeneous sphere, which, with considerable theoretical difficulty, has been ordered by some social scientists into three culturally distinctive segments. Putting aside taxonomic arguments, this three-part scheme illuminates the complexity of the area and indicates the lines of development of the series itself. One subdivision includes the territories and countries of the Antilles and the Circum-Caribbean. Characteristically, these societies contain institutions that bear the imprint of a long colonial heritage and a social legacy from forced connection with the metropoles of Western Europe. The populations derived primarily from Africa, but they also include socially important pockets of people with origins in Europe, the Indian subcontinent, China, and the Middle East. A second subdivision includes those countries, most often located in the highlands of South and Central America, which contain large, culturally viable populations of Amerindians and in which the process of social and cultural integration of native peoples has dramatically influenced the course and form of nation-building. The third subdivision encompasses the societies of the southern, temperate zones of the Western Hemisphere, which demographically and culturally are dominated by the descendants of migrants from Europe.

Within each of these subdivisions south of the Rio Grande, the distinctiveness of historical events, the particular patterns of economic exploitation, and the size and complexity of the indigenous population have led to structurally similar forms of social organization and articulation. Social institutions in each of these areas, including those related to education, have taken distinctive forms and carry specific social significance. It is the aim of this series to explore these general considerations and to pursue the theoretical, methodological, and practical questions which they raise.

Lambros Comitas

Contents

Introduction

There exists a rich and varied literature about Latin America written by travelers and temporary residents coming from other parts of the world. The earliest such accounts are the migratory histories of the indigenous population, once regarded as mythology but now given considerable credence as a historical source. If one questions the appropriateness of including such accounts in the "travel literature" of Latin America, no such doubt can be raised about the chronicles of the explorers and conquerors, the reports of governmental officials during three centuries of colonial rule, and the writings of distinguished foreign scientists, like Alexander von Humboldt, sent to the New World by more enlightened Bourbon rulers toward the end of the colonial era. The list is long and the material content impressive—from the letters of Cortés and the history of the conquest of New Spain by Bernal Díaz del Castillo to the writings of missionaries and the *memorias* of viceroys. The amount of literature by the traveler and foreign resident observer and reporter increases greatly in the nineteenth and twentieth centuries, with contributions by soldiers, writers, businessmen, diplomats, and governmental agents.

In the case of Mexico, travel books and eyewitness accounts are particularly numerous. The list of writers includes D. H. Lawrence and Graham Greene, the first United States minister to Mexico, Joel R. Poinsett, and his English rival H. G. Ward, sympathetic traveler Erna Fergusson and the critical Sybille Bedford, long-time resident Waddy Thompson and diplomat's wife Edith O'Shaughnessy. Much of the literature, like an outdated travel guide, proves to be ephemeral and of only limited subsequent interest. Yet some such firsthand accounts achieve the status of minor classics, like *Life In Mexico* by Madame Calderón de la Barca, wife of the first Spanish minister to Mexico, and *Viva Mexico* by C. M.

Flandrau, one of the finest pictures of Mexico on the eve of its twentieth-century revolution. And then there is John Kenneth Turner's *Barbarous Mexico,* recently reprinted a half century after its first appearance, which by exposing the evils of the Porfirian dictatorship contributed to the ferment that led to its overthrow.

In the case of Central America, invaluable light is shed on the early days of the region by E. G. Squier's *Travels in Central America* and by the incomparable John Lloyd Stevens' handsomely illustrated *Incidents of Travel in Central America, Chiapas and Yucatán.* The latter has been called the finest travel record in American literature.

Latin American travel literature that is considered significant and readable is presently being reissued in a series edited by Professor C. Harvey Gardiner and published by the Southern Illinois University Press. In the Introduction to a new edition of Fanny Chambers Gooch's *Face to Face with the Mexicans,* which was based on the writer's experiences between 1880 and 1887, Professor Gardiner noted:

Dozens of other accounts of Mexico of the period were published by foreign observers but generally they were more of the same: overwhelmingly the short-term observation and superficial appraisal of Mexican life; commonly the word of the linguistically ignorant and the culturally arrogant. Unprejudiced outsiders were unusual, and sympathetic inquirers and balanced reporters were met even less frequently. The final proof that most writers went to Mexico as narrowly selfish individuals was the mirroring of that narrowness and selfishness in their writing.

Consequently, it is all the more pleasing to find an author of the 1880's who epitomizes breadth and magnanimity—to find a work based on long-term residence, unchanneled and ranging curiosity, and linguistic competence.[1]

Paul Kennedy's *Middle Beat* belongs to another time, very, very close to the present. To his account of his experiences as a reporter in Mexico and Central America, Kennedy brought sympathetic understanding, literary grace, and the trained reporter's experienced and penetrating eye. The book is not only a readable journalistic account of recent events—which, all too often, results in ephemeral literature—but also represents raw material for the future historian. Here is an account of key events and political and socio-economic trends by an experienced observer with an understanding of the historical background and a familiarity with the milieu.

[1] C. Harvey Gardiner, "Introduction," in Fanny Chambers Gooch, *Face to Face with the Mexicans,* ed. by C. Harvey Gardiner (Carbondale, Ill., Southern Illinois University Press, 1966), pp. ix–x.

My first contact with Paul Kennedy was indirect—through reading his dispatches from Mexico in *The New York Times*. With the usual hypercriticality of the specialist, I read the earliest Kennedy-signed dispatches datelined Mexico with a certain impatience and even irritation. However, as time went by, I was impressed by the fact that the reportages not only became increasingly informative but also were written with greater understanding. Having devoted years to the study of modern and contemporary Mexico, I could not help but admire one who so efficiently and effectively managed to penetrate the background and appreciate the *ambiente* that is Mexico's.

I did not meet Paul Kennedy until he returned to New York, already engaged in the grim struggle against cancer which was to prove fatal. He had taken over the night desk at the *Times* while undergoing treatment. We spent a whole day on the shores of Long Island Sound, swimming, drinking, and talking of our beloved Mexico. Kennedy was one of the best informed persons I have talked with regarding the current Mexican political situation. His appraisal of leading personalities was perceptive and his estimate of the politics of the moment penetrating.

Paul Patrick Kennedy had served *The New York Times* for twenty-two years at the time of his death in 1967. A native New Yorker, he had attended Fordham and Columbia before completing his undergraduate career at the University of Oklahoma. An apprenticeship on several Midwestern newspapers preceded assignments with the *New York World-Telegram* and the *Times,* which he joined in 1944.

In addition to serving the *Times* on its New York City and Washington staffs, his reportorial duties carried him to Spain, England, the Caribbean, Central America, and Mexico. For two years, beginning in October 1944, he served as the *Times* correspondent in Madrid. The government-controlled press tiraded against the newspaper and its correspondent, describing Kennedy as "the one-eyed observer" and "the Jules Verne of journalism." Apparently a notice went out after his departure in December 1946 that under no circumstances was he to be readmitted to Spain. To make the instruction effective, a picture of Kennedy was posted with the designation "unwanted." After serving with his paper's London Bureau, Kennedy returned to Madrid for another year. He reentered the country only after some difficulty, which Kennedy later humorously explained was due to the fact that "as usually happens in the lovely land of *'mañana',* the authorities had forgotten to revoke the order."[2]

Of more immediate concern to the readers of this volume was Kenne-

---

[2] Paul Kennedy, "On a Span Near Spain," *Times Talk,* 11:6 (February 1949), 2.

dy's assignment as chief correspondent for *The New York Times* in Mexico and Central America from October 1954 until December 1965. It was a period of lively and significant events, and Paul Kennedy had the fine reporter's instinct for turning up where the action was. He carried out his assignments with verve and consistently evidenced a capacity for growth in understanding.

The measure of the man is the affection which he engendered in those with whom he dealt; the measure of the reporter and journalist is the judgment of his colleagues and peers. Henry Goethels, who worked with Paul Kennedy in the field, expressed the view that the *Times* "never produced a better companion-correspondent or a more accurate, efficient chap than Paul."[3] Charles Foltz, now Foreign Editor of *U. S. News & World Report* praised Kennedy's work in press conferences.[4] And Tad Szulc, another excellent *Times* correspondent covering the Latin American beat, offered one of the warmest and most revealing characterizations of Paul Kennedy:

> To his friends who may have been Mexican and Central American presidents, cabinet ministers, ambassadors, generals, revolutionaries, editors, bartenders, cable and telephone operators, ambulance lushes, smugglers and fellow newspaper correspondents he was variously, "Paul," "Uncle Paul" or "Pablito." This is by way of saying that in the long years of covering that part of the world for the *Times* . . . Paul Kennedy was known, liked and enjoyed by just about everybody who ran into his joyfully loud and infectiously jolly presence. That he was a hell of a good reporter, whose judgment and responsibility could be trusted, was, of course, a factor. But to be a complete man in this profession, you have to be a damned good newspaperman and a nice human being. Paul, whom I called "Pablito," was both. . . .

And Szulc recalled that "the approach of Paul P. Kennedy to a conference, a presidential office, or a bar was always preceded by the sonic boom of his voice. In most cases the president, ministers, bartenders, and co-drinkers knew the voice."[5]

His colleagues recall incidents in Paul Kennedy's career that may be as much legendary as biographical, but nevertheless provide insight as to how he is remembered by them. In 1960 Kennedy covered the anti-United States riots in the Canal Zone during the Panamanian Independence Day celebration. His dispatches gave no clue that he had been any-

---

[3] Letter, Henry Goethels to Diana Kennedy, February 5, 1967.
[4] Letter, Diana Kennedy to Stanley R. Ross, June 19, 1968.
[5] *Times Talk,* 19:8 (February 1967), 11.

thing but a spectator. However, a colleague later reported that Kennedy had been roughed up by a group of Canal Zone "invaders." When questioned about it, Kennedy limited himself to saying, "They pushed me about a bit and spit on me and took my billfold with all my identification papers and $65 in cash."[6]

It was in Panama that an incident occurred which for Tad Szulc best epitomized Paul Kennedy, the working newspaperman and the human being. Szulc recalled that it was

the afternoon of a day in 1956 in the lobby of the Panama Hotel when several of us, including Paul, awaited the arrival of President Eisenhower for a meeting with his Latin American presidential colleagues. The commander of the Panamanian National Guard had resolved to clear the lobby of all newsmen to make Mr. Eisenhower's passage quicker and easier. Paul took exception to this. "I am covering the President," he said, "and I intend to remain here to see him arrive." Paul placed himself squarely in the middle of the floor and sat down crossing his arms. "If you wish to carry me out bodily you may do so," he said to the colonel. At that point President Eisenhower swept into the lobby. Slightly startled, he looked at Paul in his lonely splendor in the middle of the floor and said, "Hi, Paul, what are you doing here?" The tension broke, and Paul carried the day.[7]

During his years of reporting the Latin American scene, Paul Kennedy experienced everything from riots to coups to armed rebellions. His efforts to keep his readers informed encountered difficulties which ran the gamut from censorship of news to blackouts affecting the use of electricity. He even differentiated once between blackouts as experienced in Costa Rica and Guatemala: "In San José a guard asked you to turn out a forgotten light and invariably added *'por favor.'* Guatemalan guards resorted to the effective method of shooting out the light (and anyone standing in the light's way) and then adding the local equivalent of 'Dope'."[8]

Kennedy, like every good journalist, used his wiles to get around censorship and carry out his assignments. His efforts not only made him *persona non grata* toward the end of his initial stay in Spain, but also resulted in expulsions from Haiti and Guatemala. Characteristically, he tried to persuade his press colleagues that ridicule could prove an effective weapon against unreasonable censorship. Kennedy wrote that, while talking to the Fourth Annual Caribbean Press Seminar, the thought suddenly occurred to him that

[6] Kennedy Obituary, *The New York Times,* February 3, 1967.
[7] *Times Talk,* 19:8 (February 1967), 11.
[8] Kennedy Obituary, *loc. cit.*

in our growing—and, I hope, increasingly successful—attack on irresponsible censorship, we had overlooked a potentially devastating
weapon—ridicule. . . . This is not to say that the fight against censorship
on ethical and moral grounds should be diminished one hundredth of an
inch. My thought is there must be some reaction among nominally responsible adults when confronted with the ludicrous and stupid effects of a
censorship born in panic and unreasoning fear. . . . Seldom does panicky
and badly thought-out censorship fail to yield a rich streak of comedy. The
woeful thing is that in the heat of a fast breaking story and the attendant
frustrations of filing, the humor of it all is difficult to see and appreciate.[9]

Turning to Paul Kennedy's book on his experiences during a decade-
long assignment to the "middle beat," the journalist's major theme is the
gradual progress which he observed in the region, primarily in the political sphere, but also to a lesser degree in the economic and social realms.
Whether he would be as confident in 1970 as he was in 1965 is hard to
say. The events over the past four years have not generally supported his
thesis very strongly, for almost all of these countries have limped along
with liberal military rule or moderate civilian administrations which have
provided piece-meal solutions to chronic problems. The exception is
Mexico, where progress in the social and economic spheres has been
steady, for the most part, despite evidences of rigidity in the continued
exercise of political control by the official party and the persistence of an
exceedingly rapid population growth.

The remarkable political stability which Mexico has experienced for
more than a quarter of a century has provided her with a decided advantage over the Central American countries. This achievement can only be
understood in terms of the historical background of the Mexican Revolution, the state of mind it engendered among Mexicans, and the social,
economic, and political changes which accompanied and emerged from
it. Perhaps most noteworthy has been the emergence of a significant middle class with vested interests in preserving political stability and with a
commitment to a policy of economic diversification with emphasis on industrialization. It is against this background that Mexico's middle-of-
the-road course, with oscillations to the right of center and slightly to the
left of center, becomes intelligible.

The editor can think of no more appropriate means for ending his effort and beginning Kennedy's than the appraisal of the journalist by another long-term observer of the scene, Víctor Alba. Professor Alba
wrote about Kennedy:

[9] Paul Kennedy, "Cloak-and-Dagger Censorship in Central America," *Overseas
Press Club Bulletin,* 12:47(November 23, 1957), 4.

In spite of the fact that I had spent many more years in Mexico than he, on more than one occasion he clarified ideas for me and provided me with information which I did not know. Not only was he a great reporter who never indulged in self-censorship, but besides—and this is very much rarer among journalists—he was an excellent interpreter who placed the news in the context of the reality from which it had emerged. I believe that he understood Mexico as well as a Mexican, but without the skepticism of many Mexicans. And I know that many Mexicans read the *Times* in order to know the interpretation which Paul was giving to the news of the country. This can be said of very few journalists. At times I think that he should have dedicated himself to scholarly investigation, but, if he had done so, we would have lost one of the few journalists who really have contributed to an understanding of Latin America in the United States.[10]

Now it is time to let Paul Kennedy speak for himself. He considered his manuscript, which includes an introduction to Middle America and sections on Mexico, Guatemala, and El Salvador, complete. But the reader should realize that, since the process of turning his manuscript into a book did not begin until after his death, he did not have the usual opportunity to review and respond to comments and suggestions.

The editor would also like to call the reader's attention to three sections which he has appended to Kennedy's text. The first is an Afterword which briefly discusses major recent developments in Mexico, Guatemala, and El Salvador and also describes the political and social situation in Costa Rica, Nicaragua, Honduras, and Panama. The second is a list of suggestions for additional reading on Mexico, Guatemala, El Salvador, and "the middle beat." The third is an Appendix entitled "The Base at Retalhuleu," in which Kennedy's role as a correspondent covering this important story is discussed. This introduction would be incomplete without an acknowledgement to Miss Heather Fowler, Research Associate of the Institute of Latin American Studies, who assisted me in editing this volume, and to Miss Geraldine Gagliano and Mrs. Martha Dickson of the Institute staff for typing the Introduction, editor's notes, and bibliography.

Stanley R. Ross

Institute of Latin American Studies
The University of Texas at Austin

[10] Letter, Víctor Alba to Stanley R. Ross, March 31, 1969.

Preface

This book, for lack of a better description, is a homogenized history fragment of an area extending from the northern border of Mexico to the northern border of Colombia. We call it "Middle America," a term that is open to challenge. But there are a number of substantiating arguments in its favor, and, besides, it is utterly convenient.

Simply put, the work is an account of a news correspondent's activities in the area, against a backdrop of enough history to bring the ten-year span into focus. It is not intended to be a formal history. The professional historians are qualified for that. Nor is it intended to be profound, at least not beyond the normal approach of any correspondent interested in reporting the passing scene with all its implications and all its vagaries.

The thoughts, philosophies, dreams, and accomplishments, good or bad, of many people in high and low office are in this book. They must be thanked. Many of them are named in the text; others are not, either because they did not want to be or it was considered wiser to leave them out. The writings of historians, geographers, demographers, economists, politicians, and political theorists have gone in. They are duly credited.

In any case there are too many involved to be mentioned individually here with all of the gratitude I sincerely feel. The only specific mention will be of *The New York Times,* with deepest thanks for allowing me to collect these offerings and to draw so heavily on the reports.

I have an abhorrence of the word "mission" as applied to a book, a news piece, or a new application of the double-wingback. Yet, for lack of a better word, the "mission" of this book can be said to be a dual one of informing and entertaining. On second thought, it must be a triple one, the final being to arouse more interest in this absorbing part of the earth, to impel scholars and students to study it more, and to tell the world more about it. And to gain an affection for it as we have done.

Paul P. Kennedy

The View from the Middle Beat

"Middle America" means one thing to geologists, another to writers, and still a third to oceanographers. Once the region was the bright dream of politicians who saw in it a potentially noble political entity. That dream might well recur, but as viewed today Middle America is a somewhat wedge-shaped area thinning into an isthmus that descends from the northern border of Mexico to the northern border of Colombia. In all of its recorded history it has been one of the most unquiet regions of the world.

The area under consideration here is around 2500 miles in length with a land area of about 960,000 square miles and a population at the moment of about 51 million [about 65 million by 1970]. It comprises seven republics, one crown colony, and one treaty concession. Spanish is the official spoken language in all except the crown colony, British Honduras, and the treaty concession, the Canal Zone. English is the official language in these two.

Middle America underwent a profound geologic upheaval some millions of years past, and it has not been fully at rest geologically, socially, or politically since. There is some indication the region is headed in this direction, the direction of stability, and that is what this book is largely about. It encompasses ten years of history in which there were three presidential assassinations, four major revolutions and a rash of minor ones, five political upheavals, and five exiles of duly elected presidents. That was the reporter's Middle American Beat between 1954 and 1964.

Some millions of years ago the continental area meandering above and below the eighteenth parallel underwent an almost total facial change.

1

Ranges that ran north and south suddenly skidded off in an east-west direction, and enormous island arcs resulted. There were assorted other geologic phenomena, such as rivers which had been flowing southward suddenly being dammed up by volcanic upheavals, earthquakes, or submarine troughs. One outcome was a series of folded and block mountains which ran from what is now Mexico, Guatemala, and Honduras eastward into the Caribbean, forming the Antillean island arc. Geologists include this in Middle America. Another of the geologic phenomena was the appearance of great girdles of fire from the newly-created volcano chain, which subsequently took over in the series of chaotic events. This was, and still is to a great extent, Middle America.

These geologic manifestations furnished a backdrop for the political and social phenomena that were soon—soon, that is, in the geologic sense—to come. The cordilleras running down from the North American Rockies and penetrated by the great northern spur of the Andes allowed few population centers, and those that developed were isolated by sheer space and by terrain and finally because large sectors of the inhabitants were unassimilable. Thus the descendants of the first Middle Americans who had drifted into the region some twenty-five thousand years past, give or take a thousand years or so, were as far away from a unification of the various tribal groups when the conquistadores appeared as they were when their forefathers had come, some hunting and some planting seeds. They were a tough breed, as a breed had to be tough to fight through what is now Siberia and over the Bering land bridge down through today's Alaska. They were tough, but not quite so tough as the breed that finally conquered and almost exterminated them, the Spanish conquistadores.

It is estimated roughly that there were about three million Indians in Middle America when Cortés landed men and horses in San Juan de Ulúa. That was in 1519, and Cortés immediately established the municipality of Villa Rica de Vera Cruz. In establishing the municipality, incidentally, he executed a political maneuver reminiscent of scores that followed over the centuries in Middle America. He installed his municipal council or *cabildo* and immediately instructed it to install him as governor and commander of New Spain.[1]

In that single, almost-ridiculously simple exercise the Extremaduran adventurer installed himself magnus of all New Spain, governor and commander of the newest jewel in the crown of Holy Roman Emperor Charles V (Charles I of Spain). Four years later Cortés sent a trusted

---

[1] Cortés' desire for personalized triumph was clearly evident in the creation of such independent administrative institutions and partially fulfilled two years later in his remarkable conquest of the Aztec capital, Tenochtitlán. [Editor's Note]

lieutenant, Cristóbal de Olid, to subdue Honduras, a task the latter accomplished with such neatness and dispatch he made plans to linger on as a conqueror in his own right. In swift marches Cortés soon put a stop to this insurrection, which was blunted anyway before his arrival by the death of Olid. Cortés, somewhat of an insurrectionist himself, had little patience with it in others.

Also in 1523 the handsome, impetuous, cruel, and palpably stupid Pedro de Alvarado, another of Cortés' lieutenants, led a band into Guatemala, subduing it in a matter of seven years. He was killed in 1540, but not before he had established the capital city of what was to become the Captaincy General for nearly all of Central America. That was the birth of Middle America.

The region was a child of pillage, with quick profits the sole guideline. There was no expectation that the indigenous population or the slave population that followed merited treatment at much higher than a subhuman level, and that is precisely what they got except in the rare cases when such stout humanitarians as Bartolomé de las Casas and Juan de Zumárraga fought for reforms[2]. But by that time the mold was set, and for all the years since, until very recent ones, the law of the region was that of the fastest draw, the hardest blow, and the hold on the treasury.

But century by century, decade by decade, and in recent times year by year the picture has changed. The only way to achieve change is no longer, as it was even when I began covering the region, the assassination of a president. In some countries they are actually being voted out of office. In others they experience a genteel heaving over the border.

There was a sort of tenuous political stability in Middle America from the days of Cortés and de Alvarado. The viceroy in Mexico City ruled the

[2] Bartolomé de las Casas was a Dominican friar who dedicated his life to the Christianization of the Indians in the Caribbean and on the coasts of Colombia and Guatemala during the first half of the sixteenth century. He fought persistently against the conquistadores' practice of brutally enslaving the Indian and for establishment of protective Spanish royal policies, while preaching pacific conversion. His insistent efforts resulted in a series of investigations and experiments which culminated in the famous New Laws of 1542.

The Spanish colonial administration had a formalized bureaucratic structure designed to assert royal authority and exercise royal control over the territory and population of the New World. New Spain, or what is now Mexico, parts of the United States, and Central America, was organized as one of the two original viceroyalties in Spanish America, ruled by a personal appointee of the king assisted by an *Audiencia* or court. However, from time to time the king would designate captains general to govern outlying parts of the viceroyalty which, for reasons of inaccessibility and security, were more easily ruled virtually independent of the viceroy in Mexico City.

As the first bishop of New Spain, Juan de Zumárraga, defender of the Indians, opposed the policies of the first *Audiencia* by creating schools to promote their general education and endeavoring to prevent their destruction. [Editor's Note]

various captains general of Central America, including the captain general of Guatemala. Panama was under the New Granada viceroyalty, consisting largely of present-day Colombia. There was stability of a sort, enforced as it was by the boot and the saber.

That stability became still more tenuous when the dissolute son of a Spanish father set himself up as emperor of Mexico: Agustín I, as Agustín de Iturbide made himself known.[3] A few days earlier, in mid-September 1821, the Central American countries, represented by wealthy landowners and clergy meeting in Guatemala, had declared Central America independent of the Spanish crown. It was a bloodless operation largely because the Spanish were in no position to interpose. Guatemala took over leadership, but was supported with only slight enthusiasm by El Salvador, Honduras, Nicaragua, and Costa Rica.

Thus, in January 1822, when Guatemala accepted the invitation of Agustín I to come into his empire, there was no unanimity of the Central American nations. El Salvador even made a bungling attempt to annex itself to the United States. Agustín's military commander, General Vicente Filisola, soon put a stop to that by occupying El Salvador. To most of Central America the meaning of the proposition quickly became clear: they were breaking away from a faraway overlordship only to accept another quite a bit closer to home. The ensuing bitter argument was academic inasmuch as Agustín was overthrown before decisions could be made.

That, then, was the last all-out attempt by Mexico to intervene in the affairs of Central America as a whole.[4] In fact, Mexican presidents, usually fond of making state visits, never visited Central America until the incumbent Gustavo Díaz Ordaz accepted several invitations to visit the five Central American states and Panama in 1966.

A second declaration of independence, independence this time from Mexico as well as Spain, was issued in July 1823, and at that time in

[3] The independence movement in the northern segment of the Spanish empire was initiated in Mexico as early as 1810, when the parish priest Miguel Hidalgo y Costilla gave his famous *grito* ("cry") in the village of Dolores. However, it was not until 1821 that the ragged revolutionary bands, bolstered by the defection of the commander of the Spanish armies in the south, Iturbide, were able to defeat the royalists and proclaim the independence of Mexico. In contrast to the populist characteristics of the movement under Hidalgo and Morelos, independence was finally achieved under the Three Guarantees of the Plan of Iguala which, excepting the rupture of the tie with the Spanish empire, was dedicated to the preservation of the *status quo*. [Editor's Note]

[4] This is not to say that there have been no conflicts with individual neighbors over specific matters—for example, frontier differences with Guatemala and rivalry with that nation over the future of Belize or British Honduras. There also has been considerable Mexican interest, particularly in recent times, in Central America as a market for Mexican manufactured goods. [Editor's Note]

Guatemala the Provincias Unidas del Centro América was born. A short time before Panama had declared its independence from Spain and attached itself to Greater Colombia. There was little in the way of a bright future for the Provincias Unidas, a loosely-knit federation held together mainly by a modicum of good faith and the common bond, negative as it was, of being equally adrift in a voracious world. Manuel José Arce, the first president of the federation was forced to resign, and civil war swept the entire area.

Francisco Morazán, a young Honduran, headed the liberal cause in the conservative-liberal struggle in the federation and was sworn in as president in 1829. Later a semiliterate Guatemalan Indian, Rafael Carrera, led an Indian revolt. He was defeated but later dominated in dictatorial fashion not only his native Guatemala but Honduras, Nicaragua, and El Salvador as well. He had one further distinction, dubious as it was. He became the first of a long line of hard-bitten Central American strongmen, most of whom held on through compounded native cunning and ignorance of decent behavior. These inbred qualities have been the hallmark of all Central American dictators, and of virtually all Latin American ones too. Occasionally a sardonic sense of humor surfaces, as in the case of General Anastasio Somoza, the elder, of Nicaragua, but it is never wide enough or deep enough to soften appreciably the personality.

Finally the five Central American nations of the federation went their individual ways. Panama, with the assistance of the United States, finally set itself up as a republic free of Colombia early in the twentieth century. Mexico boiled over into its bloodiest, and hopefully its last, revolutionary war. And the Middle American region drifted on, sometimes ignored, sometimes all too much in the public eye.

In December 1954, shortly after taking over the Middle America beat I wrote from Mexico City: "Immediate and real problems, both economic and political, are keeping practically all of Central America in a state of nervous tension. A tour of all Central American republics just concluded has, on the basis of the best information available, left certain indications that the period between January and sometime in March will be a crucial one for the entire area. There are constant rumors, of course, that in some of these states, particularly Costa Rica and Guatemala, and to a lesser extent Honduras, political upheavals are possible even before January. These rumors however have been omnipresent over the past several weeks.

"Whatever their foundation and validity, these rumors affect every Central American republic. The historic awareness in all of these republics that factors affecting one nation inevitably affect all others seems to be growing keener day by day. Thus daily street gossip of the newest phase in Nicaragua's war of nerves with Costa Rica runs about the same in all these republics. The constantly shifting balance of political and military power is followed closely by millions of citizens of all these countries. For instance, when Nicaragua closed a deal for its twenty-five Mustang fighters and thus established itself as Central America's foremost air power, the effect was enormous in every Central American country.

"The feud between Nicaragua and Costa Rica appears at the moment to be the most potentially explosive element in Central America. The insults being hurled daily between presidents José Figueres of Costa Rica and General Anastasio Somoza of Nicaragua[5] create very little impression. But common knowledge in these two republics is that telling pressures are being exerted from without as well as within on the Figueres administration. And this does make an impression just as does the common knowledge that at any moment another attempt might be made on Somoza's life as happened last April."

This story is given ample space here because it provides some background for the ten years of Middle American history from 1954 to 1964.[6] It went on to note that new treaty discussions over the Canal Zone were creating difficulties in Panama. In Honduras the one-man rule of Julio Lozano, it was noted, was causing tension as Dr. Ramón Villeda Morales sought to get his Liberal Party presidential campaign off the ground.

Guatemala, the story continued, "is still not recovered from its revolution of last summer and it presents the most serious of problems. As one wag expressed it, 'It is too bad there is no world market for problems because we have plenty for home consumption and for export too.' The centrist government of President Carlos Castillo Armas is under the heaviest pressure from both the political right and left. Rising prices, serious unemployment, enduring resentment by the armed forces, and a failure to get his economic and social programs in motion are factors plaguing Castillo Armas."

In conclusion the story observed that El Salvador appeared to be the

---

[5] Presidents Anastasio Somoza of Nicaragua (1939–1947, 1950–1956) and José Figueres of Costa Rica (1954–1958) had a long-standing dispute, which arose from their contrasting types of government and political philosophies. Somoza, product of a long dynasty of dictatorial rulers, was intent on maintaining his control through traditional means, including the use of force. Figueres, who had been democratically elected, was one of the foremost champions of free elections in Central America. [Editor's Note]

[6] Kennedy's initial survey of the "middle beat," with its references to political personalities, identification of tensions and potential sources of trouble, and reports of assassinations—rumored, plotted, and achieved—should give the reader some sense of the bubbling political cauldron he had been assigned to cover. The chapters devoted to the individual countries provide more adequate identification of individuals, factions, and events. [Editor's Note]

only Central American country not under immediate pressures. Even there, however, it was seen that political tensions leading up to the presidential elections of 1956 were already being felt.

That story was filed December 22, 1954. On January 3, I was awakened at home in Mexico City by a call from the New York office informing that President José Antonio Remón of Panama had been assassinated the evening before. Later that month Costa Rica was called to arms when an invasion force from Nicaragua established a beachhead in a fortress well within her borders. In mid-January President Julio Lozano created a political uproar in Honduras by ordering all political parties to shut their offices. In Guatemala rumors abounded over assassination plots against Castillo Armas. And so it went.

Yet there was no particular prescience involved in the December story. Some months before, Sydney Gruson, my predecessor on the Middle American run, had alerted for trouble, basing his story primarily on the lack of planned policy in the area by the United States. "Governments, mainly dictatorships, came and went and little more was asked than generous treatment and protection of United States business interests," he wrote.

The last military coup in Middle America, to the time of this writing, occurred in October 1963 in Honduras, when forces led by Colonel Oswaldo López Arellano (later made general by his own instructions) overthrew the government of Dr. Ramón Villeda Morales. The reason given was that the president and his government had been "blind to Communism in their midst." This was the 136th revolution that country had undergone in the 146 years since its independence from Spain.

Since revolutions are such a significant factor in Middle American history, it is important to understand the varieties of Middle American revolutionaries. They come in all shapes, shades, and sizes, from all sectors of the ideological spectrum and from both sides of the social track. They are militarist-turned-civilian, civilian-turned-militarist, civilian remaining civilian, and militarist remaining militarist. Arthur Koestler's assessment that there is something defective about revolutionaries that keeps them from growing up cannot be applied without qualification to those in the Middle American area. The breed simply is too diverse to be put under the glass bell of absolute classification. They can be killers or gentle souls, patriots or adventurers, intellectuals or dolts.

Eric Hoffer, writing in *Harper's Magazine* (June 1965), takes moderate issue with Mr. Koestler and introduces another factor, nationalism. He writes: "Militant nationalism, too, though not primarily revolutionary in character fosters juvenile manifestations in all sorts of people.... Clearly, the childish pattern is not confined to people with 'some defective quality' which keeps them from growing up but may arise or be induced in all types."

The relevant point here is that much of the revolutionary spirit over recent years in Middle America has been triggered by nationalistic attitudes, generally with the United States as the adversary. A nationalistic drive to rid the country of North American influence in its internal affairs many times either is the spark that directly lights the fire or soon enters the scheme, no matter against whom or what the plot is originally directed. The various plots against the life of General Anastasio Somoza, one of which succeeded, were directed at the dictator primarily, but a powerful secondary motive was to remove Nicaragua further from North American orientation.

The revolutionary plots in Panama, of course, were all, with the exception of those occurring early in 1965, aimed directly at the United States. Finally President Marco Aurelio Robles achieved some sort of distinction by being despised by the Panamanian left even more intensively than was the United States. And that is despising on a grand scale.

The Central American revolutionary tends to wriggle clear of absolute identification and his methods can be baffling. One night very late I was awakened in a hotel in a Central American capital and told a group of men was awaiting me in the lobby. I dressed and went down, and one of the men said in English "We have something you might find interesting and you will be the only newspaperman. Do you want to come?"

I was eventually in a car with four of the men, and after considerable driving we entered the walled enclosure of a large residence, the car gate slamming after us. The living room could not have been better designed for the stage setting of a revolutionary plot. No electric lights. Candles illuminated the large room, and eight men including myself sat around the long table. As a final touch to the scene, a bottle of Scotch slid back and forth along and across the table. The men introduced themselves to me, not by name, but by profession: an engineer, a store owner, a laborer, and so on. Then came the main business. It was explained to me they were organizing a revolution against the chief of state and had wanted one big United States newspaper to be apprised of the developments from the beginning. After that explanation the discussion went on as if I were not there.

The possibilities were discussed and the assistance that might be counted on itemized. There was no assistance expected from the United States, which, it was argued, would support the government. There was talk of arms and of financing, and up to this time the discussion had been calm and reasonably businesslike. The bottle of Scotch continued to slide noiselessly and efficiently back and forth. Finally the subject of the disposition of the chief of state after the revolt had been accomplished arose.

"We could have the United States take him. They would give him asylum," one plotter argued.

"Too dangerous, he would be back in no time," another argued.

This went on briefly until finally a soft-spoken, expensively dressed man said "I see no other way. We've got to shoot the sonofabitch!" I gulped. Having an exclusive story on a revolution was dangerous enough, but sitting in on an assassination plot was a bit too rich for the blood.

I mentally ran through a half dozen ways of getting out of there but discarded them all. Finally, lacking the finesse of a fictional hero, I said simply and, it appeared, quite convincingly, "I want to go back to my hotel." Surprisingly there were no protestations or admonitions about silence. One member stood, led me out of the silent room to the car, and drove me to the hotel. The plot did not come off and the chief of state rode high for some more years. And then he was assassinated. Shot!

The fieriest Central American revolutionary could be a handsome, gay man-about-town. The most engaging revolutionary I knew was a debonair, well-dressed extrovert whose only interest in life besides revolutions was women. He could fit snugly into Mr. Koestler's classification of a "defective personality." He went about revolutions with a cops-and-robbers intensity and was in political exile at least five times in the ten years I knew him. He was utilized in various revolutionary movements primarily in organizing, at which he had extraordinary skill, and in fund-raising, at which he was still more adept. But when the final drive came, our friend somehow was not in the inner circle and when the revolutionary plan failed, as it invariably did, he was one of the first to be deported. He made a considerably better livelihood in exile than in his own country because, I suppose, of his ability at selling and the relief from incessant revolutionary activities. He had only to occupy himself with his work and, of course, his second compulsion.

The Middle American revolutionary (I never got acquainted with a Mexican revolutionary) could be, and a surprisingly large number were, keen-minded internationalists and intellectuals, for the most part of the ideological left. These are, when not working for a foreign cause, patriots with everything to lose and only doubtful rewards in sight. One of these, known over the years, is a prosperous young attorney, prosperous, that is, when in a position to practice, which has been seldom. A brilliant student of political history, a fine orator, and a born leader, he figures someday to be president of his country. The law of averages should be of some assistance because it seems impossible that any man could attempt so many revolutions—and be sent to jail or into exile as many times as he has been—without eventually winning one.

Least appetizing of all the revolutionaries on the Middle American beat are the disciples of the old school dictators. These are the purely ambition-ridden, power-hungry graspers and are usually found among the military plotters. To achieve the prize they invoke all the high-flown causes from fighting corruption to fighting Communist bogeymen. They are usually a humorless, hard-drinking lot, offering little to recommend them except a bludgeoning type of leadership.

Should they be able to maintain their positions of absolute power for, say, three to five years, they will have amassed sufficient funds to buy their way to safety when the blow falls and live comfortably, usually in Miami. In other days, of course, the life expectancy of this type was considerably longer than three years. Manuel Estrada Cabrera and General Jorge Ubico of Guatemala ruled twenty-two and thirteen years respectively; General Anastasio Somoza of Nicaragua lasted twenty years and General Tiburcio Andino Carías of Honduras, fifteen.[7]

Few actuaries would approve heavy life insurance policies on these dictators, and, in fact, few in the above list had policies, since the premiums would have run into the highest brackets. With these four, however, the underwriters would have done well. All but one of them lived out their years, either in loneliness abroad or at home engaging in meaningless and outdated political intrigue.

Before the Honduran coup a somewhat similar military takeover occurred in Guatemala in April 1963. Forces under the minister of defense, Colonel Enrique Peralta Azurdia (he declined to be made a general), overthrew the government of President Miguel Ydígoras Fuentes. This, followed by the overthrow of President Juan Bosch in the Dominican Republic and of Dr. Villeda Morales in Honduras, prompted a three-nation effort to head off more coups. Three Central American foreign ministers met in Managua on October 6, 1963, to seek means of putting a stop to the rash of uprisings. The participants were Daniel Oduber of Costa Rica, Alfonso Ortega Urbina of Nicaragua, and Héctor Serrano Escobar of El Salvador. Guatemala had not been invited because it was still under tight military rule following the coup in April. At the first meeting Minister Oduber sounded the keynote, declaring, "We are at the end of the line for Central American integration if we do not find some way of stopping this kind of thing." The young Costa Rican was particularly bitter about the Honduran overthrow. Dr. Villeda Morales had been sent into exile in Minister Oduber's country, and, incidentally, as a gesture of disdain for the new Honduran government the exiled president was put up as a guest in the presidential residence of President Francisco Orlich in San José. "I do not know what we can do at this meeting," Sr. Oduber

[7] The periods of domination for the cited individuals were as follows: Manuel Estrada Cabrera (1898–1920); Jorge Ubico (1931–1944), Anastasio Somoza (1937–1956), and Tiburcio Andino Carías (1932–1948). [Editor's Note]

declared, "but we all recognize the fact that we have got to do something. The world is hopping mad about this kind of thing, especially the United States."

The story filed from Managua that day stated, "There is a conviction here that Sr. Oduber analyzed the situation correctly when he observed, 'It is pretty obvious from the turn of events in the Dominican Republic and now Honduras that political maturity is not advancing nearly as satisfactorily in this area as economic maturity.' The difficulty appears to be that even states which have much the same attitude as do the three represented at the meeting here do not see eye to eye in the area of political affairs. Costa Rica tends toward strong anti-militarism in line with the thinking of President Rómulo Betancourt of Venezuela and former President Juan Bosch, deposed president of the Dominican Republic. El Salvador and Nicaragua, on the other hand, have less antipathy to militarism. The El Salvador government itself came into power after an overthrow and presently is governed by a former army colonel, Julio Adalberto Rivera. The strongest factor in Nicaraguan rule is its well-trained, well-equipped force known as the National Guard."

No results were reported from the conference, and it would not be missing the mark much to speculate that except for a vague show of alarm there actually were no results. At least one of the conferees reported that to me privately after the conference.

It is interesting to note that some two years later Guatemala originated a so-called Charter of Central American Community, which was passed around to the other four Central American countries, excluding Panama. Under the charter each country would commit itself to the renunciation of government overthrows by force. However, the charter was aimed principally at organizing joint defense against outside armed intrusions. That would open the way to all manner of maneuverings; for instance, a chief of state could call for assistance from the other four republics on the claim that his government was being threatened by subversive forces. The pact was never ratified.

Despite the various alarms sparked by overthrows in the Latin American world, two of them in Central America in a matter of months in 1963, hope is still growing that these countries are moving toward greater stability. And this hope is based on precisely what Sr. Oduber feared might be dissolving, Central American integration and its by-products.

This optimism, true enough, is only vaguely defined, but it arises mainly among, of all sectors, the financial elite. The following account could be a clue: In 1964 we attended in San Salvador an ambassadorial dinner given for a visiting member of the British Parliament. In the course of things the MP and a British-educated Salvadoran clashed over the subject of Central American revolutions, the MP holding that nothing much could be expected in the way of Central American advancement until there was some sort of deliverance from the interminable revolutions.

The Salvadoran, one of the wealthiest men in the country and a member of the so-called Fourteen Families, insisted that Central American revolutions were losing their sting and, indeed, need not impede national progress any longer. It was a first-class bit of leg-pulling, but the MP went for it, particularly when the Salvadoran averred that present-day revolutions amounted to "nothing more than a change of faces in the palace." He explained, "We in business go our ways almost as if nothing had happened." He agreed that in certain areas of commerce, such as tourism, there were momentary dislocations, but generally, he claimed, business went on about as usual.

The MP was horrified, quite properly so, at the flip manner of approaching so serious a subject, but the more he protested the more radical the Salvadoran's arguments became. "Not only are the palace upheavals getting to be without importance," he said, "but in some instances it is actually beneficial to the country. The fact is England perhaps should have a few revolutions to wake it up." That ended the debate, the ambassador stepping in diplomatically, mostly to protect the MP's blood pressure.

When things had simmered down, the Salvadoran advanced some solid arguments. "We in the financial sector are now getting some built-in protection from revolutions," he explained. The point is, and the evidence supports this, economic advancement in the entire Middle American area is giving the technicians, economic experts, and financiers an advantage over the professional politicians they had never enjoyed before, even in the rosiest days of oligarchic domination.

This is not to hold that the financial elite of old, the oligarchies of various countries, such as the Five, Fourteen, or Forty Families of El Salvador and the Rabiblancos of Panama, have abandoned their power or even any substantial part of it. Rather it would indicate that this power is becoming increasingly vitiated by the intrusion of new elements, the economic technicians. And in turn the two groups, the economic technicians and the financial elite, are having a stronger influence on political trends. The interlocking families of the oligarchies still command the major share of the wealth, but new norms are being introduced. A case in point:

Early in 1965 a meeting of the representatives of the *financieras* of six Middle American countries was held without much publicity in San José, Costa Rica. *Financieras* are investment banks patterned somewhat after the government-owned Nacional Financiera of Mexico, which are opening the way to further expansion of Central America's middle class.

Paul Kennedy, far right, and other reporters meet with rebel leaders in Honduras in 1963.

Kennedy in Mexico City in 1959.

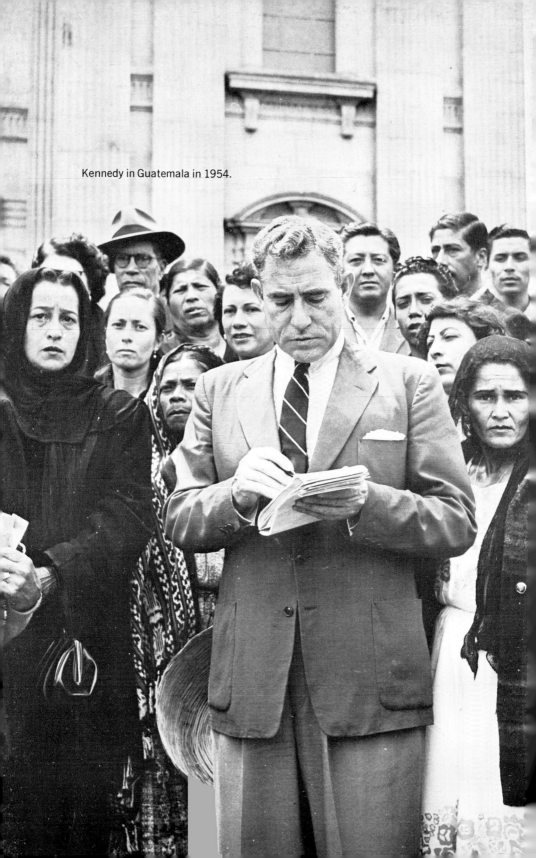

Kennedy in Guatemala in 1954.

The meeting was an initial step toward bringing a loosely related system of banks into closer integration. Aside from this integrative aspect, there are three matters of major interest to be considered in respect to these financieras: their purpose, the personnel of their executive direction; and their potential impact.

Their purpose in the main follows that of the Nacional Financiera of Mexico, to be responsible for industrial development, for borrowing and lending in the industrial sector. But there is a difference. While Mexico's Nacional Financiera is a governmental agency with considerable control over state and private capital investments, the Central American financieras are private organizations put together with a combination of private subscriptions and loans from the United States Agency for International Development (USAID) under the Alliance for Progress program. The financieras of the various participating countries entertain applications for industrial loans, furnish surveys for prospective industrial prospects, and on occasion participate in the new industry's capital and management. In some instances they place their men on the board of directors but more often not.

The six financieras, Panama included, began business in 1964 and 1965, and all but two had a minimum capitalization of $1,000,000. Nicaragua had a capitalization of $2,000,000 and Guatemala, $1,200,000. All but two had loans from USAID for $5,000,000. Nicaragua had a $3,000,000 loan and El Salvador a $5,200,000 one. All of the stock in each of the financieras was disposed of immediately upon incorporation.

As regards the second matter of interest, the directive personnel: While the entrenched financial interests, the oligarchic groups, have part of the stock, as indeed they have stock in virtually everything in their respective countries, they do not in this instance have sole interest and, in fact, in a number of cases have a distinctly minor interest. A large part of the stock is in the hands of relatively new arrivals on the financial scene in their respective countries. The organizers for the most part are of the younger financial group, owners of new money, young foreign-trained economists.

And the third matter of interest, the potential impact: At the San José meeting in July 1965 tentative arrangements were discussed for changing the various financieras to open-end mutual funds or even for eventually establishing an overall fund encompassing all the financieras, with shares distributed to the public under accepted financing regulations. This would assure a spread of Central American industrial ownership among Central Americans.

In this connection, while the various financieras are independent of each other, there are arrangements whereby one, encountering an investment application too large to handle alone and too inviting to turn down, may bring in another financiera, or perhaps all of them, to participate in that particular venture. As a result there are already instances of stocks of one industry being owned in all the other Central American republics and Panama. It appears virtually certain this will also extend to private investment organizations in Mexico.

San José was a likely locale for the first meeting of the financieras. It was there that the first experiment in financing a Central American basic industry through public stock subscription was undertaken. The story fits well the theme at hand. The Industria Nacional de Cemento, S.A., Costa Rica's first cement plant, was organized, again by relative newcomers to the finance scene, some of them Americans. The stock could probably have been oversubscribed by the usual group of established financiers, but the idea was conceived of filtering it down to the middle-class level. A block of over three thousand shares was apportioned to the public at $15 a share and was sold mainly among the professional classes, such as teachers, lawyers, doctors, and newspapermen, and also to skilled laborers. For those wishing to purchase on a partial payment basis, the first payment was $4.50, with the remainder to be paid over several months. The shares were quickly absorbed.

This has been a rather far-flung discussion of the Salvadoran's claim that the financial sector has built-in protection from revolutions. One other very important factor in this situation is the Central American Common Market (CACM). As of the present the Market comprises only the five Central American states, but Mexico and the CACM countries have petitioned the Economic Council for Latin America (ECLA) of the United Nations to investigate ways and means of closer commercial relations between Mexico and the Common Market countries. Should this relationship come about, as it probably will, and further should Panama eventually enter the Common Market scheme, as again it probably will, hopes for Middle American integration will further increase.

The Common Market is so complex and extensive that few laymen outside or inside of Central America understand it. Probably four out of five of the presidents of the member countries do not. It had its vague beginnings in the early 1950's but did not begin noticeably stirring until 1958 when the General Treaty of Central American Economic Integration was signed. The treaty has been in effect since June 1959 for all the member countries save Costa Rica, whose entrance became effective in September 1963.

This treaty was only one of many documents. In the organizing years the Central American countries signed some twenty-four instruments which, in varying degrees, contributed to the Market's final form. As the Market presently stands the member countries are committed to a gradual achievement of free trade for virtually all products originating in their respective states and the free trade includes exemption from export-import duties.

In simpler terms, the Market is gathering populations ranging from Costa Rica's 1,402,000 to Guatemala's 4,300,000 and binding them into a market of just less than eleven million persons. Its effect on trade among the member countries, on intraregional trade that is, has been electric. Between 1950 and 1954 the trade between the five countries was 13 per cent of the total trade of those countries. Between 1954 and 1960 this figure increased to 20 per cent of the total, and at the end of 1964 it stood at 42 per cent.

In shopping basket terms, this means that Salvadorans are now eating Costa Rican and Nicaraguan beef at reasonable prices, whereas before most of them were eating no beef at all. Theoretically, manufactured goods from Market countries should be considerably cheaper than those from other countries, and this must become a reality if the Central American Common Market is to succeed.

In this connection, at a Harvard Business School seminar held in Guatemala recently a hypothetical question was posed to some of Central America's businessmen asking how they would react if intraregional tariffs were suddenly withdrawn from one manufactured item, in this instance, paint. The responses were split about half and half, one half insisting they could not survive and the other half insisting just the opposite— the old versus the new in Central American economy.

And the old versus the new brings to mind an anecdote a young Central American businessman related. He said he was talking to his banker, one of the region's old-line financial figures. "Don Joaquín," our friend asked, "Why are you bankers so opposed to letting foreign banks into the country? They probably would make business better for all of you."

The old banker answered, "My boy, we are old and those people are young. They want to bring in young ideas. Why, they even practice lending money to people who haven't got money."

The Central American Common Market is not concerned solely with goods. It also concerns itself with services and freedom of movement. Ideally it should allow El Salvador's jammed populace (328.9 persons per square mile) to migrate freely to Honduras, which has a population density of 49.1 persons per square mile. In fact thousands of Salvadorans do migrate there now as farm laborers, but while there are subject to the capricious policies of both countries.

The original scheme of the Market was to grant one industry in each country a monopoly in supplying the remaining member nations, but this met with considerable opposition. Presently only two industries, a tire and rubber company in Guatemala and a caustic soda operation in Nicaragua, have been placed in a monopoly position, and they must pay normal duties when their products pass their own borders into another Central American nation.

Finally there is the financial bulwark of the entire system, the Central American Bank for Economic Integration. It was signed into existence in 1960 and became fully operative three years later. The bank, located in Tegucigalpa, Honduras, finances highway systems and development of internal industries in addition to other projects leading to fuller economic integration. Initially the bank was capitalized at $26 million, with United States agencies advancing $10 million and the member nations the remainder. The bank pays no interest or dividends and puts any profits into capital reserve.

The sustained growth of the Central American Common Market, while a gratifying thing, is not without its worrisome aspects. It is being recognized that the advanced intraregional trade is fine but that sooner or later there will be a limit to its growth, a limit dictated by the size of the market. It is agreed without argument that the market, no matter what its development, will be too small for a continued closed economy.

A much wider development base must eventually be established, and that will be one of the big problems of the near future, perhaps as early as 1970. The productive capacity in being and that in the planning stages will be sufficient for the present, but basic industries will eventually be badly needed to keep the momentum of the market from faltering. There are reasons to hope this can be brought about. Investigations are being undertaken, for example, into the production of caustic soda-chlorine insecticides in Nicaragua; soda ash and chemicals in El Salvador; steel and pulp and paper products in Honduras; mining and forest products in Guatemala.

Another export item, product of the so-called smokeless factories, is tourism, and this is expected to contribute substantially to the CACM economy. A recent survey indicated that the Central American area received 111,702 visitors from all sources in 1963. With modern planning, the survey brought out, this figure should be raised to 420,000 by 1975. The visitor expenditure in 1963 of an estimated $11,983,000 should rise to $136,000,000 with nation-wide planning plus $477,000,000 additional income from newly-generated business, the survey showed.

There is little argument that the internal production increase in the Common Market countries has been remarkable over the five-year span from 1960 through 1964. The 1960 internal production total was $2,840,000,000, and this was broken down as follows: agricultural products, $910,000,000; industry, $390,000,000; construction, $82,000,000; and commerce, $614,000,000. The internal production figure for 1964 was $3,567,000,000 and this was broken down: agriculture, $1,137,000,-000; industry, $523,000,000; construction, $104,000,000; and commerce, $772,000,000.

That is the sunny side of the picture. The somewhat less sunny side is the export-import figures. In 1960 the Central American Market countries exported $435,200,000 in goods but imported goods worth $514,200,-000. In 1964 they exported an estimated $648,000,000 but imported $750,000,000. The one favorable aspect of this overhang in imports is that the purchases consisted to a great extent of production equipment and fuel. One economist expressed it, "Central Americans are eating more canned soup and are importing more machinery to produce more canned soup."[8]

Still another built-in factor contributing to increased stability despite political upheavals has been the Organization of Central American States. This association, known by its Spanish initials, ODECA, was established in October 1951 with the objective of achieving regional integration on a political, economic, and social basis. However, the organization came into some hard times primarily because it was the child of the politicians rather than the economic technicians, and in recent years

[8] Mexico has not made any concrete efforts to become an integral part of the CACM since 1965 because its membership in the Latin American Free Trade Area has been considered so much more essential to its trade. However, Panama did decide to enter the Common Market in 1966, but making that decision effective has been delayed by protracted negotiations over the conditions for its entry.

By 1968, the achievements of the Common Market included the elimination of duties on 95 per cent of all imports originating within the area, the balance representing a handful of agricultural products. Common tariffs had been applied to 98 per cent of the list of 1,525 products on which agreement had been sought. However, the situation was not as favorable as these figures would tend to suggest. The remaining items represented 18 per cent of the total trade and the major sources of revenue.

Although trade for the region quadrupled between 1960 and 1965, principally in industrial goods, increases have leveled off in more recent years as a result of the limitations imposed by the size of the potential market and the magnitude of investment funds available. Meanwhile, certain private businessmen have been profiting from the protection afforded their particular nonessential industries by the tariff measures.

During 1968, a presidential-level conference was held to explore ways and means to bolster the sagging trade level as well as to consider multi-national projects for the Gulfs of Fonseca and Honduras and for the development of transportation and communications systems. President Johnson provided financial encouragement by granting an additional $65 million for projects contributing to the integration of the region. A plan to create a new source of investment funds for integration efforts by levying a common 30 per cent import tax on luxury items has not been implemented as yet, since Costa Rica and Honduras have yet to concur. [Editor's Note]

there have been periods in which progress, if there was any at all, was slowed to a crawl.

As it began lapsing into inactivity, a new charter was drawn up and signed in 1962, but as late as 1965 only three countries, Guatemala, El Salvador, and Honduras, had ratified it. The organization under the new charter planned several new objectives, including the establishment of a Central American Court of Justice and a Central American Defense Council. The latter is already suspect in many quarters and will probably meet increased opposition as time goes on.

In all of this it appears the most important factor, more important even than the accomplished steps toward integration, is that the Central American governments themselves are lending active support to the overall concept. This does not necessarily mean that the governments wanted it that way or that the individual presidents, military rulers, or the oligarchy as a whole wanted it that way. The pressures on all of them have been great indeed. Social change, social revolution has been in the air reaching the tiniest mountain *población.* Even the densest *político* and the most socially moribund oligarch can understand the population pressures on limited land resources and the straining of employment opportunities.

Population expansion has been faster in Middle America in recent years than in any other major region of the world, according to a survey made by the Economic Council for Latin America of the United Nations. In the years from mid-1950 to mid-1959 the annual rate of population growth in the five Central American countries and Panama was 3.2 per cent, and Mexico's present rate of growth is 3.1 per cent. With an annual growth of 3 per cent, the population will double in 23.5 years.[9]

The highest growth rate among the countries under consideration was in Costa Rica, where in the years mentioned the figure was 3.87 per cent. El Salvador was next with 3.38 per cent and Nicaragua third with 3.34 per cent; Honduras followed with 3.32 per cent. The average rate of increase for the United States in those years was 1.73 per cent.

In 1955 El Salvador led all the Middle American countries in overall density of population based on total area, with 284 persons per square mile, and Nicaragua was lowest, with 20.72 persons per square mile. Mexico in that year had an average population density of nearly 39 persons. In 1964, El Salvador's population density was 328.9 persons per

[9] More recent figures for the annual rate of population growth in the countries concerned were as follows: Costa Rica, 3.6 (1963–1967); El Salvador, 3.8 (1961–1967); Guatemala, 3.3 (1964–1967); Honduras, 3.5 (1961–1967); Mexico, 3.4 (1961–1967); Nicaragua, 3.8 (1963–1967); Panama, 3.1 (1963–1967). [Editor's Note]

square mile; Nicaragua's was 27.8 and Mexico's was 51.8 persons. The 1964 statistics are from the Social Progress Trust Fund report.[10]

The projections of the Economic Council for Latin America of the United Nations (ECLA) for the area in 1980 are the most startling of all. In 1950 the total population of the Middle American countries under consideration was 34,539,000, with a density of 36.2 persons per square mile. The prediction for the area in 1980 is 70,838,000, with a density of 74.1 persons per square mile. In that projection El Salvador would have a population of 3,556,000 and a population density of 435.1 persons per square mile. For all the Central American countries and Panama a population of 20,321,000 is seen for 1980, with a density of 88 persons per square mile.[11]

In March 1963, the presidents of the five Central American republics and Panama held a three-day meeting in San José, Costa Rica, with President John F. Kennedy of the United States in attendance. The object of the conference was to discuss ways and means of improving the social and economic conditions of the region, and at the end of the conference an eight-page joint declaration was issued. The declaration devoted thirteen lines to education, and that largely to the training of technical personnel to assist in Central America's economic integration. Yet of all the problems facing the Middle American region elementary education is possibly the most pressing. The high rate of illiteracy in nearly all of the region is inhibiting economic and social progress and of course is a significant obstacle to the eradication of political demagoguery.

It has been pointed out by educators that economic and social advancement in the region is caught in a vicious circle: the lack of education retards advancement in the economic and social spheres and the retardation of advancement in these sectors contributes to the backwardness of education.

A simple answer to the question of why illiteracy is still so prevalent in the Middle American region would be that the funds necessary to advance literacy have been spent or misspent on such things as military preparedness and industrial development and lost, of course, through old-fashioned graft. That would be a simple answer, but unfortunately there

[10] More recently Mexico's density of population per square mile was 60.3 (1967). The comparable figures for the other countries were: Costa Rica, 81; El Salvador, 400; Guatemala, 110; Honduras, 53; Nicaragua, 32 (with very extreme regional variations ranging from 367 to 3.9); Panama, 45.5. [Editor's Note]

[11] By 1970 these estimates for 1980 appear quite conservative. Because of consistently high population growth rates the projected levels had almost been reached a decade earlier than anticipated. [Editor's Note]

is no such thing as a simple answer to anything in this region. The answer varies from country to country.

In Mexico, for example, probably the greatest single factor in the way of making a sizeable dent in illiteracy is inability to bring the great indigenous Indian population into the nation's educational system. In El Salvador the feudal rural labor system has been largely to blame, a system in which the entire family, including all the school-age children, are in the labor force. This is changing but is still an obstacle, and a formidable one, to the eradication of illiteracy there. Honduras has historically been so tyrant-ridden that scant attention has been paid to education. And so it goes, with only Mexico, Costa Rica, and Panama showing any appreciable progress over the years.

Costa Rica has consistently had the lowest illiteracy rate of the entire area. The best statistics available are those of the ECLA report for the year 1950. In that year Costa Rica had an illiteracy rate for persons ten years or over of 21.2 per cent. Mexico had a rate of 43 per cent for that year. The illiteracy rates of the other countries were El Salvador, 57.8 per cent; Guatemala, 70.3 per cent; Honduras, 66.3 per cent; Nicaragua, 62.6 per cent; and Panama, 28.2 per cent.[12] The greatest disparity in illiteracy rates is between urban and rural areas. In El Salvador the rates were urban, 32.5 per cent, and rural, 73.2 per cent; in Guatemala, urban, 39 per cent, and rural, 81.5 per cent; in Nicaragua, urban, 30 per cent, and rural, 81.1 per cent; and Panama, urban, 7.2 per cent, and rural, 42.9 per cent.

The unfortunate fact is that attention is being focused increasingly on higher education as a tool for the industrial growth of the area. Elementary education is largely being left to fend for itself, and it is doing rather badly. The progress in eradicating illiteracy in the region, Mexico excepted, has not been overly encouraging in the present century.

The solution to the educational problem in the various Middle American countries depends, of course, on getting as many as possible into existing school facilities and providing more facilities for the growing school-age population. Matters appear to be improving in this respect. In the eight countries of Middle America (including British Honduras) in 1959 there was a school-age (seven to fourteen) population of 9,058,000. The school enrollment of that age bracket that year was 5,434,000. In 1962, the population in the seven-to-fourteen age bracket in the eight countries was 9,851,000. The enrollment that year was

[12] By 1961, illiteracy had been reduced further to 15.6 per cent in Costa Rica, 34.6 per cent in Mexico, 51.0 per cent in El Salvador, 55.0 per cent in Honduras, 50.2 per cent in Nicaragua, and 23.3 per cent in Panama. Illiteracy data for Guatemala is available through 1964, when that country's percentage was reported at 62.1. [Editor's Note]

6,881,000. Thus there was a deficiency in enrollment in 1959 of 4,424,000, and by 1962 the deficiency was reduced to 2,970,000.

In the early sixties the American International Association for Economic and Social Development undertook a study to determine the significance of illiteracy as a hindrance to social and economic progress in Latin America.[13] Two groups were studied: one primarily literate population and one primarily illiterate population. The first consisted of stockholders of the Costa Rican cement company mentioned earlier. The Association wanted to know why more than three thousand persons who had never before held stock in an industry, some of them only vaguely aware of what it meant, had made purchases in a cement company. Two thousand Costa Ricans were interviewed. The answers were varied and for the most part surprising. It was found, for instance, that most of the purchases were made, not for immediate returns, but as long-term investments. In a large number of instances investments for the future were intended to build inheritance for the children.

Simultaneously, another survey was undertaken among the second population, mountain Indians in Guatemala. The object of the investigation was to learn why at the time the literate Costa Ricans were buying stocks they little understood, the illiterate Guatemalan Indians were refusing to buy Incaparina for their children, a food supplement which for three cents daily assured remarkable health advancement in two or three years. A majority of the answers indicated that the Indians had no concept of life in five years or, for that matter, in even one year. Some explained they could think in terms, at the most, of one week in the future, but most thought in terms of one or two days.

A story I sent at the time from San José noted, "Time, as a useful tool or a personal resource, is completely unknown to the illiterate Indian of the Guatemalan highlands. Time, on the other hand, is considered a friendly ally by the Costa Rican, who is likely to have the equivalent of a grade school education. The conception of time as a friendly device rather than a vague foe increases in direct proportion to the decline of illiteracy, it was found.

"Similarly the knowledge of man's surroundings changes in direct proportion to grades advanced in elementary education, particularly in regard to the universe. The size of a star, it was found, increases greatly from one grade to another over the estimation of illiterate adults. To an illiterate adult the star's size is about that of a lime. In the equivalent of

---

[13] See William R. Lassey, "Communication, Risk, and Investment Decision-Making in Costa Rica" (Ph.D. thesis, Michigan State University, 1967), and Paul Deutschmann and William Herzog, *Adoption of Drugs and Foods in Five Guatemalan Villages* (San José, Costa Rica: Instituto de Nutrición de Centro América y Panamá, 1967). [Editor's Note]

the first grade the star is considered as large as a tub, and in the equivalent of the sixth to eighth grades it is thought to be larger than the earth.

"The sun to some illiterates is a fire which is put out once daily, to others it is a god, and to still others it is something bright which is left hanging in the sky during the daytime and taken in at night. These notions change rapidly from one grade to another until around the sixth to eighth grades the sun begins taking on its true character and proportions."

Another great problem facing Middle America is the landless farm laborer's need for land. Guatemala has 1,389 people for 2,470 acres (one thousand hectares) of cultivated or pasture land; Salvador, 1,328; Costa Rica, 915; Nicaragua, 510; Panama, 413; Honduras, 403; and Mexico, 205.

According to Professor Harry Kantor of the University of Florida, Costa Rica in 1959 had 47,286 farms occupying a total of 4,682,531 acres of cultivated and pasture land. There were 160 farms of 2,470 acres or more, and these totaled 1,336,924 acres. El Salvador had 174,204 farms occupying nearly 3,800,000 acres, and 145 of these farms occupied 853,592 acres. In other words, 145 owners—families or syndicates—controlled nearly 20 per cent of the land in cultivation and pasture.

In the ten-year period under consideration, six of the seven republics of Middle America witnessed agrarian reform of one kind or another through their national institutions. The seventh, El Salvador, has no agrarian reform law, but during the first six months of 1964 the administration distributed nearly one thousand parcels of land from state-owned *haciendas* through its Institute of Rural Development.

Mexico led the entire region in agrarian reform land distribution. During the six years comprising the term of office of Adolfo López Mateos nearly 40,000,000 acres of land were distributed to 128,000 families. Some 9,633,000 acres were distributed to 23,000 families in 1964 alone.

The work remaining to be done, however, is enormous and is growing steadily.[14] The Inter-American Committee on Agricultural Development (CIDA) noted in its land tenure studies that of 417,400 agricultural families in Guatemala in 1950 there were 42,000 low-income landless workers. In El Salvador at that time, of 201,900 agricultural families,

---

[14] Since 1964, land reform in the countries of Central America has been principally a holding operation, in which colonization projects of a fairly costly nature have been undertaken utilizing either federal or vacant lands. The policy appears to have the dual purpose of satisfying the most urgent land pressures without posing a major threat to the established large landholders of the country in question. The number of beneficiaries of these projects has averaged approximately one thousand families annually per country; thus only a small segment of the landless rural populations of these countries is affected. [Editor's Note]

19,400 or 9.7 per cent, were low-income landless workers. In Honduras in 1961, of the 216,700 agricultural families, 48,500, or 22.4 per cent, were low-income landless workers.

It has been estimated that in 1958, because of low family incomes, at least 15 per cent of Mexico's people were suffering from hunger and that the caloric deficiency among those affected was upward of 20 per cent. Even so, Mexico is one of only seven Latin American nations with an average level of caloric intake exceeding the ideal daily standard of 2500 calories. It barely topped that figure in 1959–1961 with 2,580 calories per capita.

The Inter-American Development Bank in the report of its Social Progress Trust Fund for 1964 said in respect to the agricultural food supply problem in Latin America, "While the population is growing at an exceptionally high rate (between 2.7 and 2.8 per cent annually) agricultural production as a whole and food production in particular are increasing more slowly if at all. Over the past five years total farm production shows an average annual increase of only 1.6 per cent. As a matter of fact, for the [Latin American] region as a whole the per capita level of food production is lower today than it was ten years ago."

Earlier mention was made of a food preparation called Incaparina prepared under the auspices of the Nutrition Institute of Central America and Panama (INCAP). Its development came about from a suggestion that the traditional dietary deficiency of children in the Middle American region could be remedied appreciably by applying new ingredients to *atole,* a traditional Central American food drink. Much of the credit for carrying out this proposal is due to a coordinated drive by Dr. Mariano López Herrarte, minister of health for Guatemala, and Dr. Nevin S. Scrimshaw, director of INCAP.

In a story from Guatemala in 1959 it was noted that "the infant mortality rate in Guatemala for children up to one year of age was 126 per 1000 live births, as compared with 26 per 1000 in the United States. The mortality rate for children between the ages of one and six years is 42 per 1000 as compared with .9 in the United States.

"As many as 90 per cent if not more of the deaths in the one-through-five bracket in Guatemala result directly from malnutrition. An infant generally is breast-fed until the age of one and one-half or two years. After that it receives only gruel of corn starch or broth of beans, meats, and vegetables, but rarely ever these in bulk form."

This *atole* is the ground corn mixture with a little flavoring added. Its nutritive value is negligible. Incaparina calls for little in the way of new experience for the Central American Indians who have been drinking atole for centuries. The exception is that Incaparina has the same quality as Grade A milk and the same amount of protein and vitamin A. And it is sold at three cents a package, each package containing enough for three glasses daily, as against five cents for one glass of milk in Guatemala, a prohibitive price for Indians and low income *campesinos* of Central America. It was found over long periods of testing that a large majority of the children wanted three glasses daily. Those who couldn't drink the formula in liquid were served it in food and ate it contentedly. Over a period of time the food preparation was found to bring about a remarkable improvement in children suffering from diet deficiencies. However, as noted earlier, Incaparina met with sales resistance from the Guatemalan Indians, particularly on the illiterate level.

Mexico

This could be Mexico:

A burning afternoon in Nuevo Laredo just over the International Bridge. A station wagon loaded with books, clothing, a worn portable typewriter.

There was also a letter from Don Manuel Tello, ambassador of Mexico in Washington, explaining that the bearer was taking up his duties as a resident correspondent in Mexico and was to be shown all of Mexico's courtesy. Don Manuel, later to become Mexico's foreign minister, was then and is now one of the most respected citizens of his country.

His recommendation could have brought gentle treatment by the Mexican customs that glaring afternoon. Instead the station wagon was ordered completely emptied. The customs inspector casually stuffed Don Manuel's letter in his hip pocket and began grimly turning the station wagon inside out. Each pocket of each piece of personal clothing was inspected painstakingly. The cartons of books were emptied simply by spilling them on the ground and each book shaken vigorously. After something over two hours the inspector walked away muttering over his shoulder to load up again.

Or this could be Mexico:

A month later at the same point of entry, the same station wagon, but this time loaded with shiny new utensils, electric kitchen equipment, new clothes. Each item dutiable. There was no letter from Don Manuel this time, no letter from anyone.

And it was a lovely, cool morning. The customs inspector cheerfully waved the station wagon on its way without so much as a glance inside. All was brotherly love, no glaring, all pleasant and cool.

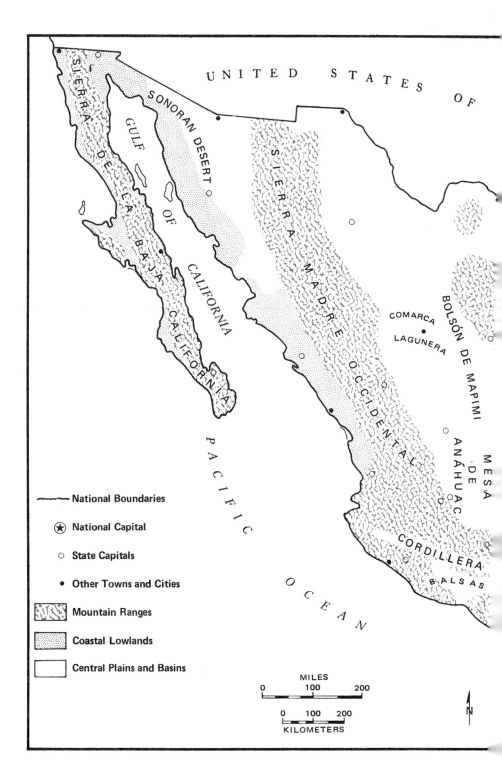

UNITED STATES OF

SIERRA

GULF

SONORAN DESERT

OF

CALIFORNIA

SIERRA DE LA BAJA CALIFORNIA

SIERRA MADRE OCCIDENTAL

PACIFIC

OCEAN

COMARCA
LAGUNERA

BOLSÓN DE MAPIMI

MESA DE ANÁHUAC

CORDILLERA

BALSAS

——— National Boundaries

⊛ National Capital

○ State Capitals

• Other Towns and Cities

Mountain Ranges

Coastal Lowlands

Central Plains and Basins

MILES
0   100   200

0   100   200
KILOMETERS

N

26

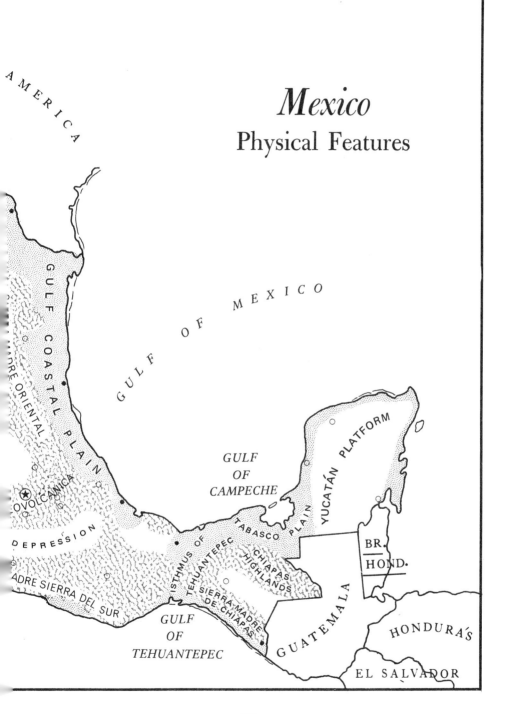

Mexico
Physical Features

A M E R I C A

GULF OF MEXICO

GULF COASTAL PLAIN

MADRE ORIENTAL

VOLCANICA

DEPRESSION

SIERRA MADRE DEL SUR

GULF OF CAMPECHE

YUCATÁN PLATFORM

TABASCO PLAIN

ISTHMUS OF TEHUANTEPEC

CHIAPAS HIGHLANDS

SIERRA MADRE DE CHIAPAS

GULF OF TEHUANTEPEC

GUATEMALA

BR. HOND.

HONDURAS

EL SALVADOR

All this was in 1954 and there could hardly have been a more instructive introduction to the sprawling, cordillera-ribbed land of nearly forty million mixed population. The area of Mexico is somewhere between 738,200 and 762,000 square miles, depending on whose statistics one accepts. The area, like the population, invites varying interpretations. It is a lovely, mutable land where the only constant is change.

The customs inspector who gave you the miserable two hours in a Nuevo Laredo customs shed is sooner or later replaced by a benign, cheerful individual dedicated to the proposition that all men should get into Mexico as quickly and as painlessly as possible.

At the cleaners around the corner a pretty girl took your clothes today and marked the ticket with, instead of a name, the description *cano,* "gray" and *gordo,* "fat." You strike up a warming acquaintance with the cleaning girl, and the next day she has been replaced by a querulous girl with a wart on her cheek.

Telephone people in Mexico City say the annual directory changes about 50 per cent each year. Big cities like the capital, Guadalajara, and Monterrey with centuries of history have very few houses of business which display proudly such signs as "Established in 18—." Mexico City, old Tenochtitlán that was, was a thriving metropolis when Cortés and his hard-bitten crew showed up at the lakefront in 1519; yet a business in Mexico City over fifty years old is almost a rarity.

One of the most fortuitous titles we know for a book on Mexico is Lesley Byrd Simpson's *Many Mexicos.* There are indeed many Mexicos, most of them greatly tempting to the writer who wants to pin them to his blank sheets of typing paper. And these many Mexicos are as elusive as they are tempting. The threadbare aphorism of foreign correspondents the world over that the best time to write about a country is about two weeks after arrival while the reactions are still fresh and uncomplicated applies to Mexico, only more so.

Geography, of course, has had a hand in shaping Mexico's bewildering history. There is an often-quoted tale, too often quoted most likely, that Columbus or Cortés or someone else was asked by someone, usually identified as King Ferdinand or Queen Isabella, about the physical appearance of Mexico. A sheet of parchment was crumpled, so the story goes, into a ball with the explanation "That sire, is Mexico." It is an entirely reasonable description and speaks well for the person, probably a writer, who originally dreamed it up.

The northern border area of Mexico is largely an extension of the United States, of the part, that is, which at one time was in fact Mexico when under the Spanish crown. It extended then over the area now comprising the states of California, Utah, Nevada, Colorado, New Mexico, Arizona, and Texas. Some tippling Mexican friends of ours spend hours during gay parties delighting each other with tales of what Mexico would presently be if it had not lost all of this territory.

The evening usually ends with an uproarious plan for Mexico's annexation of the area, often beginning with taking over the San Diego Naval Base. Additionally the plan usually calls for the forbidding of English instruction in Los Angeles schools and for a mandatory diet of tortillas three times daily in all the annexed territory. Finally, of course, the plan would call for the expulsion of all gringos from the area with the exception, naturally, of present company. The latter would be given Mexican citizenship and a liter of tequila daily.

As Mexico presently stands, the land mass extends deep into the country before the levels rise sharply. After that rise, rather than appearing to be an extension of the United States, Mexico begins to take on the geographical characteristics of Central America and the West Indies . . . Middle America, that is. As a consequence of this distinctive geographic division, the Mexicans along the United States–Mexico border of nearly 1,577 miles have over the years been more sharply oriented to the United States than to their own country.

One of my first assignments to the border was due to this northward orientation. Because of the nearly-impossible communications between industrial Mexico on the central plateau and the northern area, zones surrounding the various cities on the border had for years enjoyed a so-called free zone status; that is, they could import from the United States without restriction or tariff.

President Adolfo Ruiz Cortines, about midway through his administration, in 1955, handed down an executive decree making import licenses mandatory for certain items in the free zones. Merchants selling imported goods in the border cities were incensed at the withdrawal of their traditional privileges and were further incensed by the conviction, right or wrong, that the government had been spurred on in the new policy, not by Mexicans, but by North American business interests in Mexico.

The strategy, these border city merchants insisted, was to force Mexicans to buy goods produced by United States manufacturing interests in Mexico. These goods, it was charged, could be manufactured and sold in Mexico at a greater profit than if they were manufactured by the parent company in the United States and sold in the United States or transported over the border to Mexican customers. A dispatch from Tijuana quoting Baja California businessmen to this effect, especially in regard to such items as tires, electric refrigerators, washing machines, and other appliances, was denied emphatically by the United States manufacturers in Mexico. But Tijuana businessmen were adamant. They named names and sent a committee of border businessmen to Mexico City in June 1955 to protest the presidential decree.

The committee was successful in having 60 per cent of the affected items put back on the nonrestricted list. The entire exercise, however, was academic because in the ensuing years communications between the industrial center of Mexico and the border improved to such an extent that presently the zone privileges have largely disappeared.

Tijuana at this particular time was having more than its share of difficulties. While the businessmen were fighting to force the government to rescind import strictures, the citizenry as a whole was in the midst of an anti-vice drive, one of the drives that city undergoes periodically. This particular drive, like the ones before and after it, fizzled, and vice continues to be the chief commercial enterprise.

It was the same old story of any city where a few vice lords commandeer a large army of followers, who are opposed by only a few forlorn crusaders. Logically the grim crusaders should eventually win the struggle, but they have been losing consistently for well over a century. In fact, not many of the righteous of Tijuana care to discuss their families more than two generations back. A large part of the present-day fortunes in Tijuana originated in the steaming fleshpots, gambling-halls, and narcotic pipelines.

Doing a crime story in Tijuana was a newspaper police run revisited. In the city's burrows and warrens, most of them only a tunnel's length away from the mainstreet nightclubs, deviltry throbs and thrives. At the time I did a crime story there in 1955 there were statistics produced before a United States congressional subcommittee showing that at least ten thousand of the city's then total population of seventy thousand lived directly off traffic in prostitution and narcotics.

Ten years later the picture had not changed much. Prostitution and narcotics were still the city's most thriving industries. In fairness, however, it should be noted that condition did not apply exclusively to Tijuana. Just as Tijuana is "joytown" for lower California, so is Ciudad Juárez the overflow area for El Paso's sinning and Nuevo Laredo for that of Laredo across the border.

Narcotics addicts in the United States go across the line to Tijuana for their daily "fix." In fact many of them live the year round in San Isidro just across the line in California. At the Tijuana crossing, just as at border crossings in all the other states, there are signs warning that narcotics addicts must register with immigration before going into Mexico.

Traveling east from Baja California the Sierra Madre Occidental introduces an arid plateau. This plateau extends eastward with relatively unimportant declines until it reaches the coastal plain, which extends southward to Campeche on the Yucatán Peninsula.

The northern plateau is known as the Bolsón de Mapimí. It is a land mass of nearly 40,000 square miles. It is, roughly, hemmed in between the parallel mountain chains of the Sierra Madre Occidental, which runs down through Panama, and the Sierra Madre Oriental. In the area between the two mountain chains much, if not most, of Mexico's cattle industry and a lot of the nation's steel manufacturing are located. The entire area is oriented toward Monterrey, one of the country's three largest cities and its northern industrial hub.

Monterrey is apt to appeal to the North American, during his first visit to Mexico at any rate, more than the other cities. It presents the nearest thing to his homeland of all the cities south of the Rio Grande.

Parenthetically, the term "North American" is used herein with the full knowledge that it technically does not differentiate Mexicans from citizens of the United States of America. The Mexicans can quite rightly claim they too are "North Americans" as differentiated from "Central" and "South Americans." To complicate matters still further, Mexico is "the united states" too, its formal title being Estados Unidos Mexicanos. And finally, to beat a dead horse, many Latin American nationalists resent the appropriation of the name "American" to denote a citizen of the United States of America. They maintain, and again correctly, they are as much "American" as we are.

Monterrey, something of a cross between Pittsburgh and Chicago, has enormous drive and is completely oriented to big ideas and big money. Its residences are not walled-in against prowlers, as are virtually all other residences throughout Latin America. Doors of parked cars are left unlocked. The incidence of petty crime is probably the lowest in Mexico and possibly in all Latin America. And its citizens are known to be adept at making a fast dollar and to have the devil's own problem of not being able to part with a dollar once they have pocketed it.

Monterrey and the state of Nuevo León, of which Monterrey is the capital, also have distinctive attributes in regard to major crime. The direction of the state penitentiary in Monterrey is considered one of the most progressive and enlightened in the world. Some of the penological practices used there are so broad and humanitarian as to cause eyebrow-lifting in the rest of Mexico, which in its own right is noted for approaches to penology undreamed of generally in North America.

As in most Mexican and, for that matter, most Latin American penitentiaries, the wife of an inmate of the Nuevo León penitentiary is invited to visit her husband privately in his cell. Unmarried inmates have the privilege of receiving private visits from medically inspected women, some of them sweethearts, others prostitutes. The incidence of homosexuality in this prison ranks, so far as can be determined, very low among the prisons of the world. The inmates who refer to themselves as "interns" have their own theater and produce shows with visiting Monterrey women taking the female roles. The "interns" have their own orchestra and, additionally, a locally famous dance combination. This latter is given regular liberty to play Monterrey nightclubs. It was mentioned casually to the warden that this particular combination would be making a fortune when it was finally given full freedom. The warden agreed this could have been so, but said that unfortunately they were not all to be released at the same time and quite possibly the first released would be on their way back by the time the last got freedom.

Citizens of Monterrey are known as *regiomontanos* (people of the royal mountain). Although their traditional frugality is the basis of many vaudeville jokes, they are generous in taking care of their own destitute. They look sternly on begging or panhandling, keep their city clean, and lead the entire nation in progressive labor relations.

Mexico's broad coastal plain runs along the Gulf of Mexico from the United States border through the entire Yucatán peninsula. The plain has abundant water, as is seen from its swamps and marshes, and the heavy rainfall in the area swells the many rivers, usually to unmanageable proportions, during the rainy season. Some of these rivers, like the Pánuco, are among the greatest in the hemisphere. There are annual floods, especially in the Tampico area, with great losses of life and property.

The land begins rising sharply at the southern tip of the Bolsón de Mapimí and after traversing the mountainous mining regions of San Luis Potosí and Zacatecas eventually levels off into the central plateau or Mesa de Anáhuac. This central mesa comprises only 15 to 20 per cent of Mexico's land total but it is the true heartland of the nation commercially and in terms of population, as well as geographically. Its principal basins range in altitude from 5,000 feet for Guadalajara to 8,600 for Toluca.

The Federal District, a political division of Mexico vaguely similar to the District of Columbia has an area of about 580 square miles and a population probably over 5,000,000.[1] The District, almost completely surrounded by mountains, is the nation's industrial and cultural center. It houses Mexico City, the national capital, with a 1965 population of over 3,000,000 as compared with the 1963 population of Washington, D.C. of about 800,000.

South of the central mesa there is rugged mountain terrain with the altitudes dropping, falling away to the east to the low-lying Isthmus of Tehuantepec and the Yucatán Peninsula. During much of Mexico's ancient and some of its modern history the isthmus and the entire peninsula were cut off from the nation's body. Travel and commercial transportation in modern times were, until fairly recently, confined to water, and Cuba and

[1] According to official census figures in 1970, about 15 per cent of Mexico's 48,313,438 people—or some 7,000,000—were concentrated in the Federal District. [Editor's Note]

the gulf ports of the United States were as easily accessible from the peninsula as was Veracruz, the port of entry and departure between the rest of Mexico and Yucatán.

As a consequence the culture, the dress, the food, and even the beer, thought by many stout beer-bibbers to be the best in the Western Hemisphere, were and still are more alien to the main body of Mexico than are those of any of the nation's other regions. And many, including me, view with a certain sadness the opening up of this mysterious, fascinating area by modern automobile, water, and air travel. At a time not so far in the past its people referred to themselves as *Yucatecos* ("Yucatecans") rather than "Mexicans". They felt so hopelessly separated from the Mexican mainland that there was once an application to annex themselves to the United States, or so the story goes at least.[2]

The Spanish tongue on the peninsula is more attuned to the Caribbean than to the Gulf, and unless one has a sharp ear it is difficult to distinguish a conversation on the streets of Mérida from one on the streets of Havana. Mérida, the capital of the state of Yucatán, proudly refers to itself as the "White City." Its wide, clean avenues and stately mansions have a fading character and charm dating back to the days of the wealthy, haughty, and feudal henequen planters. Henequen, a member of the cactus family, is peculiarly adaptable to Yucatán's limestone soil.

In the days following the conquistadores named Francisco de Montejo (there were three of them with the same name), enormous acreages were staked out for henequen, and the foundations of great fortunes were laid. These fields of sisal-hemp provided the hemp and the cordage used on the sailing ships up and down the world, and the society built on the returns from their export was a glittering one indeed. The offspring of the planters were schooled in New Orleans, where they became trilingual, speaking English and French besides their own Spanish, or were sent to Europe for finishing. They looked down on the nouveau riche of Mexico City and even evidenced disdain for the regal citizens of Guadalajara.

But then the sailing ships slipped over the horizon never to return, and following this came the final blow, synthetic fibers. The hemp industry slipped disastrously, and the great homes along Montejo Boulevard in Mérida sank into shabbiness. The children of the haughty peninsula families went to the capital to get jobs, and now the White City is still white but has become a modern city that is rapidly losing its centuries-old charm. The area probably has a higher percentage of English-speaking residents than any other region of Mexico.

---

[2] Yucatán did indeed seek foreign adoption, its petition to the United States being made in 1845. Parallel gestures toward Europe prompted the issuance of a corollary to the Monroe Doctrine. [Editor's Note]

The indigenous population remains, the descendants of the great Mayas. Many went into commerce, others into law or allied professions, and many remain as guides to tell the thousands of tourists annually, usually incorrectly or exaggeratedly, of the the cities of their ancestors strewn over the entire peninsula. The archeological ruins of Chichén Itzá, Uxmal, and Tulum are among the most spectacular in this part of the world.

Before leaving the peninsula and the isthmus, at least a glance should be taken at one of the most grandiose schemes of this country, the famous, long-studied, and much-discussed Tehuantepec Canal. One of the great rewards of reporting from Mexico is that when things get dull someone invariably comes up with a scheme so audacious and magnificent it catches the breath and certainly overwhelms the imagination. These ventures, "dreams" if that's a better word, invariably make good stories.

A more fascinating assignment could not be picked up than to go over the plans and tour the area for the Tehuantepec Canal with José S. Noriega, a respected and highly successful hydrological engineer. Sr. Noriega had been dreaming of and working on plans for the canal some twelve years before I caught up with him in 1960. He had used as his springboard studies of other planners as far back as 1871. And even earlier, the conquistador Hernán Cortés had had a few private dreams of his own of cutting through the isthmus from the Gulf of Mexico to the Pacific. After Cortés came a host of others, including Baron Alexander von Humboldt, Johann Wolfgang von Goethe, and even our own Daniel Webster.

Sr. Noriega, however, had some telling advantages over these early dreamers. First, his studies had the support of the Mexican government, or rather Petróleos Mexicanos (PEMEX), which is the government-directed nationalized petroleum industry. Secondly, he would have some greatly advanced techniques at his disposal, and possibly even nuclear assistance, for drilling the canal. Finally, in recent years there has been serious talk of financing the job, which, Sr. Noriega estimates, would cost from $500 million to $600 million.

According to the Noriega plan the canal would proceed up the Coatzacoalcos River from its mouth at the hot and dusty town of Coatzacoalcos. The river could easily be made navigable the 60 miles to the village of Hidalgotitlán. From there a series of artificial lakes are contemplated stretching another 50 miles to the town of Matías Romero, and from there there would be a cut to the navigable Laguna Superior on the Bay of Tehuantepec, which opens onto the Pacific ocean. The distance, excluding the 13½ miles across the Laguna Superior, would make the canal about 135 miles in length as compared with 91½ miles for the Suez Canal and 44¾ miles for the Panama Canal.

Spice is added to this particular dream by further contemplation of a series of lagoons extending almost unbrokenly from Tampico, 250 miles from the United States border, to the mouth of the Coatzacoalcos. This series of navigable lagoons, connected with the Brownsville-Tampico Canal, which in turn connects with the United States inland waterway system, would provide protected barging from the Great Lakes to the Pacific Ocean. The canal, Sr. Noriega proudly explains, would reduce the distance from New York to San Francisco from the 5,263 nautical miles of the present Panama Canal route to 4,250 miles and the distance from New Orleans to San Francisco from 4,689 nautical miles to 3,000 miles. Indeed, a reporter rarely runs short of copy living around men who can dream this big.

Mexico—The Capital

The great, sprawling city of Mexico, the nation's capital, is to some extent to the United Mexican States what Washington is to the United States of America. Actually the comparison, admittedly not a very compelling one, would be in Mexico City's favor. *Capitalinos,* as the residents of Mexico City are known to the remainder of the nation, have been on the scene for more than six centuries, while Washington's population is a conglomerate body neither Kankakee nor Pocatello.

Of course the population picture in the capital is changing rapidly and relentlessly. In 1963, 8 per cent of the Mexican population, or about 3,000,000, lived in the capital city. In 1950 the capital's population was 2,234,800. From 1950 to 1960 the capital's percentage of population increase was nearly 27 per cent.[3] The Federal District, which encompasses the capital city rose in population from 3,050,400 in 1950 to 4,870,800 in 1960, or a percentage change of 59.6 per cent.

What will happen to the capital city in the next twenty-five years is a matter that preoccupies the planners. The district is dotted with satellite cities. There have been plans advanced for burrowing through the mountains to allow highspeed commuting to the valleys beyond where bedrooms can be established for the burgeoning number who work in the city. And added to the concern over population expansion are the twin worries of air pollution and water shortage.

The Mexican capital is known simply as "Mexico," not Mexico City or Ciudad de México. A maid answering a telephone informs that the master of the house is *"fuera de México"* if he has left the city. If he is out of the country, she says *"fuera de la república"* and employs a special tone because to the average servant anything out of the republic is well out of the world.

Mexico as it now stands was settled by the Aztecs in the early part of the fourteenth century, most historians placing it about 1325. The principal part of the city was known as Tenochtitlán. In all probability early

[3] The Mexican capital's population is currently estimated to exceed 5,000,000. [Editor's Note]

36

Aztec capitalinos knew more about their empire as a whole than did the modern capitalinos before advanced communication become widespread. The early men were warriors who had fought their way down from the north, and they continued fighting from Tenochtitlán, continued it as ruthlessly and effectively and with the same cruelty that made them feared and hated. They were pressed regularly into military service to pursue the war aims of their emperors and fought periodically in the various kingdoms now comprising the Mexican republic.

But with the advent of the Spanish conquistadores in 1521, the capitalino settled down to being first a citizen of his capital and secondly a rather vague citizen of his *tierra,* or the region from which he and his forebears came. Until comparatively recently he knew little of his country as a whole and cared considerably less. Successive governments for at least the past half century have sought to overcome this provincial outlook.

They succeeded rather poorly until modern communications began pulling the nation together. This was followed by the magnetic urbanizing which has transformed the capital into a conglomerate mass. The capitalino is still inclined to look down on his countrymen below from his lofty altitude. But in recent years a nationalistic transition has taken place, in that he considers himself first a Mexican and than a capitalino.

Even the Chihuahuans (who call themselves "Chihuaguenses" rather than "Chihuahuenses," the latter denoting the Chihuahua dog breed) have relented a bit in their stiff-necked state pride, enough at least to give Mexico an even break with Chihuahua. And that leaves only the Yucatecans clinging to their lone grandeur.

In any case, it is somewhat startling to read in a Mexico paper about a sudden acceleration in tourism and find at the end that the writer has been referring to Mexicans visiting their capital city.

The tourist's view of Mexico, this time referring to the foreign tourist, is more or less the tourist's view of Paris, Rome, London, or Istanbul. Parenthetically, there are upwards of one million of these visitors each year, and in 1963 they left around $900 million in the republic, about one-third of the national budget.[4] The tourist in Mexico, as in other cities, has few opportunities and, in most cases, little desire to become acquainted with the vignettes which provide the color and spice of one of the oldest cities in the Western world.

*   *   *

---

[4] In 1969, more than two million tourists visited Mexico, and the *industria sin chimeneas* ("industry without smokestacks") contributed more than two billion dollars to the nation's economy. [Editor's Note]

An old cobbler living in a basement in the heart of the city crawls out onto the sidewalk with his awl, hammer, and some badly worn shoes left with him by maids and laborers in the neighborhood. He goes about his mending and the greeting of neighborhood strollers. His view is of a struggling tree which the city has installed. But more important, in the two-feet-square bit of earth delegated to the tree he has grown two giant stalks of corn.

They are there solely for him to tend and watch grow. They mean to him maize, the real meaning of life from which his ancestors hundreds of years back got their tortillas and *tijotle*.[5] In his tierra he spent his youth grubbing and harvesting. He looks at the two stalks and gives the impression that he finds in them the beauty a Finn finds in a giant fir or a former Irish cotter finds in a vagrant scent of burning peat.

*   *   *

Opposite an apartment in which we once lived about twenty blocks from the heart of the city there was a gynecological clinic about which all sorts of rumors grew in the neighborhood. On the roof about on a level with our apartment an old lady used to lay out the surgical instruments to dry and be aired on sunny days. On that roof there was an enormous commotion one night. A cauldron had been set up and beside it a scaffolding from which were suspended two butchered full-grown hogs.

The hogs had been scalded in the still-steaming cauldron and now two men were hard at scraping and disemboweling them. A giant searchlight played on them, throwing huge shadows of the scene on the side of a white-walled apartment building adjacent to the clinic. The cauldron's steam and smoke arose in shadows high on the wall; the men, twenty-five feet tall, were hacking away at hogs five feet taller. "A Daumier drawing of hell, my wife whispered.

The next morning the roof was clear, a bad dream dissipated. The old lady was laying out her surgical instruments.

*   *   *

[5] It would appear that Kennedy has reference to *jilote (xilotl),* which Robelo in his *Diccionario de aztequismos* defines as "an ear of tender corn," "tassell of corn still milk, but already edible," and "silk of the tender ear of corn." The only possible variant reading of the term in the text would be *tiljoche* (or *tlilsuchitl* and about half a dozen other variants in spelling) which Santamaría's *Diccionario de mexicanismos* defines as an Aztec term for the tropical vanilla plant—a definition which hardly fits with the sense of the remainder of the sentence. [Editor's Note]

Understanding the Mexican capital is greatly facilitated if it is remembered that anything any large city in the world has, this capital city has too. The old cobbler and the gynecological clinic were only a few blocks from one of the greatest anthropological museums in the world.

Crime? In 1963 the Mexican republic as a whole ranked third in the entire world in number of crimes. In that year, said the director of the Institute of Special Investigations, there was a major crime in the country every eighty-nine minutes and there were thirty-nine homicides for every ten thousand people. This was in the republic. Mexico itself, the capital, reported for that year a murder for every one and one-third days and 17,000 orders for arrest issued in car thefts. In petty crime the capital, if not the actual leader year in and year out, was high on the list. In 1960 there were 40,320 crimes recorded.

Sports? The National University stadium, designed by the painter Diego Rivera, is jammed week after week to its 110,000 capacity for soccer-type football (Mexico will be the center for the world championships in 1970) and for North American-type football. A giant sports city is to be erected for the Olympics to be held in Mexico in 1968, as well as many new hotels. The city has a triple-A baseball team and in the spring brings in National and American major league teams to play in exhibition games. And the local nine wins a respectable number of them.

Culture? The city has two symphony orchestras, two ballet companies, and a university that is the second oldest in the hemisphere and certainly one of the most spectacular in the world. It has a world-famous library, two art galleries, and the already-mentioned anthropological museum, ranking with that of Cairo.

Traffic? Ghastly! Again, on a par with that of the great cities of the world. Certainly driving in Mexico City compares to driving in Paris or Lisbon. Some years ago we reported to a magazine, "The guiding principle in driving through traffic here is to utilize the French military strategy 'l'attaque, toujours l'attaque.' There is no room or survival for the weak of will or the soft of heart."

The great hurdle to a smooth traffic system in Mexico, as in all parts of the world, is simply that there are too many vehicles for too little street space. In 1963 there were close to a million motor vehicles of all types operating throughout the nation. Accurate percentages are difficult to come by, but the best estimate available was that 40 per cent of the passenger cars that year and 33 per cent of the trucks were confined to the 579 square miles of the Federal District.

This disproportionate mass of trucks, cars, and buses, the latter completely unregulated for diesel exhaust, is creating a problem for the capital far more perplexing than its traffic snarl. An authority on atmospheric contamination staggered the capital recently with the blunt statement that the health of the population was being endangered and actual poisoning was widespread because of automotive exhaust. The location of the capital in an intermont basin is the key factor The interstate trucks and buses with abnormally rich fuel mixtures to cope with the altitudes into the basin spread billows of smoke so drivers behind them are forced to close their car windows, that or choke.

Although automotive exhaust is the chief culprit, it is by no means the only one. Industries in control of powerful political and financial forces contribute greatly to the contamination. Commission after commission has been assigned to study wind currents and the various factors contributing to the growing crisis, but the industries still spew their smokes and gases. Visitors coming over the mountains from Cuernavaca or Puebla and looking down on the valley from altitudes of 8,000 to 10,000 feet are more often than not greeted by great domes of haze, smoke, and smog covering the entire capital.[6]

In the early sixteenth century Bernal Díaz del Castillo, a foot soldier in the company of the conquistador Hernán Cortés, tells of seeing the valley for the first time: "We were amazed and said that it was like the enchantments they tell of in the legend of Amadis, on account of the great towers and cues and buildings arising from the water. And some of our soldiers even asked whether the things we saw were not a dream."

Marquesa Frances Calderón de la Barca was still more ecstatic. She was the American-born wife of Spain's first ambassador to Mexico after the latter had won its independence from the Spanish crown.[7] She first saw the valley in December 1839 and wrote, "Standing in the midst of the great lakes, upon verdant and flower-covered islands, a western Venice with thousands of boats gliding swiftly along the streets . . . the

---

[6] For centuries travelers marveled at the clarity of the atmosphere of Mexico City. Carlos Fuentes, internationally respected Mexican novelist, titled one of his books *La región más transparente,* which appeared in its English edition with the very appropriate title, *Where the Air is Clear.* A few years ago, experts estimated that the capital had lost one-third of its atmospheric clarity due to a combination of denuded soil, industrial haze, and vehicular exhaust. [Editor's Note]

[7] Although Mexican independence was first proclaimed in 1810 and became an established fact eleven years later, Spain did not recognize Mexico's independence until 1836. Actually, Mexico was the first of her former dependencies which was accorded such recognition by the former mother country. The process of recognizing the political independence of other parts of Spanish America dragged on until almost the end of the century. The quotation is taken from Madame Calderón de la Barca's *Life in Mexico,* which was referred to in the Editor's Introduction. [Editor's Note]

whole fertile valley enclosed by its eternal mountains and snow-covered volcanoes. What scenes of wonder and beauty to burst upon the eyes of wayfaring men!" Mexico, the capital, has come a long way since those days.

Everything in the capital, in fact everything in the nation of Mexico, begins at the Zócalo, or Plaza of the Constitution, which is the Zócalo's formal name. This great square, which on occasion holds more than 100,000 spectators, has been the center of national events ever since the founding of Tenochtitlán. When Cortés arrived in November 1519, the square accommodated magnificent Aztec temples and the palace and gardens of Emperor Moctezuma and was the marketing center of the empire. It later housed the palace of Cortés. Today it is the center of the national administration. The National Palace, occupying one whole side of the quadrangle, comprises the president's administrative offices and the Ministry of Hacienda (Treasury). On another side of the square is the Ayuntamiento, or City Hall. The Monte de Piedad, the national pawnshop, is on the plaza and contributes to keeping the republic oiled and operating.

On the foundations of the Aztec temples is the National Cathedral, the center of the Roman Catholic archdiocese and the see of the archbishop primate of all Mexico. The construction of the Christian houses of worship on the foundations of pagan temples was practiced widely by the Spanish under Cortés. It was in part a technique of psychological warfare to demonstrate the ascendancy of the Christian religion over the pagan. A second inducement was that the temples provided ready-made foundations and building materials for the new Christian structures.[8]

Foreign correspondents get a dramatic view of the Zócalo once each year when they are invited to the annual *grito* ("cry" or "shout") ceremony. This particular ceremony triggers the national celebration of the Grito de Dolores in observance of the dawn of September 16, 1810, when Father Miguel Hidalgo y Costilla launched the revolt that eventually led to Mexico's independence from Spain. That dawn he rang the bells of the church in the town of Dolores, where he was pastor. When the crowd gathered to learn what the wild ringing of the bells meant, Padre Hidalgo read the message of revolt, called the *grito,* and thus the revolution began.

[8] The Spaniards also were capitalizing on the habits of the conquered to facilitate conversion. Yet the newly won parishioners continued to worship their old gods as well—often with new attributes—in the old places. The result was a fascinating blend of pagan and Catholic ritual with the important consequence that it helped the Indian to survive by enabling him to preserve what made life meaningful for him. [Editor's Note]

On the night of September 15 each year, the president of the republic steps onto a balcony of the National Palace, rings a small bell, and repeats the exact words of Padre Hidalgo. This brief ceremony sets off the ringing of the ponderous bells in the National Cathedral and in all the churches of the nation. On that night the Palace is so jammed with invited guests jostling for position on the various Palace balconies to look at the throng below that only a fortunate few see the president in person. Of late, television sets are scattered throughout the presidential offices so that the chief executive, a few feet away, can be seen on television.

The old Zócalo has witnessed its share of turbulence. Some of the most violent demonstrations in the country's history have taken place there, many of them in recent times. The most awesome of these in our coverage was in August 1958 when university students initiated a series of demonstrations which ended in rioting and in what appeared to be an all-out attack on the government. The National University students, ostensibly protesting increased bus fares in the capital, began that day by holding up buses, forcing passengers off and driving the pirated machines out to the National University. The university in Mexico, as in all Latin America, is an autonomous institution into which no city or national police are allowed entrance.

The Zócalo was in the process of renovation. Streetcar lines and flower gardens had been ripped out and the entire area paved. The concrete was still fresh when the caravan of about seventy kidnapped buses weaved drunkenly down the main thoroughfares of the city and started skidding onto the wet concrete in the Zócalo.

A scene of frightful confusion followed, with the student drivers playing games of sending the ponderous buses slithering toward each other in the six-inch mush. The vehicles were loaded with students, some of them hanging from the windows and others clinging desperately to the rooftops. As the buses ripped into each other the students fell from the windows and the roofs and extricated themselves as best they could from the slush and out of the way of the careening juggernauts. Those who missed were run down amidst great howling and shrieking and were carted away in ambulances. The latter had descended on the Zócalo in force, and with their siren-wailing and careening in their own right they added to the general bedlam.

That demonstration, as if by plan, set off several days of rioting in the city, finally culminating in a nationwide railroad strike which virtually brought the nation to its knees. It was eventually broken by the government and most of the leaders were jailed. This was in March of 1959 and proved to be the first real test of Adolfo López Mateos, who had taken over the presidency in December 1958. His arrest of the strike leaders, members of the newly-elected union for the most part, brought down on him the wrath of the left from moderate to extreme, and their anger followed him through his entire administration in spite of the fact he himself caused considerable commotion by announcing that his government was "of the left."[9]

But back for the moment to softer and more romantic matters. Shortly north of the Zócalo is the Plaza de Santo Domingo, a favored locale of many capitalinos that is little known to casual visitors. Not only is it a little jewel of a park, but it is the home of one of Mexico's more famous and romantic institutions, the Evangelistas.

The Evangelistas, and none including the members themselves appear to know the origin of the name, have their stalls along one side of Santo Domingo Plaza. From the time of the earliest recorded history, these artisans have sat at their desks and taken on all sorts of tasks, from writing love letters to composing stern notices of overdue bills. Before they got their rickety typewriters, which appear to be as old as Mexico itself, they wrote in fine florid hands, beginning with quills and graduating to steel points.

Year after year these sturdy scriveners ground out their romantic pleadings for suitors who were either illiterate or had no polished phrases at hand. The writers had varying fees: an I-wish-you-were-here type letter cost so much, and the costliest of all was a full-blown letter of love. This latter was expensive, but, excluding unusual complications, the results were virtually guaranteed—the girl or your money back. Progress, however, caught up with the Evangelistas. As illiteracy waned and telephones came in, the lovelorn found they could negotiate their own courting. The writers, who for generations, son succeeding father, had worked at their little desks in Santo Domingo, dwindled from more than one hundred to less than forty.

Eventually the writers changed over from writing love letters to typing themes for students of the medical school, which was across the Plaza until it was recently moved out to the National University. Some of the more ambitious Evangelistas learned to keep a simple set of books, and some even picked up enough rudimentary law to write collection letters

---

[9] Student demonstrations have continued to plague more recent administrations. Compounded of legitimate concern for politically sensitive issues and agitation for its own sake, the violent and bloody events of July and October 1968 (the latter at the Plaza of the Three Cultures) brought strikes and demonstrations in which protests against police brutality, violations of university autonomy, and the imprisonment of student leaders played a prominent role. The staging of the Olympics in October and the upcoming presidential election in 1970 were background elements not without significance. [Editor's Note]

and draw up simple contracts. The latter almost proved their undoing. Pressure was brought by the professional lawyers to have them evicted from the Plaza. They fought their case and finally won approval from the district Department of Markets, which solemnly pronounced that the Evangelistas "performed a singular and highly valuable social function."

*   *   *

In the capital they still talk with awe of "The night the angel fell." That was July 29, 1957, when one of Mexico's most damaging earthquakes in recent times split skyscrapers down the middle, crumpled apartment houses, and caused death and destruction throughout the valley. The capitalinos surveyed the ruins in the morning more or less philosophically. There had been earthquakes before and others would come. But their calm deserted them when they saw their beloved, great gilded Angel smashed to bits at the base of its 155-foot column.

The five-ton statue, called affectionately "El Angelito" or "The Little Angel," is more than a giant figure atop a column adorned with the figures of Mexico's revolts. It is an institution that draws peasants and aristocrats alike from all corners of the republic, and it is the point of reference for most directions given visitors. The Angel monument was planned in 1877 and finished in 1910,[10] and since then it has been as important a part of the Mexico City scene as is Popocatépetl volcano, the 17,887-foot snow-covered peak that stands guard over the valley. Had Popo crumbled it would have been no more of a shock than that the Angel had fallen. A cab driver speeding around the monument at the moment of the great fall said later he had heard a noise like two freight trains colliding, but he did not look around. "I knew it was not El Angelito," he said, "I knew the angel could not fall."

The Angel was redone and restored to its pedestal about a year and a half later. The sculptor commissioned to restore the statue, José María Fernández Urbina, had many woes. A rumor that the sculptor had employed an American girl as the model for the restored angel caused a near riot. The mere hint that a foreigner could have anything to do with the refashioning of the symbol of Mexico's freedom was greeted with amazement, anger, and horror. Further, it was demanded that the sculptor use as much of the original statue as could be found and put together. So with a new wing here and a new foot there and a great amount of ar-

[10] The Monument to the Independence was dedicated in connection with the showy celebration of the centennial anniversary of the Grito de Dolores staged by the dictatorship of Porfirio Díaz on the eve of its overthrow. [Editor's Note]

Protesting students fill the Zócalo in Mexico
City with pirated buses, August 23, 1958. In
the background is the National Cathedral.
(Wide World Photos)

Mexican president, Adolfo López Mateos, center, with U.S. Secretary of State Christian A. Herter and Mrs. Herter after the "grito" ceremony marking the 150th anniversary of Mexican independence, September 15, 1960. (Wide World Photos)

Manuel J. Tello was Mexico's ambassador in Washington (1953-1957), where Paul Kennedy became acquainted with him. Kennedy carried a letter from him when he went to Mexico in 1954. During the presidency of Adolfo López Mateos (1958-1964), Tello was foreign minister.

tistic patchwork Sr. Fernández Urbina finally got the angel back together, and the whole nation breathed easier.[11]

Mexico, the capital, is one of the first, if not the first city of the Western Hemisphere in monuments. There are more than six hundred scattered throughout the Federal District. Surprisingly there are none, so far as can be learned, to the conquistador, Hernán Cortés. Writers, however, who maintain there is not a single statue of the conqueror in all of Mexico are mistaken. There is quite a flattering one in nearby Cuernavaca.[12]

The monuments of the capital include colonial buildings which have been declared by the Office of Colonial Monuments to be of sufficient historical value to be preserved under state jurisdiction. There are 331 of these landmarks in the capital alone. One is a downtown hotel which had formerly been a convent. The hotel is considered one of the better addresses in the capital and certainly is one of its more picturesque hostelries. But the great difficulty is that every time so much as a toilet gets clogged, the state has to be advised to get a plumber, and the request passes through in-out baskets interminably until help arrives.

There are more than five hundred colonial landmarks throughout the central valley, the best known of which is probably the National Cathedral on the Zócalo. Most of the other colonial monuments are church properties which were confiscated under the anticlerical laws promulgated by the Plutarco Elías Calles administration.[13] One of the most notable of these is the Seminario de San Martín at Tepotzotlán about 27 miles northwest of the capital. The seminary was established in the latter

[11] Two of the presidential hopefuls for 1958 had "Angel" as one of their given names, and the Mexicans characteristically made political jokes about "the angel having fallen" to suggest the collapse of their political prospects. [Editor's Note]

[12] There also is a monument at Cortés Pass, between the two great snow-covered volcanoes through which the Spanish conqueror and his men entered the Valley of Mexico. On the monument is a representation of the head of a Spanish conquistador who could be Cortés. The periodically-recurring proposal to place a statue of Cortés in the *glorieta* or circle on the Paseo de la Reforma at the intersection of the main boulevard with Rhin and Sena always provokes a heated debate, and, to date, no action has been taken. The circle remains a monument-free patch of palm trees and other plantings. [Editor's Note]

[13] Plutarco Elías Calles, a member of the Sonora triumvirate which ousted Venustiano Carranza in 1920 in the last successful military overthrow of a Mexican regime, served as president from 1924 to 1928. Then, after the assassination of Obregón, he was the power behind a series of presidents from 1929 through 1934. It was during his presidential term that the provisions of the revolutionary constitution of 1917 regulating the Church were implemented in a systematic way for the first time. There followed the most serious conflicts between Church and State, including an economic boycott, a religious strike which closed churches to public worship for three years, and an armed rebellion. Finally, in 1929, through the good offices of United States Ambassador Dwight Morrow a *modus vivendi* was achieved. [Editor's Note]

part of the sixteenth century by the Jesuits. The present structure, considered an outstanding example of churrigueresque architecture, was constructed in the middle of the seventeenth century. It is presently a museum with a restaurant in the courtyard and an art gallery. The church section of the monastery is used for the production of Spanish classical dramas, an unusual theatrical experience. Mexican actors, performing in the Spanish tradition, need space, which the church transept amply provides.

Mexico's Federal District is a sprawling area almost totally surrounded by the State of Mexico. As noted, the population of the District in 1960 was 4,870,800, an increase of 59.6 per cent over the population in 1950. By 1963 the population was estimated to be 5,621,000, with an estimated growth of 182,000 annually. Around its perimeter, there is a further population of about 2,700,000; in other words, there is a population of 8,310,000 in an area of 814 square miles. Thus 1 per cent of the total area of Mexico contains more than 21 per cent of the total population.

In the 1964 budget the Federal District received the equivalent of $128,000,000. In that year President López Mateos, presenting the District's record budget, explained it was $10,000,000 more than had been apportioned the District in 1963 but that the growth of the area, with attendant necessities, such as drainage, paving, and additional illumination, accounted for the increase. Of the total amount $15,120,000 was earmarked for an expansion of the District's water system. As with most burgeoning areas throughout the world, the water problem is the Federal District's knottiest at the moment. The capital, which takes preference presently, as in centuries past, over all other areas of the nation, has used water from virtually every source immediately available. There is even a plan under consideration, following the Australians, to dam up the waters from the millions of tons of melting snow on the two volcanoes Popocatépetl and Ixtaccihuatl.

In any case, the Federal District and the surrounding area are being bedevilled by the demographic problems of nearly all highly populated areas of the world. Mexico is in transition from a rural to an urban nation. This came about gradually at first and without any great dislocation, but since 1940 the rhythm has become so accelerated as to become almost unmanageable.

The rural population is being attracted to urban areas all over the nation, but the trend is epitomized by what is happening in the Federal District. Population Reference Bureau, Inc., in one of its reports, remarked, "The Federal District is to Mexicans as a flame is to the moths. It is the commercial, financial, industrial, political, and cultural center of all the nation. More and more people want to live there." Simply put, the land is

hard and the return for a day's work in the country is miniscule compared with that in the city. A maid, and this has happened more than
once in our own household, who can be assured of acceptable and steady
employment finds it feasible to send to her *tierra* and bring to the District
her sister, brother, and in some instances, both parents.

The Federal District claims as its metropolitan area six political "delegations," most of them in the State of Mexico. The area, with less than 1
per cent of the national land mass, accounts for an extraordinary proportion of the gross national product. In 1964 it had nearly 40,000 industrial units accounting for the dollar equivalent of $171,160,000 in ex-
ports. Incidentally, it invariably comes as a surprise to learn that in 1964
there were nearly 50,000 acres of farmland in the Federal District. This
land is rapidly being utilized for residential units, usually apartment
buildings.

The District, as has been noted, is the center of the nation's religious
activities, and it has been so for hundreds of years, since long before the
Spaniards came. There are 125 national and regional religious fiestas
held in the republic each year. A dedicated observer of the Mexican
scene, by the way, may derive some satisfaction from knowing that with
clever planning and good communications he could attend, in one part or
another of the republic, year in and year out, one great fiesta nearly
every other day, with an odd day here and there for recuperation and for
the long jumps. In a lifetime, however, he would probably not attend another like the annual Passion Play of Ixtapalapa, just outside the capital.
It was one of my most amazing and controversial assignments in Latin
America.

Each Good Friday some 25,000 invade the dusty, winding streets of
the ancient Aztec village of Ixtapalapa for one of the most extraordinary
depictions of the trial and crucifixion of Christ seen in the entire Western
Hemisphere, and perhaps in the world. In addition to being a bizarre and
truly remarkable performance, it annually creates a storm of debate. On
the hot afternoon I attended, I was accompanied by a woman correspondent who was alternately scandalized and frightened half out of her
wits.

The origin of the Ixtapalapa play is obscure, but it apparently had its
beginning shortly after the Spanish Conquest in the early sixteenth century. Before the Conquest the village of Ixtapalapa was the seat of one of
the most important religious observances in the Aztec empire. At the end
of each fifty-two-year period in the Aztec calendar, the ceremony of the
New Fire was observed on Cerro de la Estrella ("Hill of the Star") at the
edge of the village. All fires and lights were extinguished throughout the
Valley of Mexico. The days leading up to the festival were desolate ones,

with furniture in each house destroyed, garments torn to shreds, and the holy fires in the temples allowed to expire.

This is the way Prescott described the ceremony in his *Conquest of Mexico:* "On the evening of the last day a procession of priests, assuming the dress and ornaments of their gods, moved from the capital towards a lofty mountain about two leagues distant. They carried with them a noble victim, the flower of their captives, and an apparatus for kindling the new fire, the success of which was an augury of the renewal of the cycle.

"On reaching the summit of the mountain, the procession paused till midnight; when, as the constellation of the Pleiades approached the zenith the new fire was kindled by the friction of the sticks placed on the wounded breast of the victim. The flame was soon communicated to a funeral pile, on which the body of the slaughtered captive was thrown. As the light streamed up towards heaven, shouts of joy and triumph burst forth from the countless multitudes who covered the hills, the terraces of the temples, and the house-tops, with eyes anxiously bent on the mount of sacrifice. Couriers, with torches lighted at the blazing beacon, rapidly bore them over every part of the country; and the cheering element was seen brightening on altar and hearthstone, for the circuit of many a league, long before the Sun, rising on his accustomed track, gave assurance that a new cycle had commenced its march, and that the laws of nature were not to be reversed for the Aztecs."

The current theory is that the Passion Play was introduced by the missionaries to draw the Aztecs further away from their pagan ceremonies. There is a solid basis for this theory. The procedure introduced by Cortés was to tear down as expeditiously as possible the Aztec temples and altars and, as was noted, to erect Christian places of worship on the ruins as a symbol of Christian ascendancy. The ancient religious practices were not obliterated in their totality, but, where possible, modified substitutions were introduced. Sometimes the pagan practices were adapted so successfully to the Roman Catholic ritual that they are still being followed, as among the Mayas in mountainous areas of Guatemala.

Only in recent years has the Ixtapalapa ceremony attracted national attention and that appears to have been largely due to the furor it has been causing. The growing criticism of the play was based on protests that year by year it had been becoming more of a grotesque carnival, and totally irreverent, if not actually blasphemous.

The year we attended, something new had been added, a public address system. At the trial, held in front of one of the nation's most interesting colonial churches, a professional commentator filled in between the dialogue of the participants. The commentator had, in fact, assumed an important role in the whole proceeding. Along the route toward the hill and the crucifixion the commentator described on the public address system the events as they occurred. At the appointed places where the actor depicting the Cristus falls, the microphone was lowered to the fallen man for a person-to-person interview in which the Cristus gave a detailed and generally lurid description of the ordeal he was undergoing. And it was literally an ordeal because he was carrying a heavy cross barefoot over cobbled and jagged rock streets.

The physical discomforts do not end there for the star of the crucifixion play. For some reason never clearly explained, spectators try to break through the guards each time the Cristus falls, not to assist him, but to beat him. The actors portraying the Roman soldiers are more occupied with protecting the Cristus than with persecuting him. Often they are overpowered by the mob, and the Cristus can depend on receiving some blows before the crowd has been driven back and order restored.

Much of the confusion and, in the case of my feminine colleague, most of the fright are caused by the mounted centurians. These curiously costumed participants are dressed from the waist up in tin armor, and in cowboy levis and boots on the lower half. On the occasion of our visit they charged helter-skelter through the crowds with no other visible assignment than to send the spectators fleeing in terror. One year, or at least so the story goes, one of these mounted guards ran down the woman portraying the Virgin Mary and her role was eliminated from the play that day.

The crucifixion of the Cristus and the two thieves takes place on the Cerro de la Estrella. By the time the Cristus, after his agonizing journey, reaches the crown of the hill, he and the two thieves are bound to their crosses by leather thongs, with the commentator describing the proceedings in detail over the many loudspeakers placed on the hill. By then the Cerro is filled on all sides with spectators.

The year we were there, just before the crosses were placed upright, the Cristus was asked if there was anything he wanted to say as his last words. He adjured the audience against their sinful ways and finally, as the very last words, half-whispered "Do not forget us, boys." This last was in reference to another occasion, when as a result of the general confusion, the three who were scheduled to be taken down at sunset had been forgotten and were left suspended into the night.

All in all it was quite an afternoon. To add to the excitement, I had my first experience with *pulque*. Intermingled with the hard-riding centurians and hot-and-tired guards were the mounted pulque vendors who jogged around in the crowds with earthenware containers of the fermented juice balanced in front of them. Wherever they stopped, thirsty spectators clustered around while small clay cups were passed out at a few pennies each. The woman correspondent, who by this time was considerably shaken and in need of a drink, pressed forward with me. As is usual in such instances, we were passed along, in polite deference, a pint each. Members of the throng insisted on paying for the "gringos."

A word here about pulque. This is a white, sweetish fermented substance with an alcoholic content about that of 3.2 beer. Enough of it— and an accomplished pulque-drinker can handily knock enough back— will produce impressive results and equally impressive hangovers. Our first experience with the stuff did not, however, recommend it as a thrist-quencher on a hot and dusty afternoon. The history of pulque goes back many centuries, some maintain at least eight hundred years, placing it in the time of the Toltecs. Certainly it was one of the prized drinks on the tables of the Aztec nobles in the time of the Montezumas. It is produced from the maguey plant, a member of the century plant family, the cultivation of which is confined largely to the central plateau. The state of Hidalgo, just northeast of the capital, accounts for one-third of the national production of about 750,000 quarts daily. According to government statistics for 1961, the consumption of pulque in the Federal District alone for that year was 200,000,000 quarts, or a little over four quarts for each man, woman and child. Beer was a close second with 184,000,000 quarts, and milk a poor third with 64,000,000 quarts.

It is considered quite likely that sometime in the third quarter of the present century beer will move into first place as the national drink. Its rapid rise in national consumption is attributed to two important factors: the rise, as imperceptible as it may seem, in the laboring class income; and the traditionally excellent beer produced in Mexico, which sells for about one-fifth the price of beer in the United States.

The raw juice of what eventually becomes pulque is gathered from the maguey plant by coring it and withdrawing the white, sweetish liquid called *aguamiel* or "honey water."

The plants, ranging from 96 to 112 per acre, produce a harvestable crop in from eight to twelve years depending on their care and fertilization. The plants die after coring, but not before dropping shoots which take their places and produce after so many years. Rising production costs, a growing appetite for beer, and other factors appear to be spelling the doom of pulque as the great national drink. Hidalgo state, where there were 22,000,000 plants in 1934, reported only 8,000,000 plants in 1960. The maguey plantations, which give the hills of Mexico their most distinctive and fascinating character and are so dear to the landscape artists and Christmas card designers, are shrivelling away.

The Politics

Politically, Mexico represents one of the great modern anomalies: certain freedoms, with certain restrictions; encouragement of civic responsibility, with discouragement of the exercise of freedom of choice; overwhelming centralism in government, with determined regional overlordism, or *caciquismo*.

The *cacique* system, later more popularly known as *caudillismo,* is as old as Mexican recorded history. It goes back at least to the Aztecs of the early fourteenth century and quite possibly to the Toltecs in the midseventh century. Only in comparatively recent times has Mexico's political maturity reached a point where the country has been able to come to grips with the system, and this only in scattered areas.

In the years of turbulence in the early part of the present century, from, say, 1910 to 1917, or even in some cases much later, a strong man with enough gunmen or *pistoleros* at his command could force the fealty of anything from a village to a state. No forces of the federal government in those days were strong enough militarily or politically, or, better said, no forces had enough determination to come to grips with the well-entrenched *cacique*. In the 1930's Saturnino Cedillo, a barely literate revolutionary adventurer, held the entire state of San Luis Potosí. He was eventually brought down by the determined caciquismo-fighter President Lázaro Cárdenas, but caciquismo still remains a viable parasite on the body politic.[14]

It is difficult to determine the bedrock of Mexico's political system. It would not have been in the caves of Puebla, where the hunters lived out their backbreaking lives and ate maize or corn some five thousand years

[14] The unsuccessful Cedillo rebellion in 1938 was the last armed regional rebellion against the Mexican government. It was not without overtones of rightist and clerical opposition, petroleum politics, and the 1940 presidential election. [Editor's Note]

before Christ. A gleam of it could possibly have been found in the Aztec empire shortly before the Spanish Conquest. A stronger trace showed in the groupings of the liberal and conservative factions in the early nineteenth century. The warrior Indians and the maize-cultivating Indians had a hand in it, as did the Spaniards in their way, and the commercializing Creoles. It would be difficult to evaluate the amount contributed at each level to the Mexican political system as it has presently evolved.

Whatever the isolated contributions from the various levels, Mexico's political system as we now know it grew from the Mexican Revolution of 1910. The causes and effects of the cacique system, with roots as far back as the Montezumas, were significant factors in the evolution of the system. The enormous pressures of the *campesinos,* or landless peasants,[15] to gain back land which had been taken from them from the colonial period on was another significant factor, as were the festering sores which contributed to the final split between the Church and the State.

Mexico, a diverse and divided country, had to have, in the rambunctious beginnings of the twentieth century, a highly specialized political system or perish, as, in fact, it very nearly did on occasion. Over a long period, the system evolved into what it presently is, creakingly old before its time, dangerously balanced between interests which would not blink an eye at its destruction. It is one of the seven political wonders of the world, but despite the habitual pessimism of its detractors, it has a habit of being workable. Robert E. Scott, in his valuable work *Mexican Government in Transition* (University of Iilinois Press, 1964), says: "the country has fulfilled the most basic of all requirements for a western political system—a single system based on the needs, necessities, values, and desires of a nation—in short, a workable and working system that includes the entire country."

The genesis of the administration's all-pervasive Institutional Revolutionary Party (PRI) was the inspired announcement by President Plutarco Elías Calles in September 1928 of the creation of a single revolutionary party. A party was established in March 1929 in Querétaro under the name of the National Revolutionary Party (PNR). This party was dissolved in December 1937 by President Cárdenas and was followed by a corporate-structure organization known as the Mexican Revolutionary Party (PRM), which comprised three basic sectors: popular,

---

[15] *Campesino* is a general term used to identify rural folk, and only when usage is differentiating between the landless, on the one hand, and *ejidatarios* (shareholders in the communally owned *ejidos* or the large collective commercial *ejidos)* and *rancheros* (owners of the small, individual *ranchos),* on the other hand, may the term be equated with landless peasant. [Editor's Note]

agrarian, and labor.[16] This party in turn was succeeded by the present PRI, retaining the same structural components.

The PRI, as the administration party is known, reaches into the nooks and crannies of the nation as thoroughly and as effectively as the old Tammany machine of New York, the big difference being that the PRI is demonstrating greater overall efficiency and staying power. There is another difference, perhaps the most basic one. The PRI as it presently stands provides a continuity of participation by a majority of the more significant social and economic interests, and this is true to a greater or lesser degree throughout most of the country.

All in all the party has withstood some major and at times apparently unanswerable challenges to its authority. There was the case in point of San Luis Potosí, the capital of the state by that name. Two days after Adolfo López Mateos was inaugurated president on December 1, 1958, troops were brought into San Luis to preserve order in the face of a state-wide strike called against the last of the great caciques, Colonel Gonzalo Natividad Santos. For eighteen years Colonel Santos, a gunman in his own right surrounded by *pistoleros* who had been brought into his orbit, had dictated the municipal and state politics of San Luis Potosí. He elected the state legislators, appointed the national legislators, and put into power the highest to the lowest appointive officials in the state.

In a dispatch of October 23, 1958, I noted in respect to Colonel Santos, "The political chieftain has been a source of embarrassment to the present administration and will quite likely remain so for the incoming administration of president-elect Adolfo López Mateos this coming December. Because of his power over the state political machinery, he is one of the most influential members of the administration's Institutional Revolutionary Party."

In that same dispatch it was noted that Colonel Santos was one of the three remaining great caciques in Mexico. The other two were Leobardo Reynosa of the adjoining state of Zacatecas and Margarito Ramírez of the territory of Quintana Roo on the Yucatán peninsula. All three soon disappeared from the political scene.

The strike of December 1958 actually was triggered by the inauguration of President López Mateos. Whether it was intended to test his strength before he was well settled in office or to challenge his authority outright is debatable. The immediate objective of the strike was to re-

---

[16] The PRM, as first organized, was composed of four sectors, those listed in the text and the military. The latter sector was dropped in December 1940 since both civilian critics and the military themselves were not happy about the overt identification with direct political action. [Editor's Note]

move from office the Santos-appointed governor, Manuel Álvarez, who had gone into hiding in Mexico City. Through Santos, Álvarez asked for the intervention of the Interior Ministry. The newly-installed Secretary of the Interior Gustavo Díaz Ordaz, who six years later became president, held several extended conferences in his office in Mexico City with leaders of the strike who remained adamant that Álvarez must go. It was Díaz Ordaz who ordered the troops to go to San Luis Potosí.

The strike and its implications were so serious I immediately set out for San Luis, only to be stopped at León in the adjoining state of Guanajuato. My plane would not proceed further, and I could not even hire a cab or hitchhike a ride that night. The story filed from León that night noted: "The strike activity has been joined by students, organized labor, and businessmen of the state. It began last week, at which time the citizens of the capital and of other cities in the state were asked not to pay city or state taxes. As a consequence, it is reported here that some of the city and state employees were not paid last week."

While all this was going on, there was deep concern throughout the whole of Mexico and particularly in the national capital because, firstly, it involved what was known to be the desperate stand of one of the last of the great caciques; secondly, it involved a challenge to the all-powerful political party and to the new administration, and finally, it was realized that if Santos could be overthrown the other state dictators would topple. That is what actually happened. The situation was given relatively little attention in the United States and my paper was only mildly interested.

On December 5, I got into San Luis. I filed that day a story stating, "Twenty-three truckloads of federal troops from the Twentieth Infantry Batallion in Mexico City arrived here last night. Immediately afterward a huge demonstration in Plaza de las Armas, the city's principal square, was broken up. Several leaders of the Potosina Civic Union, which is directing the strike, were arrested."

The state capital was virtually paralyzed, with business houses, schools, factories, and even gasoline stations closed. The railway shops in the vital railway junction for north-south freight traffic closed down, as did a part of the telephone system. More troops eventually were brought in. Local police fired into demonstrating crowds and one fatality and several casualties resulted. The federal troops used gun butts and truncheons but did not fire.

On December 15, I filed a story from Mexico City pointing out that San Luis Potosí, the capital of that state, was essentially a "dead city." There appeared at that time, as mentioned in the dispatch, "little likelihood that even a reasonable percentage" of the demands of the state insurrectionists would be achieved. In that I proved to be unduly pessimistic. The state governor was eventually removed from power and finally Colonel Santos himself was.

Álvarez, under pressure, asked for and received permission to resign. Santos was given a face-saving job as federal fisheries supervisor, a strange sop for a mountain man in an interior mining state. For a vigorous personality who had been virtual king in his domain, this proved to be too tame, and he went into private life immensely wealthy.

In the decade from 1954 to 1964 the Institutional Revolutionary Party witnessed a series of self-imposed reforms. But the observer who was beguiled into thinking that the party in those years was prepared to ease the final hold on municipal, state, and national machines would have been badly mistaken.[17]

Time and again the political student, for his own orientation, must return to the basic concept that while the administration party constitutes a corporate entity it does not now have, nor has it ever had, the power of ultimate decision. The final power in Mexico is reserved to the presidency. The president could, if he felt so inclined and found time enough, put his stamp of approval on the shortest bridge of the most backward farm-to-market road. And yet his course of action continually is circumscribed by the party, the self-same party which has given him complete domination. Little wonder then that correspondents assigned to Mexico after experience in all areas of the world confess complete confusion as they delve deeper into the Mexican system. It does not fit any known pattern, but, as has been noted, it works. Up to the present at least.

One of the wonders of Mexican politics is the presidential campaign. It is still evolving, and indeed changed considerably in the two campaigns we covered. Basically, however, the official candidate, that is the nominee of PRI, devotes his campaign speeches to a great extent to regional affairs, rarely mentioning the opposition. The speeches are, in fact, only a

---

[17] During the 1968 gubernatorial and municipal elections, the PRI, under its new president, Licenciado Alfonso Martínez Domínguez, who had been an outstanding legislative leader, tried to stress the policy of democracy from the "periphery" rather than from national party headquarters in Mexico City. However, this policy to allow more local decision-making in the selection and election of individuals to local governmental positions seems to have been more apparent than real and its implementation was complicated by a real challenge to PRI domination on the local level. Two state capitals, Mérida in Yucatán and Hermosillo in Sonora, elected opposition candidates. Although the president permitted the election results to stand in Yucatán, they were annulled in Sonora on the grounds of procedural irregularities. When it was announced in early January 1969 that the opposition National Action Party (PAN) mayoralty candidate had triumphed in Uruapan, the second largest city in Michoacán, it represented the nineteenth municipal government won by the PAN in a two-year period. [Editor's Note]

minor part of the campaign. The candidate spends at least three-quarters and probably eight-tenths of his time in the hustings listening to complaints and ascertaining the economic and political difficulties of the area. He knows, as does everyone else, that he is the future president learning his job.

The opposition conducts an old-fashioned grassroots campaign and takes far greater risks of personal danger to their candidates. In both the campaigns we covered the opposition was the National Action Party. Their campaign speeches, in contrast to those of the administration party, are fire-and-brimstone denunciations of the PRI and of the ineptitude of its local leaders. Last but not least, they invariably dwell on the dishonesty and the stupidity of the governor of whichever state they happen to be speaking in. The governors, of course, are invariably of the PRI. The national government time after time warns that the opposition speakers are to be treated with respect, which is all well and good for the people sitting at ease in Mexico City. But the local dignitaries, hearing themselves lambasted unmercifully, cannot muster the same detachment. The opposition candidates share none of the responsibility of the administration candidates, and they pull no punches. Their attitude is often, "what can you lose if you have already lost!" Their speeches become so vituperative at times that the PRI sympathizers attending the opposition meetings, for the most part to heckle, eventually become so overwrought that mob actions ensue, and sometimes fatalities. A government official in Mexico City said proudly after the last election, "What an election! We didn't have one killing, and that is better than you can say of the United States!"

On one occasion we were traveling with the opposition presidential candidate and his party in an automobile caravan through the state of Veracruz. In a fair-sized city the speakers, including the candidate himself, were more devastating than ever in their attack on the state government, and it soon became clear there was going to be difficulty. Sporadic fistfights were breaking out at various places in the crowd. Eventually one of the candidate's men found me in the crowd. He led me away with the explanation that they had learned PRI adherents were planning to intercept the candidate's caravan as it left the city.

The opposition strategy was for the main section of the caravan to leave in one direction and the candidate, his wife, the campaign manager, and myself to sneak out in another. We were guided out of the city and onto the highway far out of the city limits by a local guide. Later we found the main caravan, which had been stopped and searched. It was allowed to proceed when it was learned the candidate was not present. There was no indication of what might have happened had the candidate been there, but some weeks later he was arrested on a charge of inciting to violence and was held until the government in Mexico City ordered his release.

This particular candidate, Luis H. Álvarez, was thirty-eight years old, a member of an industrialist family in Chihuahua. He was a quiet, mild-mannered person, but he waged one of the most aggressive and violent campaigns the country had seen since the system of one predominant party had been introduced. From early December 1957 up to election time in July 1958 he addressed 520 political gatherings in all parts of Mexico. Aside from having been jailed, he and his entourage, including his wife, were held at gunpoint, and on another occasion the entire state committee of the opposition was held in jail during the candidate's visit. At that time I sent an article noting, "These incidents are being received with great enthusiasm by the candidate and the fiery young orators in his entourage. They heap upon the local authorities, all of whom were installed through the administration party, a type of invective not approached even in the most violent campaign speeches in the United States."

All of this is mentioned at some length to underline a point: while the political system in Mexico is propelled by a monolithic device there is room left around the edges for some opposition, as ineffectual as it may be. Which calls to mind a news conference with General Alfonso Corona del Rosal prior to the 1964 campaign. The general, a witty, genial personality, was then president of the Central Committee of PRI, the highest job in the party and probably next to that of the presidency in power. At the news conference the committee president was asked what he considered to be the greatest problem facing his party in the coming campaign. He answered with a grin, "Finding an opposition candidate."

But returning to the 1958 campaign, it ended on a note of bitterness when a twenty-seven-year-old National Action Party worker of Chihuahua died of gunshot wounds received while helping decorate the city for the candidate's arrival. Under the direction of the then president Adolfo Ruiz Cortines, a special investigator was sent to investigate. At that time I wrote, "Since Sunday the political air has been charged with increasing bitterness. There have been mass demonstrations here in Mexico City asking for prompt government action in the killing. An official of the National Action Party declared 'We do not wish violence but it does not frighten us.' The party headquarters in the downtown business district has been draped with a banner declaring 'Mexico will not vote for a party of assassins.' "

The PRI candidate, Adolfo López Mateos, who the next month was elected president of Mexico, was asked by his closest advisors to cancel his public appearances until after the election. He declined to do that, but he did make a compromise by agreeing to stop driving his own car.

In September of 1958 I dispatched a weekend story beginning, "This capital has regained most of its normal calm, but it is still breathing heavily from violent demonstrations of the past week. A series of student riots interspersed with acts of violence by dissident factions in the Petroleum Workers Union brought out riot squads, firemen, and federal troops to quell the disorders."

These eruptions had nothing to do with the campaign or its aftermath. Violent demonstrations of one kind or another continued to the end of the year and it was explained the primary reason was that the country was at that moment in what might have been termed an interregnum period. The incumbent president Adolfo Ruiz Cortines was approaching the end of his term and Adolfo López Mateos was preparing to take over the presidency in December. The interim period is traditionally one of political and social dislocation.

Actually from the time the party has named its new candidate, usually a year or more before he takes office, the incumbent president increasingly loses his power and prestige. That takes a bit of explaining. The party is broken down into three basic sectors: agrarian, popular, and labor. The popular sector consists of members of the party not belonging to either of the other two sectors; it is something of a catchall. The agrarian sector is represented by the National Peasant Confederation (CNC) and the labor sector by the Mexican Labor Confederation (CTM).[18] Each of these divisions expresses itself through its leaders on the choice of president, governors, legislators, and down the line, eventually even to village chiefs. Their points of view are given serious consideration, particularly as regards the president-elect. The incumbent president assumes the responsibility of pulling together the divergent views of the three sectors of the party. Further, he confers with the more powerful of the ex-presidents.

This task of bringing together the various views and of finally making a decision is far and away the greatest responsibility and the greatest exercise of power the president assumes in the six years of his administration. And when all the opinions are in, sorted and balanced one against the other, they are thrown into the hopper and out of it will come the president's own choice, the final choice, of the man to succeed him. Obviously it is not quite that simple but this amounts to the general outline.

[18] The CTM (Confederación de Trabajadores de México) still dominates, despite some recent challenges, the Mexican labor scene, overshadowing its half dozen smaller rivals. The CTM is the "official representative" of organized labor within the PRI. The FSTSE (Federation of Government Workers) is the second largest grouping of organized labor and is the key element in the party's popular sector. The CNC (National Peasant Confederation) and the UFCM (Union of Peasants Federations of Mexico) similarly represent agrarian interests in the party. [Editor's Note]

A dispatch sent *The New York Times* November 4, 1963 said: "Gustavo Díaz Ordaz, Minister of the Interior and chief officer of the López Mateos cabinet, will be the presidential nominee of the administration's Institutional Revolutionary Party and the next president of Mexico, it appeared virtually certain today. The labor sector of the party declared itself in favor of the Díaz Ordaz nomination last night. It is expected the agrarian and popular sectors will declare for him within the next twelve hours. When any one of the three sectors comprising the party declares in favor, it is a certain indication the other two sectors are in agreement. (Actually it is agreed among the three groups which one will have the honor of declaring first.) The party is so dominant in political affairs from the lowest precinct worker to the highest office that nomination as its candidate signifies certain election. The formal nomination will not take place until the party holds its convention, probably ten days from now. The Central Committee of the Party went into conference this afternoon to decide the exact date. The convention, however, will merely confirm the accomplished fact."

The system up to this point has one quite serious flaw: From the time it becomes evident the incumbent president is gathering information preparatory to making up his mind, the period of *futurismo* sets in and the wheels of the government begin slowing down. Regularly, every six years, government officials sternly warn the remainder of the country to avoid *futurismo* like sin, and just as regularly the selfsame officials desperately begin a *futurismo* program of their own. The *futurismo* system is simply the jockeying for position along the paths the president must take in coming to his final decision.

Futurismo has its own elaborate code. A candidate, for example, who shows too blatantly his eagerness to be selected becomes *quemado,* or "burned out." If he, and the "he" in this instance is almost invariably a cabinet minister, begins making too many speeches throughout the country, appears late at a bullfight and commands attention with his entrance, or issues too many profound declarations concerning his friendship with and professional attachments to the incumbent president, then indeed he is a "futurist" and is, in fact, well on the way to quemado-land.

The person on whom the president eventually places his mantle of approval is known as the *tapado* or the "hooded" or "veiled one." Who he is, is not known for certain until the late autumn or early winter of the year before the elections. He is usually known, as in the case of President Díaz Ordaz, some days before the PRI convention. In any case, the tapado system has the same basic flaw as futurismo in that it is reflected in the life of the nation, economically as well as politically. Industrial programs are held in abeyance in much the same manner as they are in the United States or any other country in which there is doubt over the coloration and texture of the incoming administration. Foreign investments, in the case of Mexico an extremely important factor in the national economy just now, dry up to virtually nothing. Among the thousands of rumors, invariably there is one that a minister known to favor strong federal control will be picked for a key portfolio by the candidate, who is still more than a year away from the presidency. Money for private initiative balks. Another rumor invariably begins the rounds that a committed radical leftist is to be selected for an important cabinet post. Man the lifeboats and bring along the petty cash drawer!

For these and other reasons the tapado system has been coming under increasing attack in recent years, but with little result. In a talk in New York in 1963 I noted, "It may be only a notion on my part, but it seems there is a stronger than usual resistance building this year to the present system of choosing the candidate. There appears a growing awareness that the selection will be of such vital importance for the future of the country that the responsibility is too grave for the few who still make the primary decision and the one who will make the final choice." That observation appears to be as valid now as it was then.

The campaign, in the case of the newly-announced PRI candidate, begins a few weeks after his nomination and continues until the Christmas holidays, when all activities stop. After the holidays the campaign is resumed and continues until about a week before the elections in July. As was observed before, the campaign is merely a *pro forma* affair for the official candidate, that is so far as the election itself is concerned. He is a certain winner, and the candidates in the districts in which he is speaking are equally certain of being elected. The presidential candidate's campaign is nevertheless a highly intensive one, combining the usual radio and television appearances with exhaustive travels throughout the republic. And this is not just window dressing. It has a real purpose.

Primarily, it gives the population an opportunity to see at first hand the man who is going to control their destinies to a great extent for the coming six years. But more importantly it gives the candidate himself an opportunity to see his people in the aggregate, an opportunity he has never had before, no matter what his past experience has been. His campaign speeches, as many as five a day, are the least demanding part of his program. In the evening and into all hours of the night, he receives delegations of local agrarian and labor political leaders in order to learn about local conditions, the shortcomings of the local government, and the relative weaknesses of the party machine. He usually keeps a couple of secretaries busy taking notes to be transcribed and studied at his leisure.

President Díaz Ordaz was one of the more arduous and interesting of the campaigners. A slender, wiry person, he took the rigors of the campaign in stride and with an unexpected sense of humor for one so utterly serious. There were endless jokes about his appearance—one of them that he looked like the motion picture comedian Jerry Lewis made up as a Chinese detective. He himself capitalized on his features while campaigning, telling the crowds on occasion, "You can tell immediately I am not two-faced, because if I were I certainly wouldn't be wearing this one!"

The PRI is broadly enough based ideologically to cover the entire spectrum, with the exception of a large part of the right and the relatively narrow segment of the extreme left. The right can be more or less accounted for in the National Action Party and the National Sinarquista Union, a falange-type organization created during World War II.[19] The extreme left can be accounted for in the three Kremlin-accredited parties and the National Liberation Movement created with the sponsorship of former president Lázaro Cárdenas.

Of the three Kremlin-accepted parties only two were in undisputed favor with the radical left as this was written. These were the Mexican Communist Party, whose head, Dionisio Encina Rodríguez, was jailed in 1960 and sentenced to fourteen years' imprisonment under the highly controversial "Social Dissolution" Law, and the Mexican Workers and Peasants Party, whose chief, Valentín Campa, was arrested a few months after Encina and also sentenced to fourteen years on the same "social dissolution" charge.[20] The third, the Popular Socialist Party (PPS), is the

[19] The Sinarquista movement had its beginnings in the 1930's. During World War II its activities were a source of governmental preoccupation. In 1949 a segment of the movement which had organized as a political party was denied ballot status under the provisions of the electoral law. [Editor's Note]

[20] As indicated, during World War II the Sinarquistas became a source of concern for the Mexican government, which took action to preserve internal security against the activities of Axis sympathizers. President Ávila Comacho in 1941 issued a decree modifying Article 145 of the Penal Code making it a criminal offense for a foreigner or a national to speak, write, or act in any way which spread ideas, programs, or methods of action to disturb the public order. Disturbance of the public order or sovereignty of Mexico was defined as an act to produce rebellion, sedition, or riot, placing the territorial integrity of Mexico in danger, or preventing the functioning of the legitimate institutions. In 1950 President Miguel Alemán reformed Article 145, now entitled "Penalties and Types of Crimes of Social Dissolution." The article, widely known as the "Law of Social Dissolution," doubled the maximum penalties and broadened the definition of public disturbance to include acts of sabotage, provocation, and subversion of institutions. Presidents Alemán and López Mateos both applied this law against leftist agitators. The administration of Díaz Ordaz avoided applying this Article in the judicial proceedings against the student demonstrators of 1968, probably because the Article has been the object of serious criticism, including challenges to its constitutionality. In July 1970, on the recommendation of the Permanent Commission of the Congress, President Díaz Ordaz called for a special session of the Chamber of Deputies to abolish Article 145 and to draft a new article defining "Crimes against the Security of the Nation." [Editor's Note]

only relatively strong and cohesive organization of the three. Yet it fell into disfavor with the radical left when it endorsed the candidacy of the PRI presidential nominee Gustavo Díaz Ordaz in 1963. Since one of the basic rules of the extreme left is to be in opposition to the PRI as a "hopelessly bourgeois" creation, the PPS and its leader, Vicente Lombardo Toledano, were virtually read out of the radical sector.[21] Lombardo Toledano, however, makes periodic pilgrimages to Moscow and Peking, and the party's director of campesino activities, Jacinto López, never gave up radical agitation in the rural areas despite having been given a seat in the national legislature under an arrangement created by the PRI.[22] A severe blow was dealt the Popular Socialist Party in 1961 when its mouthpiece, the morning paper *El Popular,* was discontinued in bankruptcy proceedings. In a front-page editorial published on the final day, it was explained that the paper was being forced to discontinue because it was no longer receiving what amounted to government-subsidy in the form of advertising by the state-directed national lottery.

The National Liberation Movement (MLN) is not a political party as such but rather, as the name implies, a political concept. It was created as a result of the pro-communist Western Hemisphere Peace Conference held in Mexico City in the winter of 1961 under the co-sponsorship of Lázaro Cárdenas of Mexico, Alberto Casella of Argentina, and Domingos Vallasco of Brazil. Out of the MLN came the extreme left campesino organization, Campesina Central Independiente (CCI) and a further offshoot, the Frente Electoral Popular, an extreme left splinter group which ran a write-in candidate for president in the 1964 elections.

This write-in candidate, Ramón Danzos Palomino, was expelled from the CCI in 1964, along with ten others of the twenty-two-member board of directors. The expelled directors led a large sector of the CCI away and established the rival Frente Electoral Popular, which, in turn, ex-

---

[21] Vicente Lombardo Toledano was the key figure in the Mexican labor movement during the Cárdenas period. As the Revolution moved to the center and the right, his political influence declined. A key figure in the leftist, hemisphere-wide Confederation of Latin American Workers (CTAL), he was the prime mover of the PPS. Lombardo's death in November 1968 dealt a severe blow to the "pepistas" of the Popular Socialist Party. With his passing, the ideological orientation, and even the survival, of the party is in doubt. [Editor's Note]

[22] By 1968 Jacinto López had aroused so much criticism within the Popular Socialist Party because of his extremist views, as voiced through his Unión General de Obreros y Campesinos de México (General Union of Workers and Peasants of Mexico), that he was expelled from the party's national direction in February of that year. Subsequently, he organized a new political party, the Mexican Labor-Agrarian Party. The Marxist agrarian leader's following is estimated at less than 5,000, a figure far below the 75,000 registered members required to qualify nationally as a political party. [Editor's Note]

pelled the other half of the directors of the original board. Frantic attempts by the radical left organizations throughout Mexico to bring about a reconciliation failed. In the ensuing confusion Danzos Palomino led a series of communist-supported demonstrations in the city of Puebla in October 1964, as a result of which several demonstrating University of Puebla students were wounded by police gunfire. Danzos Palomino and several other demonstration leaders were arrested.[23]

The entire CCI episode represented one of the major fiascos of the Mexican radical left in recent years and quite naturally was a source of some jubilation for the rightist groups. The CCI, ostensibly created to take up the slack of the National Peasant Confederation, soon revealed itself to be an organizing and agitating body. It was pinpointed early in its history by Vicente Lombardo Toledano as a "divisive force" in the leftist peasant movement. It did join in some demonstrations in the northern states with the General Union of Workers and Peasants of Mexico, the peasant branch of Lombardo Toledano's Popular Socialist Party, but it was never accepted by the party leader himself.

Soon after the CCI's creation, former president Cárdenas said he had no more than an academic interest in the organization. It evolved, however, out of the National Liberation Movement, with Sr. Cárdenas' assistance. The former president sat on the platform at the organizing meeting of the CCI as did his son Cuauhtémoc, the latter being listed as one of the directors. The former president defended his attendance at the organizing meeting. He issued a statement through the leftist daily paper *El Día* in January 1963 terming the charges of his connection with the organization "fallacious and articulate calumnies." Emilio Portes Gil, another former president of Mexico, joined the polemics by charging General Cárdenas with being a "committed Communist" but "without enough courage to admit it." The National Liberation Movement and the CCI, Sr. Portes Gil contended, were instruments of "international Communism, which in Mexico is dedicated to the undermining of the government and the starting of a new revolution."

There was gathering evidence toward the end of 1964 that General

[23] Despite the persistence of the division within the CCI during 1968, the faction led by Alfonso Garzón and Humberto Serrano agreed to support the PRI in the gubernatorial elections. Most of the support for the CCI is to be found in the richer rural areas where the level of discontent seems to be higher, perhaps because of a rising level of expectations. In many cases the peasants turn to the CCI after having experienced the inability of the CNC-affiliated organization to resolve their complaints. The CCI tends to encourage more extreme measures, including land invasions, since its growth is associated with dissatisfactions which are difficult to resolve. [Editor's Note]

Cárdenas' political influence was waning although few would have denied that he still had enormous influence in the provinces among agrarian labor. In the ten-year period from 1954 to 1964, however, the former president increasingly vitiated his influence in the liberal and moderately left areas and, of course, placed himself completely beyond the pale of the right, both moderate and extreme. This, incidentally, was an orientation wholly acceptable to the former president and one he had long ago become comfortably accustomed to. In the summer of 1964, furthermore, the former president lost a great amount of prestige built up over long years in the extreme left.

The coolness between Cárdenas and the extreme left, where he had been consistently held up as a leader, developed in earnest when in June 1964 he met publicly with president-elect Gustavo Díaz Ordaz and offered his commendation and political support. Sr. Díaz Ordaz in turn conceded that the former president, with whom he had never before had anything in common, occupied a "distinguished place in Mexican history." The effect was immediate and electric. *Política,* the recognized organ of the extreme left, challenged Sr. Cárdenas to clarify his motives in endorsing the PRI president-elect. The magazine complained in a three-page editorial that the act was "inexcusable." The *Política* reaction was the more intriguing in that a short time before Cárdenas had written a highly laudatory letter to *Política* commenting that it was especially "invaluable in its assessment of national and international affairs." It later developed that *Política* suspected General Cárdenas of having entered an agreement with Díaz Ordaz to lend his endorsement in return for leniency toward the leftists serving time in federal penitentiaries on the "social dissolution" charges. The magazine did not flatly state there had been such a deal but did say that if there was any secret understanding between Cárdenas and the president-elect it was the former's duty to clarify the matter.

General Cárdenas was born in the village of Jiquilpan de Juárez in the state of Michoacán on May 21, 1895. Because of his habitual inscrutability he has been generally referred to as the "Sphinx of Jiquilpan." He was one of eight children and his family was, by the standards of small Mexican villages, moderately well off. In a profile sent my paper in 1961 I noted, "His was an age of revolt and there has hardly been a time in his life in which he has not been a rebel with or without cause. While still in his teens he and some friends in Jiquilpan published a crudely-printed pamphlet in defense of Francisco I. Madero, who later was assassinated while in the presidency. He later fought with the peasant leader Emiliano Zapata and still later fought against him. He is recognized by friends and enemies alike as fearless, resourceful, and a tough and conscientious fighter." His friends and enemies, incidentally, have shifted sides constantly both during his revolutionary days and during his later political life.

In his early twenties the revolutionary, who had already become the equivalent of a brigadier general, was made provisional governor of Michoacán and following this was successively secretary of the interior and secretary of the army and navy. At age 39 he became president of the republic. He tightened up the party which later became the PRI. He drew up a nationalization law and, under his determined leadership, his administration expropriated foreign petroleum interests.

Foreign correspondents of late have found him far and away the most difficult man in Mexico to reach. He has a relatively few trusted friends who somehow get in contact with him in a matter of moments, whichever of his several houses he is in. But to reach him through the normal channels is next to impossible even for most of his political followers.

In all the years on the Middle American run, I saw Cárdenas but once at a conversational range, and that was at a small press conference held in Mexico City in 1961. The former president explained to a group of us that we had been called so he could tell us about the coming Western Hemisphere Peace Conference because it was not being written about in the domestic press. There was no way of ascertaining the validity of his accusation that the Mexican press had been instructed by official sources to suppress information on the conference. It was a serious charge, coming as it did from a former president who obviously had informants in the inner circles of the government. But nevertheless he insisted the government of President Adolfo López Mateos was at fault, and certainly there was little or no press coverage, whatever the cause. We mentioned this to a government official during the conference, and he dismissed it with the curt comment that "Cárdenas was being made a fool of."

Close friends of the former president in fact were disturbed over his involvement in the peace conference. Almost to a man they were convinced that he had been duped into his co-sponsorship role by Latin American Communist groups and that he refused to see he was being used. This was difficult to believe, but credence certainly had to be given his friends, who knew the former president as well as he could be known. They were wholly convinced he had been betrayed by his own deep convictions and did not recognize that the so-called peace conference was a Marxist-Leninist organizational meeting and a taunt to the United States some seven hundred miles away.

At first impression General Cárdenas is a man of enormous strength and great reserve powers although he speaks in a tone so subdued one has to strain to hear him in a crowded room. He is of medium height and sturdily built, but the two principal characteristics one remembers most are his extraordinarily long head with its exaggerated, sloping forehead and his deep green eyes. Women with whom I have talked about the former president maintain that his eyes have an intensely hypnotic quality. Certainly they remain in the memory.

Much space has been devoted to General Cárdenas here because of his unusual place in Mexican history. In a dispassionate evaluation—and it must be agreed that few can be dispassionate about him—he must emerge as Mexico's outstanding figure in this century. His influence on the national scene appears to be waning, but it would be a serious mistake to write him off at this date.[24] Lesley Byrd Simpson has put the matter succinctly and adequately: "Lázaro Cárdenas ended his remarkable term as one of the most controversial figures in Latin America, but it must be acknowledged that he rescued Mexico from the dismal corruption of Calles and spoiled caudillos of the revolution. He was a builder. Roads, public works, dams, irrigation projects, and the like went forward with his full support. Thousands of schools were built. He inaugurated the change in peasant land toward larger and more efficient communal ejidos. Indeed he never forgot his own peasant origin and his constant preoccupation with the good of the small farmer made him the best beloved of all revolutionary presidents."

General Cárdenas made a multifaceted imprint on the country's history. Probably the deepest as well as the most controversial imprint was in the role he played in accelerating the dormant agrarian reform program and expropriating foreign-owned petroleum interests in Mexico. The first, agrarian reform, was inadequately planned and has not fulfilled the revolutionary's expectations, but it did bring more land under cultivation than had ever been before. The second, petroleum expropriation, has fulfilled some of its expectations. With the creation of a nationalized petroleum industry, it achieved one of its goals. As a resource for meeting the country's needs, the petroleum industry is adequate but expensive. As a viable commercial enterprise, it has only an uncertain future unless, as seems immediately unlikely, it finds facilities for increased production and more foreign markets.

---

[24] Some observers have found it difficult to reconcile the history of Cárdenas's administration, his support of the Cuban revolution, and his participation in the so-called peace conference with his silence as the Ávila Comacho administration moved to the center of the political spectrum, his endorsing appearance with Miguel Alemán, whose candidacy and subsequent administration carried the Mexican government to the right of center, his endorsement of Díaz Ordaz, and, most recently, his condemnation of disruptive violence by the student movement. However, these seeming contradictions become intelligible if one recognizes the importance which Cárdenas attaches to the peaceful, orderly development of the country. That his power is considerably less than before was dramatically demonstrated when a PRI gubernatorial candidate not of his choosing was nominated and elected as governor of Michoacán in 1962. [Editor's Note]

The Land and the People

Agrarian reform was begun following the Mexican Revolution, before which about 3 per cent of the population owned around 90 per cent of the land. The Constitution of 1917 took cognizance of the growing demand for land reform by giving the government the right to expropriate and distribute property.

Dr. Edmundo Flores, professor of agricultural economics at the National University and former visiting professor at the Woodrow Wilson School of Public and International Affairs, Princeton, has maintained that from 1915 to the early 1960's 108,000,000 acres of land in Mexico have been distributed to about two million peasants. Approximately 20 million acres were distributed in the years between 1915 and 1934, the latter being the year Cárdenas came to power. In the six years of the Cárdenas administration 34,187,784 acres were distributed. Adolfo López Mateos in the first five years of his administration (1958 to 1963) distributed nearly 30 million acres. Between the administrations of these two, during the successive administrations of Manual Ávila Camacho, Miguel Alemán, and Adolfo Ruiz Cortines, there was a total distribution of slightly over 31 million acres.

Virtually all of this distribution was under the ejido system. Ejido lands are held as the property of a town or village, either for collective use or for distribution among ejidatarios for cultivation in small plots. These properties, usually around 16 acres, cannot be sold or mortgaged. Again according to Dr. Flores, there were 57,000 properties in Mexico before the land reform and presently there are 2,700,000. Improved techniques, better credit facilities, and other factors account for greatly increased agricultural production in the past twenty years or so. The volume produced has increased 33 per cent or more, it is true, but the population in that time has increased about 75 per cent.

The ejidos, however, have not pulled their weight in the productivity increase, not yielding as much as private enterprise as a general rule. In a majority of instances the private farms produce upwards of 20 per cent more than the ejidos. The reasons underlying the discrepancy are many and far-reaching. There is not enough cultivable area for the ejidatario and his family. The plots or "farms" run from 10 to 16 acres and do not lend themselves to mechanized cultivation. In addition, probably less than 5 per cent of the ejidos receive fertilizers as against nearly 10 per cent of the private holdings.

General Cárdenas has been criticized both at home and abroad for having pursued the single purpose of reanimating land distribution under the reform laws without first drawing up a careful plan about how production could be increased or at least sustained. His defenders, however, maintain that he dedicated himself more than any other single person in Mexico's history to fulfilling the promises of the Revolution through land distribution and development. They further maintain that had not Mexico been caught up in a revolutionary maelstrom beyond the control of his predecessors and, indeed, of Cárdenas himself, he could have devised better methods to free the farm laborers and to raise agricultural production.

There are presently tendencies to incorporate the small holdings into cooperatives for more efficient cultivation and increased production. But the distribution phase of the reform program appears to be nearing its end. President Díaz Ordaz in his campaign speeches warned repeatedly that land was running out.[25] In November 1964, Javier Rojo Gómez, chief of the National Peasant Confederation, declared that all distributable land would be dealt away within three years. He said the time was nearing when the rural sector would have to enter the second phase, that of training for the technical development which would increase production.

It was officially estimated as early as 1960 that the rural overpopulation in the states of Michoacán, Guanajuato, and Querétaro exceeded 5,000,000 men, women, and children. It was thought at that time that this overpopulation could be handily absorbed among such states as Campeche, with a population density at that time of about fourteen to the square mile, and Chiapas, with about ten to the square mile, and the territory of Quintana Roo (pronounced "row"), with from seven to eight persons per square mile. In 1960 I wrote, "The problem of colonizing the isolated and sparsely settled states, most of them with a difficult tropi-

[25] President Díaz Ordaz initiated a national program to be completed during his administration to survey the entire Republic, using aerial photography, in order to determine the exact number of acres still available for distribution. Although this enormous undertaking has not been completed, on the basis of the work done through 1968 certain of the sierra states (Morelos, San Luis Potosí, Colima, Aguascalientes, and Zacatecas) were officially declared to have finished the initial stage of agrarian reform. During the Díaz Ordaz administration, from 1964 through September 1, 1969, 16 million hectares have been distributed to 301,364 beneficiaries, primarily in the arid northern states. [Editor's Note]

cal climate, is an old one here. It has been such a difficult task that it has been abandoned time and again after repeated failures. It was in July of last year that the latest and by far the most ambitious plan thus far was undertaken. Since that time an estimated 18,000 families have been removed from the densely populated rural areas to prepare communities in the state of Veracruz. President López Mateos in his most recent order has asked that the program be extended into the peninsular states."

Three years later, in March 1963, another article stated, "Despite the enormous funds put into colonization by the federal government the program has been persistently bogging down. This has been due largely to sociological factors, according to the agrarian authorities. A Mexican family transplanted from the Laguna, according to these authorities, suffers as much sociological shock as an Arizona Indian would suffer being planted into the Louisiana bayou country."

In 1963 a plan had been advanced by the Department of Agrarian Affairs and Colonization to remove families from the Laguna area. That was to be the first of several transplantations in which, within a period of six months, 3,000 families would be moved from drought-stricken and worn-out regions into sparsely populated virgin lands in the state of Campeche. An official of the Department of Agrarian Affairs painted such a dramatic picture of the transplantation program that some of us became deeply interested in the plight of the entire area and in the fortunes of the families who were to be hauled nearly the length of the nation to their new homes.

The Laguna is an area of about 500,000 acres located in the valley of the Nazas River, taking in parts of southwestern Coahuila and northeastern Durango. It was once the agricultural pride of Mexico, producing the nation's finest cotton crops and, to a lesser extent, wheat. It was a showcase of the Cárdenas distribution program, an area he had hoped to use as a model for the remainder of his distribution scheme.[26]

The region has run into difficulty for a number of reasons: lack of proper irrigation, parcelization into very small farms, improper credit facilities for fertilizing and marketing, and a host of other things. A further difficulty was common to many of the areas carved out in the Cárdenas distribution scheme: the ejidatario could transfer his acreage to his heirs

---

[26] The Laguna area represented Cárdenas's most ambitious agrarian reform project. It involved the expropriation in 1936 of some 600,000 acres, largely foreign-controlled, and the organization of some 30,000 peasants into a number of large cooperative farms. Some five hundred such cooperative undertakings were established throughout the country, principally in areas concentrating on commercial cash crops. The Laguna cotton-growing effort near Torreón was a showcase until successive years of drought recently prompted resettlement efforts. [Editor's Note]

but could not sell it. Thus a family rapidly outgrew the cultivation potential of the acreage.

In the Laguna, as with other similar projects, the population expansion clashed with a growing water shortage and consequent crop shortage, and although extraordinarily detailed plans were devised to rehabilitate the area, the results at best have been less than adequate thus far. The final desperate effort, the transplanting of large parts of the surplus population of the area proved equally painful. "What do I know about this new place?" one campesino of the Laguna replied on being questioned about his prospective home. "I lived here all my life, my parents lived here all their lives, and I thought my children would too, but now we go to Campeche and God knows what."

In January 1964 I wrote: "Of the original 700 colonizers [to Campeche] about 40 found the unfamiliar climate, vegetation, and fauna too much. They abandoned the project and returned to their arid homeland. The remaining 660 formed seven communities along the banks of the Candaleria River. Each community covers 12,651 acres, about half of which is set aside for common grazing grounds, public buildings, and roads. The rest is divided into 123-acre farms for each family. The principal crops, at least in the beginning of the venture, will be beans and corn."

The next goal of the Colonization Department is in the state of Tabasco, where the El Limón project, financed as an Alliance for Progress project by the Inter-American Development Bank, is being prepared. It will comprise 50 communities and eventually should support 5,000 families from the Laguna area.

The El Limón project deserves special mention here because it seeks to avoid many of the mistakes of the earlier colonization plans and is easily the most ambitious program of its kind undertaken thus far in the agrarian reform program. The project comprises some 130,000 acres in the rich Ola de la Chontalpa region. The cost of the project, the first of several contemplated, is $65 million. All the area will be either irrigated outright or accessible to irrigation. Its principal products as presently planned will be cattle, cacao, bananas, and rubber.

This project will be the first completely integrated rural development that Mexico has attempted. In this connection the government has invited teams of Israeli technicians to assist in the groundwork of the project, which in its overall scope parallels the kibbutzim developments. Under the present plans there will be twelve population centers in the area, each supported by a pre-planned number of land parcels to be worked by the campesinos.

If all goes according to plan, six more areas will be similarly developed in the states of Tabasco, Campeche, and Chiapas, all in the sparsely settled Yucatán peninsula region. These areas, as presently planned, will provide an additional 742,546 acres in addition to the 130,139 acres in the El Limón project.

Despite these ambitious projects, the argument over the efficacy of the colonization system as a solution to the pressing problems of Mexico continues to rage. There was a definite campaign conducted in 1962 to abandon the colonization schemes in favor of renewed efforts to put new life into the old ejido system. At that time the government put up a strong defense for colonization. As part of its argument the Department of Colonization maintained that there were around 45 million acres of utilizable land available to the burgeoning population. The creation of new centers of population was proposed at that time, but, as has been seen, the results were not satisfactory in the beginning. Now, however, with the runaway population rapidly shifting from rural to urban centers, the problem is being given high priority in Mexico. It appears certain the colonization plan will be given a lengthy trial before any new attempt is made to pump new life into the old ejido system.

Two interesting official announcements were made in this connection in March 1963, one by the Department of Agrarian Affairs and the other by the then governor of Campeche, José Ortiz Ávila. Roberto Barrios, chief of the Department of Agrarian Affairs, announced on March 2, 1963 that new centers of population would be created on national lands, most of them in the state of Campeche. Three days later Sr. Ortiz Ávila announced that his state could offer the federal government 7,680,000 acres of land for purposes of colonization.

These and similar announcements are not unusual in the Mexican newspapers and give some indication of the population movements. The transplantations were by 1963 becoming a real problem. Shortly after the Campeche announcement a news item appeared from the Candaleria region of that state reporting that 49 newly colonized families were "dying of starvation" and had appealed to state authorities for assistance.

Finally for a few statistics. Mexico has a total land area of 487 million acres. Of these 15 per cent, or 74 million acres, are cultivable, of which 31 million are under cultivation. Grazing land accounts for 44 per cent of the total, or 214 million acres, and forest for 85 million, or 18 per cent. Nearly 85 per cent of Mexico is in the semi-dry or very dry regions.

Again citing the Population Reference Bureau Inc., "The relationship between agriculture and developing industry is circular: the agricultural sector must be able to expand production to feed a growing urban population and, in turn, must be able to furnish a domestic market for industrial products. Self-sufficiency in agricultural production, with something left over for export, is equally important in the transition from traditional to modern economic organization."

The population problems of urban areas are perhaps even drearier than those of rural areas. Mexico City, Monterrey, Guadalajara, Tijuana, and Mexicali have in recent years been the principal centers of urban concentration. All of them have the same problems, and the solutions have been equally inadequate. The runaway population growth of recent years would have taxed the capabilities even of cities with adequate long-range planning, if indeed there are any such in Latin America. But in the case of Mexico, the struggle has been a consistently losing rearguard action.

For example, in the national capital the area of *jacales,* or shacks, clustered around industrial suburbs contains more than 10 per cent of the city's population. The jacales are lacking in running water, electricity, and the elementary sanitary facilities. In 1958, according to a review by the National Bank of Mexico, 12 per cent of the land area of the capital's metropolitan district was occupied by overcrowded tenements accounting for 34 per cent of the population, which at that time had reached around 5 million. The first-class residential areas of the Federal District occupied 36 per cent of the land area but provided dwelling for only about 14 per cent of the population.

Private initiative in the principal cities of Mexico, such as the national capital, Monterrey, and Guadalajara, has been making sporadic attempts at a solution by building satellite areas. At best, these satisfy the needs of only the upper economic levels. In addition, no matter how far removed from the city itself the satellite areas are, they must draw upon the city for many services. This drain became so pronounced recently in the capital that an ordinance was invoked freezing satellite construction pending a solution to the problem of a water supply.

The city governments themselves, particularly that of Mexico City, have been initiating crash programs to build mainly *familiares,* or highrise, low-cost family units, in order to meet the burgeoning population problem. As costly as these have proved to be, they are not even remotely meeting the housing demands.

Urban concentration is, of course, a worldwide problem, but it is particularly acute in Mexico, with its current dedication to industrialization. The National Bank of Mexico explained, "The underlying economic basis of inordinately rapid urban concentration in Mexico lies in the extreme contrast between the opportunities for regional and agricultural labor on the one hand and the attraction of urban employment on the other. The problem is aggravated by the fact that the impetus to urban expansion, rather than being diffused, appears likely to continue concentrated in the present centers of growth."

Now that that "concentration" is an accomplished fact, there are various remedial measures underway, although, as indicated earlier, they are often like rearguard actions. Plans are constantly being advanced to make regional and agricultural labor more palatable. Such projects as El Limón attempt to give added dignity and security to rural living. But with white-collar and semi-skilled labor earning over 1,500 pesos ($120) a month and the farm laborer struggling to earn that much in half a year, no way out is presently in sight.

There is the possibility, and the Díaz Ordaz administration appears to be planning in this direction, of expanding industrialization in the agricultural areas. Tentative programs have been under consideration for concentrating several of these pilot industrial projects in the highly agricultural state of Morelos adjoining the Federal District.

There appears to be no question that the population problem is the chief preoccupation of the Mexican government. Why this should be so was underlined by the revelations of the 1960 census. It was shown that the economically active population (15 to 60) declined appreciably from 1950 to 1960, while the economically dependent groups (under 15 and over 60) increased appreciably. In 1940 there were 865 dependents for 1,000 economically active persons; in 1950 there were 897 and in 1960 there were 1,008 for every 1,000 economically active. These figures take on added meaning in comparison with other countries: In France in 1946 there were 609 economically dependent persons for 1,000 independent and in Denmark there were 593; in 1950 in the United States there were 647 per 1,000.

Nationwide hygiene programs and the almost total eradication of such endemic diseases as yellow fever and malaria increased life expectancy in Mexico from 36.27 years in 1930 to 48.3 years in 1950. The projection for 1965 is 58.4 years for men and 62.3 years for women.[27]

The indigenous Indian population is a considerable factor in any discussion of Mexico's population. The 1960 census reported 3,638,000 Indians, but that figure could well be low. Missionaries, both Catholic and Protestant, who devote all their efforts to the Mexican Indian have estimated the population at over 6 million. Whatever the figure, the plight of

---

[27] Mexico's population was estimated at 45,671,000 by 1967, and at the end of 1969 the official figure was 48,313,438. The rate of growth has remained fairly constant over recent years at a phenomenally high 3.5 per cent annually. The increase has been greater in the cities, although the rural population still composed 49 per cent of the total. The death rate declined between 1960 and 1965 from 11.2 to 9.5 per 1,000, but this was still higher than several of the Central American countries. Illiteracy, which had declined nationally to 34.6 per cent, was still much higher in the rural areas. Educational enrollments increased substantially between 1960 and 1967 at the preschool and primary level (from 5.1 million to 8.2 million) and at the secondary level (from 351,000 to 1.3 million), but even these striking advances hardly kept pace with the burgeoning population. [Editor's Note]

the indigenous Mexican represents one of the country's most serious problems. Administration after administration has wrestled with the task of incorporating this segment into the political, economic, and cultural body of the nation. And each, in turn, has failed.

During his campaign, Sr. Díaz Ordaz promised that the integration of the Indian population would be given high priority in his six-year administration (1964–1970). In one of his campaign speeches he told the Indians of the Mezquital Valley that Mexico's program of economic and social development could be subject to doubt as long as progress was not made in bringing the Indian into the national mainstream. He was speaking to the Otomíes, who inhabit the Mezquital, and are one of the most economically depressed and socially backward of all of Mexico's Indian tribes.

Without exception, however, the tribes, some of whom were at one time the guardian of this hemisphere's literature and science, are now in a state of social and mental lethargy. The chief tribes are the Otomíes, Nahua, Tarahumara, Zapoteca, Maya, Tzeltal, Mixteca, Totonaca, Mazahua, Mazateca, Tzotzil, and Huasteca. A majority of the Indian population speak nothing but the native dialect of their respective tribe. Most of them have little intercourse with Mexican life, and those that do come into contact with present-day Mexico do so only on market days, and then only at the *pueblo* nearest them.

The problem was regarded with such seriousness that a special Apostolic Congress was called in Mexico City in 1961 to deal solely with the Catholic missionaries' plans for the Indian. The Catholic Church in Mexico devotes a large part of its work to Indian missions. The congress was called and presided over by Monsignor Luigi Raimondi, apostolic delegate in Mexico. It was attended by twelve Mexican bishops, and deliberations dealt mainly with the Church's program in such areas as medical assistance, housing, education, and social adjustment. The apostolic delegate urged the clergy: "Draw near to these people, not in the sense of superiority but with humanity and in the fraternal spirit."

During the congress, incidentally, the apostolic delegate passed on the somewhat startling information that in present-day Mexico, where clerical laws prohibiting the activity of religious orders are still on the books, there are twenty-seven Catholic religious orders carrying on missionary work among the country's indigenous population.

The Indian is as isolated economically as he is socially from the Mexican life flowing around him and his tribe. He eats what he produces, mostly maize and beans; and he resists technological development and is illiterate unless he is one of comparatively few now being given some education by the missionaries. The economy is conditioned to family-unit production; labor relations are personal. Money is a secondary consideration except among some of the tribes which have achieved specialization in weaving and carving.

Another note, not entirely relevant. In mid-1960 the editorially staid morning paper *Excélsior* published a considered opinion on the subject of "Matrimony and the Free Union." The editorial noted with surprise that the census revealed "at least half of the Mexican population lived outside matrimony or, that is, it was preferred, through ignorance in most cases, to live in so-called free union, or to be realistic, in concubinage." The editorial continued by saying the real sufferers from such unions were "the children who are deprived of many of their rights and all too frequently are abandoned by irresponsible parents without home, without education, and almost without bread. They take their places in long lines of pariahs and constitute one of the most serious burdens our country faces."

The editorial told only half the story. The other half could well have been witnessed in an auditorium one morning when 1,000 couples were joined in a gigantic wedding ceremony. Large numbers of them were Indians who had come from their tribal areas, many accompanied by their children of various ages. Most of the women held young babies. There was an atmosphere of barely suppressed fiesta, probably arising from the certain knowledge that the pulque and tequila would be stoutly flowing in a thousand gatherings following this simple ceremony.

These were not the "irresponsible parents" described in the newspaper commentary. For the most part they were couples who had never been able to afford the time or money for the type of marriage ceremony they had wanted. In fact, many years ago this same kind of ceremony could have been seen in the West and Southwest of the United States, where the Indian population, with generation upon generation of Catholicism in their background, were on hand with their children when the priest finally reached their out-of-the-way villages. The marriage ceremonies and the baptisms were performed the same morning, followed by a right lively party.

On the other side, however, the newspaper's position was in some respects solidly based. There are no reliable data on the number of desertions in these "free unions." The figure must be a towering one, particularly in the urban areas. In the long line of maids we have had over the years, young and middle-aged women who were supporting children from babyhood to grammar-school age, few had not been deserted by their husbands, some of them two or three times.

Quite possibly the incidence of desertion of children by the mother as well as the father is appreciable, but the far more remarkable thing is the deprivation and hardship a Mexican mother will go through to protect her young, either providing some sort of shelter for them herself or paying for their care elsewhere.

Another interesting observation in the *Excélsior* editorial was that the problems of "free union should not be left in the hands of the clergy, who, because of their inadequate numbers are unable by themselves to resolve this very deep problem." There is considerable conviction that public morality began breaking down with the first, somewhat minor, anticlerical offensives in 1833 and has become increasingly lax ever since. There is some argument, of course, that the problems of modern living, increased population, and economic pressures have had a hand in moral disintegration. Many of the followers of both these theories are genuinely convinced that the only return to morality will be through a rekindling of Mexico's old religious fervor.

President Lyndon Johnson greets President Gustavo Díaz Ordaz of Mexico in the center of the International Bridge between El Paso, Texas, and Ciudad Juárez, Mexico, on December 13, 1968. The two presidents met to inaugurate the Rio Grande channel project, which diverted the river back to its original course and settled the Chamizal dispute. (Wide World Photos)

General Lázaro Cárdenas, former president of Mexico, addresses a pro-Castro rally in Mexico City on April 18, 1961, the day after the Bay of Pigs invasion of Cuba. (Wide World Photos)

The Economy

The years from 1954 to 1964 were the cinderella years for Mexico's economy. There were rags-to-riches overtones and from time to time hints of disaster, but once the pitfalls were skirted and the plateaus traversed the national economy lunged upward and still further upward. In a year-end review of the economic situation in December 1964 it was noted, "In evaluating economically the year past the key word probably would be 'confidence'. In September last President López Mateos in his final State of the Union message predicted that the previous year's gross national product increase of 5.4 per cent would be topped by at least 1 per cent at the year's end. The final figures when adjusted probably will show an increase of at least 7 per cent and perhaps more." The increase for 1964 was actually 10 per cent, unprecedented for Mexico.

The economy had come a long way from the dreary days of the spring of 1954, when despite ample reserves President Adolfo Ruiz Cortines devaluated the peso from 11.5 cents (U.S.) to the dollar to 8 cents. There were boom days for awhile, but the reaction soon set in with prices soaring and discontent throughout the land, particularly in the rural areas.

President Ruiz Cortines met the slump head-on with an accelerated program of spending in public works, and things began shaping up. The president was in a good position for this type of program. Mexico's zeal in meeting her international commitments when they were due, an old-fashioned approach, had given her an excellent credit rating. Although in speeches early in his administration the president emphasized his desire to refrain from resorting to foreign loans, when it was finally necessary he borrowed on a large scale and with effectiveness. The programs he pursued were devoted largely to social services and rural development projects, with the result that land cultivation increased markedly and the value of agricultural production more than doubled, from about 7,000,000,000 pesos ($560,000,000 U.S.) to 16,000,000,000 by the time he left office.

In the 1959 to 1961 period, the economic rhythm slowed down almost to a walk, the gross national product growth reaching a dangerously low point of 3.5 per cent for 1961. Private investment fell off markedly and so did the demand for Mexico's raw materials. The 1960 excitement over President López Mateos' classification of his government's ideological position as left and the succeeding incidents probably had much to do with this. So the government again resorted to heavy investments in the public sector, and again, as in the instance of President Ruiz Cortines, the strategy worked. Confidence began returning in the private sector and there was a slight reawakening of interest among foreign investors. The year 1963 wound up with a 6 per cent increase in the gross national product.

It was in the summer of 1962 that Mario Ramón Beteta, one of Mexico's bright young economists and manager at that time of the Bank of Mexico, laid the ground rules for foreign investment in an address to a convention of attorneys from Mexico and Texas. The Mexican economy wanted and needed foreign investment, Sr. Beteta noted in what at the time was considered something of an understatement. Nevertheless, he observed, Mexico's economic and social advancement was primarily the responsibility of Mexicans themselves. He warned that the country was not prepared to give foreign capital advantages over Mexican investment. Conversely, he explained, foreign capital would be guaranteed the same rights and privileges as Mexican capital. Some foreign investors have often complained since then that the policy sounded fine but the practice was not always such. Yet despite complaints, the foreign investments continued to multiply.

And the investments continued to be needed. Nacional Financiera, the government's borrowing and lending agency, estimated that the country would need $3,000,000,000 (U.S.) to bring its industry up to the growth level of 6.5 per cent considered necessary by 1972. The priorities specified for investment between 1964 and 1972 were, in order of their importance: manufacture of machine tools and transportation equipment; chemical and petrochemical manufacture; petroleum and natural gas extraction and refining; steel and metal products manufacture; and the manufacture of paper and paper products.

The decade from 1954 to 1964 was perhaps the most significant period in Mexico's economic development, and by all odds it was the most interesting. The entire economic structure underwent a profound change in that span of years. The Social Progress Trust Fund, in its admirable report for 1964, noted, "Between 1950 and 1963, manufacturing output increased by 145 per cent, raising its share of the national product from 11 to 24 per cent, with industrial employment increasing from 12 to 14 per cent of the labor force."

With the increase in industrial activity, however, there was a corresponding decrease in agricultural activity, resulting in an economic dislocation which Mexico will probably spend many years adjusting to. Population shifts, with the thousand-and-one accompanying problems, can tell one part of the story. In 1930 Mexico's urban population was 5,500,000, or 33 per cent of the total, and its rural population was 11,000,000, or 67 per cent. By 1960 the urban population was 17,700,000, or 51 per cent of the whole, and the rural, 17,200,000, or 49 per cent.

Employment presented its own problems, not as startling as those of population but equally important. In 1950 the number employed in agriculture, livestock, and forestry was 4,823,901, or 58.3 per cent of the total. In 1960 the number was 6,144,930, but the percentage had dropped to 54.2 per cent. In 1950 the number employed in manufacture and construction was 1,197,054, or 14.5 per cent of the entire work force. In 1960 a total of 1,964,717, or 17.3 per cent of the work force, was employed in manufacture and construction.

In addition to the population dislocations, there has been severe unevenness in agricultural productivity in recent years and with it an unequal distribution of income between urban and rural populations. The income of the average rural family in most Mexican states is at best one-third that of the average urban family. In the northern desert areas the discrepancy is still more pronounced. Up to 1964 the rural population did not participate in the general economic upturn of the rest of the nation.

During his presidential campaign Gustavo Díaz Ordaz dwelt mainly on the necessity of bringing the rural population into the national scheme. He repeatedly sounded warnings between his election and his inauguration in December 1964 that the rural sector was certain to be the greatest problem of his six-year administration.

In 1964 it was estimated that the per capita gross national product was between $400 and $500 in the urban areas but remained below $100 in some of the rural sections. The picture of Mexico's development tends to become blurred unless one keeps constantly in mind that, while agriculture contributes less than one-quarter of the gross national product, almost one-half the Mexican people live off the soil.

There were spectacular advances in agriculture over the decade despite dislocations. Irrigation, in operation in 1964 over almost 12 million acres, accounted for heavy advances in cotton production, which rose from 1,138,000 bales in 1950 to over 2,230,000 bales in 1964. The country for the first time in its history became a wheat exporting nation in 1964, with most of the surplus going to Communist China.

In the economic roundup for 1964 I noted, "There was little worry over agricultural production as such, but the past and present governments have indicated real concern over the agrarian problem. President Díaz Ordaz in his inaugural address devoted a brief paragraph to agricultural production but many paragraphs in repeated references to rural population, its problems, and their possible solutions. There are about 6,000,000 Mexicans directly engaged in farming. There are about the same number directly engaged in farming in the United States.

"One of the great disparities, it has been explained here, is that some 54,000,000 North Americans derive their livelihood directly from the active farmers in providing goods and services to them," the year-end report noted and continued, "In Mexico there is scant livelihood for the rural population in providing goods and services to the active Mexican farmer. In other words, when the farmer is in trouble, as he nearly always is, the entire rural population is in difficulty, as it presently is."

Mexican leaders in government, finance, and labor are keenly aware of this. Industry in the ten-year period from 1954 to 1964 made the news because of the spectacular role it played in the national advance. But no responsible Mexican or, for that matter, no well-informed foreign investor overlooks for long the somber shadow of the disheartened campesino. In Mexico's history the intellectuals fomented Mexico's revolutions and uprisings of varying intensity, but the humble campesino furnished the backbone.[28]

---

[28] Since 1964, according to the Social Progress Trust Fund Reports, the Mexican economy has continued to show consistent progress, with the gross national product increasing at the average rate of 6.2 per cent annually. The government has tried to restrain the growth rate by means of strict control of credit in order to lessen the possibility of inflation. In 1968 public expenditures were up only 7.6 per cent despite enormous outlays for public works connected with the Olympic Games and the construction of the Metro, or subway system, for the capital. The balance of trade has shown steady improvement, although a deficit still was being registered in 1968. In terms of the principal sectors of the Mexican economy, industry continues to record the most significant advances, although efforts to diversify export items have not greatly changed the ratio of manufactured goods sold abroad (22 per cent). The decentralization of industry, especially in the direction of such states as San Luis Potosí and Puebla, has been encouraged by means of tax incentives. While cotton, coffee, sugar, and minerals remain the prime export products, there has been little increase in agricultural production. This is due, in part, to the low prices of sugar and coffee on the international market, but also is a reflection of the basic reluctance on the part of the government to stimulate the total agricultural sector in any substantial way. Instead emphasis has been placed on large-scale irrigation projects, rural education, and guaranteed prices for corn, beans, coffee, and, in some instances, sugar. [Editor's Note]

The Church

There are two fundamental points to keep in mind while considering the role of the Roman Catholic Church in Mexico: (1) it has been one of the principal forces in Mexican life since shortly after the conquest and (2) the Church and the Mexican State have never been able to get along together for any length of time. This latter should be qualified somewhat, however, by the increasing evidence that there has been a greater rapprochement between the Church and the State in the past decade than in two centuries before. In many assessments, the first deep healing of the ancient enmity occurred at the death in 1956 of Monsignor Luis María Martínez, archbishop primate of Mexico.

Archbishop Martínez died February 9, 1956 at the age of seventy-five, one of the most respected and beloved men in the Mexico of his time. The president, Adolfo Ruiz Cortines, had called twice during the illness and in the final hours had had his personal physician attend the dying man. It was estimated by police that more than one hundred thousand mourners passed the bier of the dead primate as the body lay in state in the National Cathedral, and among the many were former presidents of Mexico and virtually the entire diplomatic corps. The column-long obituary I sent my paper on him at the time of his death gave some explanation of why he was such a powerful factor in bettering, for the time at least, Church-State relations.

The archbishop was a boyhood friend of former president Lázaro Cárdenas in their native state of Michoacán. The friendship continued as the two men advanced, the one in war and politics and the other in affairs of the Church. During his administration, between 1934 and 1940, President Cárdenas sought a rapprochement of sorts between Church and State, and although their political views were 180 degrees apart, the archbishop assisted in the effort. While he consistently fought the extreme left, the archbishop fought the extreme right with equal vigor and brought down showers of abuse when he thundered from the pulpit against the various fascist-type movements seeking to align Mexico with the Axis cause in World War II. His adherence to the democratic cause in that period was the more remarkable in that some of the most active and influential pro-Axis groups were Catholic in composition.

By that time, however, the archbishop had become accustomed to violent criticism. He took the brunt of it when during the Cárdenas regime he advocated support of the government's oil appropriation program. His course of action at that time was notable in that the Church itself was smarting under recent expropriation measures. He also flaunted every known taboo of the time for Church dignitaries, when the rule was to remain far in the background in civic and social matters. He was an enthusiastic socializer, even prominently in attendance at the dedication of the United States Embassy, and he assisted at ceremonies surrounding the visit of the then vice-president Richard M. Nixon to Mexico.

When he died, the great cathedral, the scene of so many ceremonies in the centuries of its existence, did not have sufficient facilities to accommodate the crowds. Lines three-abreast wound before the bier and stretched from the cathedral for blocks around the Zócalo. His bank account at the time of death contained $455, and in a three-line will he requested that this amount be distributed among several adopted children he had supported from infancy.

The tensions between Church and State in Mexico began with the indignation of early friars such as Bartolomé de las Casas and Vasco de Quiroga at the treatment of the Indians by the earliest conquistadores. This tension could just as well be said to have been between Church and Church, inasmuch as the conquistadores were as interested in advancing the cause of the Church as the indignant friars were in protecting the cause of the Indians. It can probably be truthfully said that since those early days the world has never quite understood the true status of the Church in Mexico and, for that matter, probably Mexico itself has not quite understood. There have been too many contradictions at play.

My first experience with Mexico was in the mid-thirties, when I was there to do a series of articles for a newspaper chain in the United States. The pieces were mine-run, "roving reporter" affairs and did not cause any unusual interest, with the exception of a story about visiting various churches in Mexico City. This story caused a furor in the United States, where the prevailing conviction was that all Catholic churches at that time were locked and barred. By the time the condemnatory letters to the editor had reached flood tide, there appeared not much use in explaining that the Cárdenas regime had begun to moderate anticlerical measures.

Further, during the regime of Plutarco Elías Calles, from 1924 to 1928, when the anticlerical campaign was at its hottest there were dozens of churches open for services throughout Mexico.[29] There was then, however, as there had been for years, a shortage of priests. In fact in most of Mexico at that time there were no priests at all remaining.

As implied by a number of historians and pinpointed by Frank Tannenbaum in his classic *Mexico—The Struggle for Peace and Bread,* the religious conflict in Mexico belonged essentially to the Mexican people and not to Rome, Madrid, or Mexico City. It came to a head in a clash between the then meager ranks of more or less liberal intellectuals and lawyers on the one side and the city or city-oriented clergy and the wealthy on the other. The latter included the urban-oriented *hacendados,* or landowners. The lawyers and the liberals, including the professional branches of medicine and a smattering of scientists, won. But the Indian in his *pueblo* neither knew nor cared much about the strife except when the *iglesia* which he helped build or the statue of the saint-patron of the village were affected.

In the buildup toward the first great clash between the Church and State, the Church became so closely identified with the crown through its many privileges that it was virtually a captive of the state, a voluntary and moderately happy captive. The rebellion against the State in its preliminary stages was in effect rebellion against the Church, and in this rebellion parish priests such as Miguel Hidalgo y Costilla and José María Morelos took the lead, and eventually lost their lives, both of them being captured and executed.

The roots of the struggle between the Church and State were buried deep in Mexican history and correspondingly entangled, as in fact they still are. The first head-on clash, however, came in 1833–34 during the temporary administration of Vice-President Valentín Gómez Farías, a liberal physician of Guadalajara who was administrating the country in the absence of the president, General Antonio López de Santa Anna. The record of the period in which Gómez Farías ruled until Santa Anna returned and eventually drove him into exile is blurred and interpreted variously by accepted historians. The essentials remain, however, that in the period the Church, whether at the direction of Dr. Gómez Farías himself or his officials, came under effective attack from the government. Education was secularized and clerical influence in the university was suppressed as, indeed, the university itself very nearly was. There were

---

[29] To protest legislation embodying the anticlerical provisions of the constitution, the hierarchy suspended public religious services for three years, from 1926 to 1929. Private services were held, and churches remained open for individual prayer, but public conduct of the Mass and administration of the sacraments was suspended until Dwight Morrow assisted in the establishment of the aforementioned *modus vivendi* between the Church and the administration of Portes Gil. [Editor's Note]

various attempts, with some success, to disrupt the monastic orders, laying the initial groundwork for the eventual complete elimination of these orders.

Other attacks followed this first effective offensive against the Church undertaken by the Mexican state.[30] The succeeding attacks reached their peak in the administration of President Calles. In June 1926 Calles issued a decree putting the religious laws then on the books into full effectiveness. They had until that time remained there in a dormant state. These laws provided for the closing of all religious schools, the expulsion of foreign-born priests, and the registration of all priests, whether foreign or national.

The impossibility of his position should have been apparent to Calles, but he persisted in it until the end of his time in office. Or, to put it another way, while President Calles failed to bring off successfully some of the more vital aspects of his program, he at least succeeded to the extent that as late as 1960 desperate attempts were still being made by pro-Catholic groups to regain some of the lost ground.

In June 1960, almost thirty-four years after the promulgation of the Calles decrees, the rightist, pro-Catholic National Action Party forced the all-powerful Institutional Revolutionary Party (PRI) into a debate on the teaching of religious matter in public education. The National Action faction claimed that education had become a state monopoly instead of a representative institution and that the article dealing with it in the Constitution of 1917 was a contravention of the Declaration of Human Rights in the United Nations Charter and, finally that the heads of families had lost influence in directing the course of elementary education. For the first time in the party's history the PRI deigned to recognize such a direct challenge. It answered the National Action charges point by point.

In answer to the contention that the administration was imposing "dangerous statism" through restrictive educational policies, the PRI replied that this was "inaccurate and deceitful." It continued, "There

[30] The most systematic attack on the institutional and societal role of the Church occurred during the Reform Era (1853–1872), when Indian lawyer Benito Juárez and his Liberal contemporaries issued decrees which separated Church and State and nationalized all property of the religious orders and secular clergy after prohibiting religious corporations from holding real estate. Ecclesiastical courts and religious orders were banned, while laical primary education and civil registration of births, marriages, and deaths became compulsory. Although not all of these measures were fully implemented, the anticlerical attitude and the specific restrictions were incorporated into the Constitution of 1857, which, although allowed to fall into almost complete disuse during the Díaz dictatorship, remained on the books to serve as the point of departure for the framers of the Constitution of 1917 and post-revolutionary governmental policy toward the Church. [Editor's Note]

would be statism if our education were obliged to inculcate in the child and the youth the concept of the superiority of the state over man." On the contrary, the reply continued, education in Mexico was designed "to develop harmoniously the faculties of being human and at the same time to foment a love of country and a consciousness of international solidarity in the advancement of independence and justice."

The situation following Calles began easing off somewhat under Emilio Portes Gil, and in 1929 the priests were back at their altars. President Cárdenas quietly modified the anticlerical laws, and his successor, General Manuel Ávila Camacho, startled a good share of the populace with his famous declaration "Soy creyente" ("I am a believer"). It was a statement gratifying to many, but tantamount to treason to others.[31]

In the intervening years the Church has been gradually reassuming some part of its influence. This is evidenced in many small ways, such as the reappearance in public of nuns in their habits. It is not unusual to see such celebrities as Fray José Mojica, the former opera and motion picture star, appearing in the garb of an order. He is seen frequently on the streets wearing his flowing Franciscan habit. Of course Fray José is so well known and admired by the Mexican public there would be little thought of challenging him even though he is breaking a law prohibiting clerics to appear in public in their robes. Nuns too are forbidden to appear in public in their religious garb, but the garments they wear are so close to the traditional robes they cannot be distinguished. Curiously, the first publicly expressed concern over this increased relaxation of the apparel regulations for clergy was expressed by former president Portes Gil, who first began relaxing the Calles anticlerical regulations.

As a side-note to the clerical garb topic, hundreds of vacationing Roman Catholic priests visit Mexico each year. They scrupulously observe the garb regulations, so scrupulously, in fact, that once they discard their churchly grays many appear in public in the wildest combinations of colors known to man.

The gradual re-emergence of the Church was noted in a dispatch sent in October 1958. Some excerpts: "A general religious resurgence noticeable here over past years was highlighted in the death this week of Pope Pius XII. This country, as a result of the liberal political victory in the 1910 revolution resulting in the presidency of Francisco I. Madero, was swept into a strong anticlerical attitude. From that time until the advent

---

[31] Ávila Comacho, consistent with his spirit of national unity, restored Article 3 of the Constitution to its pre-1934 form. This article, providing for secularized education, had been modified in 1934 to require that education also be "socialist" and combat "fanaticism." His successor, Miguel Alemán, publicly embraced the Archbishop of Mexico at the Shrine of Guadalupe. [Editor's Note]

of the administration of Manuel Ávila Camacho over thirty years later few if any men in public office dared espouse the cause of any religion here.

"Catholics and non-Catholics alike recall that at the death of Pius XI in 1936 the reaction was not comparable to that of the death of his successor. For two days, Thursday and Friday, the capital newspapers devoted most of their front pages to news of the death. There have been special services in the several hundred Catholic churches here. By Friday night the telephone company reported 2,000 telephone calls had been placed to Rome.

"By sundown Thursday not only had the majority of the diplomatic corps paid visits of condolence to the apostolic delegate, Monsignor Luigi Raimondi, but both President Adolfo Ruiz Cortines and former president Miguel Alemán had sent messengers with their personal condolences. Mexico does not have diplomatic relations with the Vatican.

"The most unusual reaction of all, however, was that of the Mexican legislature. As recently as ten years ago, observers agree, it would have been political suicide for a Mexican legislator to express the slightest sentiment in connection with the death of a pontiff. In this instance leaders of both houses, the Chamber of Deputies and the Senate, have given public expression of their sorrow at the death of the pontiff. A majority of those expressing such sentiments, however, made it clear they were impelled to do so by the stature of the man rather than his position of leadership in a religion."

A year after that story had been sent President López Mateos reasserted the liberty of religious belief in Mexico. He remarked, "I assert that religion need not be an obstacle in the constructive march of the Revolution. With emphasis, I exhort all Mexicans to maintain within their own convictions a spirit which cannot be overshadowed by time or intrigues or by diverse opinions." The president's remarks were made in an unscheduled talk to textile workers in the village of Villa Cayetano Rubio in the state of Querétaro. They were in response to the complaints of textile workers that their union was being discriminated against because of their religious beliefs.

In the past fifty years the Church has been in the ambivalent position of trying to remain aloof from mine-run politics while at the same time being more or less forced into clarification of its position vis-à-vis politics. In 1961 a political storm developed over the appearance of the Church as an active participant in the struggle between Communists and anti-Communists in Mexico. An article filed May 6 of that year noted: "The Church emerged from its heretofore self-imposed position of non-participation in political affairs. Indications over the past weeks have been that the Church was going to assume a less passive role in the ideological dispute. These indications materialized this past Sunday when an estimated 100,000 persons gathered before the Cathedral of the city of Puebla to protest increased Communist activity in the community."

Puebla is a militantly Catholic community and is also the center of violent pro-Communist demonstrations. Time after time riot squads have been called out to quell demonstrations of leftist student organizations generally led by seasoned agitators.

Through some still-unexplained chain of events the United States embassy in Mexico City became involved in the sudden reawakening of political activity in the Church. Shortly after the Puebla meeting, *Últimas Noticias,* a strongly anti-Communist afternoon newspaper, published a report that the embassy was assisting the Catholic Action group in organizing still more anti-Communist demonstrations. The morning paper *Excélsior,* which publishes *Últimas Noticias,* published the next morning on its front page an apology for the article, explaining it was without foundation. But by that time the damage had been done. The embassy spent the entire day answering irate telephone calls and explaining it had nothing to do with either the Catholic Action group or with any planned demonstrations. The morning paper, *El Popular,* then the mouthpiece of the Marxist Popular Socialist Party, took a strong view of the report despite the embassy's embarrassed withdrawal from the whole business. The paper accused the United States of intervening in Mexican political affairs and deplored the Puebla anti-Communist mass meeting. It noted, "Each day demonstrations are being carried out with increased virulence."

Política, a magazine of the extreme left, reported in its June 1 edition of that year, "The embassy in charge of the newly-arrived United States ambassador Thomas G. Mann announced a public anti-Communist meeting by Catholic Action." Finally some of the facts began coming to light. It appeared a newly-appointed public information officer at the embassy had acceded to a request by a Catholic group to place in the embassy bulletin a notice of the scheduled mass meeting. All in all the chain of events provided a rather hair-raising welcome for Mr. Mann, whose line of approach in his previous ambassadorial posts and, indeed, in all of his previous diplomatic assignments, was to keep well out of the public eye and beyond the glare of publicity.

A year later, in July 1962, the Church again entered the anti-Communist campaign, which in the meantime had been rapidly gathering momentum. In an article filed to the paper it was noted, "The Roman Catholic episcopacy in Mexico formally counselled members of the Church to enter a nationwide campaign against Communism in this country. A ten-page declaration of Catholic principles vis-à-vis the growing influence of Communism in Mexico was distributed last night, and it was made plain that membership in the party, distribution or reading of Communist literature, or showing or even indicating favorable response to Communist activities was ipso facto cause for excommunication.

"The document, published in book form, was distributed widely throughout the capital today. It was signed by forty-eight members of the Mexican Roman Catholic hierarchy beginning with José Cardinal Garibi Rivera, archbishop of Guadalajara and the only cardinal in Mexico's history, and by Archbishop Miguel Dario Miranda y Gómez, primate of Mexico.

"The importance of today's declaration is twofold: It is considered in most quarters to be the beginning of a prolonged offensive by the Church against Communism not only in Mexico but in all of Latin America, and, secondly, it marks the first time since the Church's rights were curtailed in the anticlerical decrees of President Plutarco Elías Calles (1924–1928) that the Mexican hierarchy has declared itself in matters of politics."

Finally, in February 1963 the Church, through a Diocesan Conference of Mexican Catholic Action, announced that Mexican Roman Catholics who joined voluntarily any one of several movements considered by the Church to be Communist would automatically be excommunicated. The announcement singled out specifically the then newly-organized Campesina Central Independiente, the Popular Socialist Party, and the Communist-led General Union of Workers and Peasants of Mexico.

There were some intriguing overtones in the decision of the Church, particularly as it applied to the Campesina Central Independiente, an offshoot of the National Liberation Movement. The campesino organization had been formed only a month before, and although, as mentioned, former president Lázaro Cárdenas maintained he had nothing but a nominal interest in it, he had some time before been actively interested in organizing the National Liberation Movement and had actually assisted with his son Cuauhtémoc at the organizational meeting of the CCI.

Earlier the Right Reverend José G. Anaya y Diez de Bonilla, bishop of Zamora, forbade communicants in his diocese, under penalty of excommunication, to become members of either the campesino organization or the National Liberation Movement. The pronouncement placed hundreds of campesinos of Zamora diocese in a grave predicament. There had been a growing antipathy in that area to the administration's National Peasant Confederation for its failure to recognize the deep needs of the peasant farm laborers. Zamora is a predominantly rural diocese, and campesinos there as well in most of the other rural areas gravitated to the CCI, not ideologically, but as to a beacon in an economic storm.

Matters were made more tense in that the Zamora diocese is in the state of Michoacán, the home state and political stronghold of General Cárdenas, and wherein, above all areas, he is idolized by the rural population. It was long recognized that the CCI would sooner or later be challenged by the Church because the campesino organization's potential membership was among the rural Indians who are presently the strongest element in the Catholic Church in Mexico. While the organizers of the CCI persistently denied that the campesino organization had ideological significance, most of its leaders of that time were associated with Communist causes. Later non-Communist elements rose in rebellion within the organization and voted out the militant Communist leadership.

The arrival in Mexico of Eugene Cardinal Tisserant, dean of the College of Cardinals, in August 1964, created one of the most provocative Church-State situations in recent years. The aged cardinal was, in addition to his exalted rank in the College, president of the Superior Council of the Ecumenical Council and obviously was carrying instructions from Pope Paul VI. Whether or not he was empowered to enter firm agreements in Mexico, his visit created a storm of controversy.

It was emphasized at the outset that the eighty-year-old prelate's visit was to be of a purely private nature, but that explanation was not accepted by either the devout or the anti-Catholic left. There had been ominous warnings in the leftist press for days that this visit might be the first step toward discussions leading to a renewal of diplomatic relations between Mexico and the Vatican, relations which had been broken off in 1861 under the presidency of Benito Juárez. The papal nuncio of that time, Monsignor Luis Clementi, and the archbishop of México, the Right Reverend Lázaro de la Garza, a Spaniard, were both expelled.

Estimates were that about 10,000 of the faithful were on hand to receive Cardinal Tisserant, but there were probably more than 300,000 along the route from the airport to his place of residence in the home of a Mexican industrialist. There were no official government representatives, naturally, at the airport to receive the visiting prelate who had come by commercial plane by way of Paris and who had repeatedly emphasized he was coming on a private visit. The Church delegation receiving the visitor was headed by Cardinal Garibi Rivera, Archbishop Dario Miranda, and the Right Reverend Luigi Raimondi, apostolic delegate to Mexico and titular archbishop of Tarsus. Twelve of Mexico's forty-one bishops were also in the receiving delegation. The secular diplomatic corps at the reception included the ambassadors of France, Belgium, Haiti, and the United States. In the light of what occurred or, rather failed to occur, during the visit of Cardinal Tisserant the entire affair appeared to be a classic example of a tempest in a teapot.

Controversy persisted throughout the eighteen days of his stay in Mexico, revolving around the hypothesis that the purpose of the visit was solely to explore the renewal of diplomatic relations between the Vatican and the Mexican state. There may actually have been some deeply shrouded exploratory talks in this direction, but nothing appeared during the visit or after to indicate that approaches, if there had been such, were even reasonably fruitful.

The Mexican government refused to be drawn, except in an indirect way, into the controversy. Manuel Tello, former foreign minister who had relinquished his post to become a senator from his native state of Zacatecas, questioned the advisability of exploring the possibility of a renewal of relations. A Catholic himself, the former foreign minister and former ambassador to the United States reasoned, "In my opinion it is premature to talk of the matter of new relations with the Vatican." It was presumed he was being utilized to express unofficially the official sentiment of the government.

Whatever the outcome, the visit furnished all sorts of surprises. The leftist magazine *Siempre* commented editorially, "If in this moment a plebiscite were arranged, we may be assured that 90 per cent of the citizens would decide in favor of closer relations with Rome." René Capistrán, editor of the later-deceased morning paper *Atisbos,* argued throughout the visit that the Mexican government should reappraise its attitude toward the Vatican. *Atisbos* was considered the mouthpiece of the Roman Catholic hierarchy, but if it was that, it received scant support because sometime after the visit it encountered such severe financial difficulties that it ceased publication.

The Tisserant visit also stirred discussion in Mexico of the Vatican's relation with Cuba and other nations, including Franco's Spain. Responding to a newsman's question in this area, the Cardinal commented, "The Church does not interfere in the forms of government a nation has," and ended that part of the interview by quoting the biblical admonition of Christ to render unto Caesar the things that were Caesar's.

To close out the Church's activity in the ten-year span, the final newsworthy event came in the early part of October 1964. At that time a convention of seventy-five Catholic organizations, representing, it was claimed, 4 million practicing Catholics, issued a statement claiming that although the country's social, cultural, and economic progress had been outstanding, unfortunately a large segment of the population had been neglected. The convention, known formally as the First Congress for the Integral Development of Mexico, stirred up quite a bit of interest in Mexico at that time for a variety of reasons, the principal of which was that it represented the first nationwide move in the social area by a sector of the Catholic Church since the anticlerical laws had been put into effect. In the general interpretation, it also indicated a more liberal attitude on the part of the Church than was recorded in the pre-Calles era. "We have a great technical development but we lack human development," the convention's final pronouncement declared. "We observe that in Mexico the advance of industrialization, of agricultural production, and of education once initiated does not always include the harmonious and satisfactory development of benefit for man."

There was widespread speculation at the time about why the convention was organized in the first place and why the final statement was drawn up for public consumption. My own story in this respect commented, "One line of reasoning is that the political situation here is such that virtually all forces in the nation are asserting themselves prior to the change of administration this coming December when Gustavo Díaz Ordaz is to be installed as president of Mexico."

A postscript to the convention was added by the previously mentioned *Atisbos,* which commented editorially, "We have emphasized an infinity of times that the social justice proclaimed by the Mexican Revolution was not in contraposition to but coincided with the social justice defined and demanded by Catholic doctrine." The paper concluded, amidst much eyebrow-lifting, "Therefore it was absurd to consider the revolutionary movement as being essentially anti-religious."

An account of religion in Mexico, no matter how sketchy, would be incomplete without some attention to Mexico's patron saint, the Virgin of Guadalupe. On December 12, 1964, the country celebrated the four-hundred-thirty-third anniversary of the saint in what was probably the most fervent observance in Mexican history, although admittedly these annual observances have become so huge over the years that any attempt to judge the relative sizes from year to year becomes increasingly ridiculous.

Beginning as early as a week before the event, pilgrims, or *peregrinos,* in lines up to a mile in length begin their exhausting walk to the Guadalupe shrine on the outskirts of Mexico City. They have just enough to eat to keep them going. They carry their banner of the patron saint just as Father Hidalgo carried it when he led the first march of the revolt against Spain. The long line is led by the parish priest. The way is made less tedious by hymns and prayers, and there is very little levity, even among the children, who are brought along by the thousands.

The levity begins on the night of December 11, when the greatest religious observance of the year gets underway. By this time hundreds of thousands of pilgrims from all parts of Mexico have converged in the area before the basilica. There is singing and dancing throughout the night, and at dawn the great names of the entertainment world gather to sing *mañanitas,* the "little good mornings" traditionally sung by the courting youth beneath the window of his sweetheart on the latter's birthday.

As usual with gatherings so large, the evening and night are marked with fights, sometimes to the death; with innumerable plunderings of the meager belongings of exhausted pilgrims snatching a few hours of sleep on their mats in the jammed plaza; and with picked pockets. The night is one of color-wheel intensity, with dancers in native dress from all corners of the nation, of noise and of grandeur and of tragedy, with ambulances charging in and out of the crowds to pick up peregrinos who were not able to stand the rigors of the pilgrimage. But the fiesta goes on throughout the night and the whole of the next day, after which the weary pilgrims begin the journey back to their villages.

Masses in honor of the Virgin begin early in the day and continue far into the night. Beginning with the first Mass, long before daybreak, an unceasing procession winds through the basilica to venerate briefly the patron saint, and the procession continues in single file for as long as thirty-six hours.

The story of the Virgin of Guadalupe goes like this: On December 9, 1531 an Indian shepherd named Juan Diego was passing the bottom of Tepeyac Hill, which at that time was far outside the capital near the village of Tepeaquilla. The site is now well within Mexico City, of course. On two successive days, according to the story, the Virgin appeared to Juan asking that he tell the bishop of Mexico to build a shrine on that site. However, each time that Juan described the apparition to Bishop Juan de Zumárraga he was commanded to bring some proof.

Finally on December 12 Juan returned to the site, having missed a day because of the serious illness of his uncle Juan Bernardino. On that day the Virgin informed Juan that his uncle had been cured, and she commanded him to cut some red roses and bring them to her. The roses materialized suddenly in the scrubby land, and Juan cut them and placed them in his *tilma,* a poncho-like cloak still worn by Indian peasants. When the tilma was taken to Bishop Zumárraga and spread before him, the roses were gone, but the tilma is said to have borne the imprint of the Virgin herself.

A church was begun on the site of the apparition on December 26, 1531, and Juan Diego, by this time one of the most famous men in Mexico, was named its sacristan, a position he held the remainder of his life. There is some evidence, but no positive proof, that he was buried in the original church. The tilma originally was preserved in the church, but then was placed in the National Cathedral. In 1695 it was taken back to the original church and in 1709 to the newly-constructed basilica, where it is presently on display. The Virgin, of coppery complexion, is affectionately called by the Indians *La Virgen Morena* or "the dark virgin."[32]

In 1956 the original church of Santa María de Guadalupe, sometimes known as "the old church of the Indians," was declared unsafe beyond repair and there was talk of tearing it down. Not much larger than a average-size room when it was dedicated by Bishop Zumárraga, the original church was enlarged in 1791 and again in 1836. These alterations probably hastened the deterioration of the original structure.

Over the years the veneration of Our Lady of Guadalupe has created widespread controversy sparked by skeptics who have questioned the authenticity of the apparition, of the miraculous healing of Juan Diego's uncle, and of the imprint on the tilma. This skepticism follows the reasoning that the Spanish hierarchy in Mexico felt the need of an ethnologically persuasive virgin to capture the imagination of the Indian worshippers and that, considering the superstitious nature of the Indians, it would not have been difficult to obtain the account of the apparitions, the miraculous cure, and the imprinted tilma.

The only extant factor from the series of events, the tilma, is gravely studied from time to time to see what it might yield up in the way of substantiation. The latest examination to gain attention was one to determine if the reflection of Juan Diego had not been left in the cornea of one of the Virgin's eyes on the tilma. The result of the investigation must have been inconclusive for nothing more was heard from it. In 1963 Archbishop Miguel Dario Miranda designated a commission to study the life of Juan Diego, with the study to serve eventually as a basis for the process of beatification and canonization of the Indian shepherd.

Of the dozen or so sects which over the years fled the United States and Canada to Mexico, the Mennonites have probably made the deepest imprint. Certainly they have caused the most heated controversy. In the mid-1950's the nationalist temper ran so high against them that there was talk of invading their rich and calm farmlands. This sentiment ran its course and died away, and toward the end of the 1950's several thousand members of the sect left their overcrowded property of their own accord to move to large, uncleared tracts in British Honduras. Here, making good use of their ancient gift for industry and frugality, they cleared the jungles and began producing the finest vegetables, butter, and eggs in the

---

[32] Bishop Zumárraga died in 1548 at age eighty, beloved and respected by Indians and Spaniards alike. But not by all, it would appear, because in 1527 he had been appointed inquisitor for the Holy Office, more popularly known as the Inquisition. Certainly one Indian who would not have cared much for him was a cacique of Texcoco who had been sentenced by the Bishop to be burned at the stake for having relapsed into paganism and practiced human sacrifice. [Author's Note]

Caribbean. But, at last report, their project was not doing too well because although their produce was fine there were few to purchase it.

The Mennonites were originally invited to Mexico by the president, Álvaro Obregón. Some two thousand of them accepted the invitation and established themselves between 1921 and 1923 in inhospitable desert areas in the state of Chihuahua near what at the time was a small village named San Antonio de Arenales. The name was later changed to Ciudad Cuauhtémoc after the Aztec warrior-emperor. The first arrivals of the Mennonites had purchased 100,000 acres of land around San Antonio, and at that time the acreage appeared ample for at least a century.

The procreative potential of the sect, once in the wild and barren desert, however, had been sadly underrated. By the early 1940's it was evident the sect would soon be confronted with an insoluble population problem. It was then that negotiations were begun with British Honduran authorities, negotiations which ended in agreement in 1956. The migration began in 1958.

When the Mennonites accepted the Obregón invitation to come to Mexico, they demanded and received certain guarantees which aroused envy among the Mexican population: exemption from any type of military service; exemption from the taking of oaths for any reason; and, finally, an unqualified guarantee of complete freedom to practice their religion. These three guarantees caused great wonderment because at the time a Mexican was likely to be constantly on the verge of being conscripted into somebody's roving warrior-band; to have to take an oath of one kind or another almost daily, and finally, if not Catholic, to be forbidden periodically to practice his religion. Since those first days, there has been hardly a month when the sect has not been under fire for some reason.

The new settlers made the land bloom and yield beyond the wildest anticipation of Obregón. They kept to themselves except for their visits to the market place and were known as a peaceful group if not molested and the producers of the finest vegetables, eggs, and dairy products Mexico had ever known. And they were deeply envied and cordially hated.

The intensity of this resentment reached its high mark when in the mid-1950's an official of the Federal Commission of Electricity demanded the sect explain why all attempts to push federal electrification lines through the Mennonite territory had been sabotaged. Manuel Jesús Villanueva, assistant director of the commission, complained that whenever poles were planted, whether of wood or concrete, and high-tension lines installed, they were invariably found on the ground a few days later.

There was nothing unusual about the attacks on the Mennonites. All the various sects settling in Mexico sooner or later came in for persecution. The electrification incidents, however, became so sharp a matter that the Mennonites finally agreed to let the lines go through their territory. This came about after long and painful debates in the sect councils, where electricity was considered an invention from the netherworld. It was at this time that some of Mexico's demographic authorities demanded the government take action against the sects. Moisés T. de la Peña, one of the country's outstanding demographers, declared in reference to the Mennonites, "They are a demographic tumor. . . . nothing is more undesirable for a country than to have people who accept its hospitality and enrich themselves while assuming conduct inimical to the state."

Yet the Mennonites, of course, saw nothing even remotely inimical in their conduct. All they wanted was to be left alone with their land on which they produced milk, butter, eggs, and cheese for a large part of northern Mexico, all of which is much prized, particularly the famed Chihuahua cheese. The Chihuahuans, in fact, claim that a deficiency of this cheese makes them wan and listless.

International Relations

In 1956 I received a request to make a study of United States policy first in Mexico and then in the entire area extending to Colombia. The objectives of the United States in Mexico, I wrote at that time, were "about the same as our objectives the world over, but with some unusual characteristics because of geography, history, and culture. These basic objectives could, in very general terms, be classified as: betterment of international relations; betterment of economic relations; and combatting of Communism in its pure form or, further, of those forces that are thought to contribute to the increased strength of Communism here.

"At the beginning of the present administration (that of Adolfo Ruiz Cortines) a little over three years ago, the relations between the United States and Mexico were restrained. The attitude of Mexico toward the position of the United States at the Organization of American States conference in Caracas, March 1954, was, if not actually hostile, certainly antipathetic. Actually it appears this conference marked a turning point in current Mexican-United States relations.

"Some say that President Adolfo Ruiz Cortines clamped down on the mushrooming 'anti-gringoism' to such an extent he completely reoriented his country's foreign policy in regard to the United States. Whatever the cause, relations began improving almost from the date of that conference, and at present they are better, on the surface at least, than they have been in years."

Mexico's international relations, of course, are concerned for the most part with the United States. There are periods of intense preoccupation with its Latin American sister states, but even these can in a number of instances, perhaps even in a majority, be traced to some phase of its relationship with the United States.

Relations with the United States waver year in and year out between deeply troubled and more or less tranquil phases, but in the last century and more there have not been any appreciable periods in which there were not some nettling matters disturbing the peace. The heartening note is that in the last decade the tendency seems to be toward calmer relations. Each nation appears to be approaching a mature recognition of the other's position. The United States, for instance, shown signs of abandoning somewhat at least the heavy-handed tactic of throwing its garbage over its neighbor's fence and daring him to throw it back. Mexico, on its side, has been showing signs of letting up on its resentful tactic of kicking Uncle Sam in the shins at the slightest provocation. There will never, of course, be a protracted era of sweetness and light between the two countries, because of geographical proximity, the long arm of history, and the impossibility of cultural integration. But there has been definite improvement over the years and much of this appears to be attributable to the calm thinking and flexibility of a younger breed of men in high office on both sides.

The young men who have been coming into positions of influence in Mexico in recent years are for the most part products of their Mexican background plus training in foreign universities, either in the United States or Europe. They have been able to retain their deep-rooted national pride and dignity and at the same time have an international outlook. While they remain wary of the overpowering wealth and aggressiveness of the United States in international economic and political affairs, they nevertheless have become trained to evaluate the actions of the United States coolly and with an eye to their own advantage.

Further, these newer additions to the scene of Mexican public affairs are not unacquainted with a growing sentiment in Latin America, and particularly in Central America, of apprehension over Mexico's rapidly growing influence. At one Middle American conference, I was drowsing through a warm afternoon, listening with only half attention to the rousing oratory, when the phrase "colossus of the North" pierced my consciousness. "Now it comes," I thought, "Old Uncle Sam gets his beard pulled again." I was consequently astonished to learn the Central American delegate was referring to Mexico rather than the United States. I later recounted this to a young executive of the National Bank of Mexico who remarked with a grin, "Well, it looks as if we have finally arrived."

Doubtlessly the tensest moments in United States-Mexican relations in the last decade have arisen one way or another in connection with Castro's Cuba. In the late winter of 1960 our office in New York was informed by a memo that the United States embassy in Mexico City was becoming increasingly apprehensive over Mexico's attitude toward Cuban activities in the Mexican capital. It was known at that time that personnel in our embassy were furnishing the Mexican government with chapter and verse about these activities.

In April 1960, I filed a story noting, "There is growing conviction in knowledgeable circles here that the Mexican government's attitude toward Cuba is rapidly stiffening.[33] There are numerous conjectures on what action will be taken, but it is considered almost certain measures soon will be put in motion to curb the activities of diplomatic personnel assigned here by the Fidel Castro regime and also to adopt a firmer policy with elements based here in opposition to Castro."

This had been, as was learned later, about the time of the turning point in Mexican-United States relations over Cuba. Before that time there had been some lifted eyebrows in Washington over the Cuban embassy's activities in the Mexican capital, but beginning sometime in the spring of 1960 the strain began to tell. In June, a story in this respect was sent, explaining, "The Mexican government is making determined efforts to assure calm during the visit here of President Osvaldo Dorticós of Cuba." The story went on to describe the efforts of the government and all communications media to assure a peaceable reception for the visiting chief of state and added, "The left-oriented Federation of Mexican Youths was the first organization to express publicly concern over what it described as a reactionary plan to disrupt the visit. It called on state authorities to provide the 'maximum securities' to snuff out any hostile demonstrations." The story continued, "The extreme right National Sinarquista Union noted the impending visit with the question of whether it would mean the narrowing of ties between Mexico and Cuba or be a signal for leftist agitation."

The following day President Dorticós arrived. A news story dictated to New York that day noted, "He was greeted at the International Airport

[33] Mexico, like most Latin American countries and the United States itself, was clearly elated when Castro gained power in January 1959. The removal of General Fulgencio Batista from office after his long dictatorship was greeted with enthusiasm and new hope for the future. Mexico's sympathies with the revolutionary government not only were based on ideological considerations, but also had historical roots. Mexicans have long regarded themselves as the first to have undergone a complete revolutionary experience, setting them apart in the Western Hemisphere. Although the Mexicans never tried systematically to export revolution, their dedication to the forces and ideals of the cause has continued unabated—for some in earnest and for others in a purely nominal sense. The Mexicans took a kind of proprietary pride in the seeming Cuban emulation of their example. However, the Cuban movement was viewed as a distinctly national movement, not directly inspired by either the Mexican or Russian examples, but one which merited encouragement for its goals of social and economic reforms. The Mexicans could identify with the Cuban revolutionaries, who were undergoing analogous experiences, particularly with respect to the achievement of economic independence through severing the bonds with American capitalism.

In regard to subsequent developments, Mexico has tread the difficult path of trying to maintain an independent foreign policy vis-à-vis Castro's Cuba without antagonizing the United States. The Mexican policy has represented a devotion to traditional principles—national self-determination, sovereignty, and nonintervention—more than to ideology. [Editor's Note]

by about 15,000 persons." The story continued, "The atmosphere at the airport when the Cuban president arrived for a five-day state visit appeared to be more anti-American than pro-Cuban. Hundreds of spectators set up the chant, 'Cuba yes—Yankees no' as President Dorticós, accompanied by President Adolfo López Mateos of Mexico, headed a procession through the throng. Some of the cheering for the visiting dignitary and against the United States was led by the Mexican Communist David Alfaro Siqueiros, one of the country's greatest muralists. The artist stopped his chanting long enough to give a statement to the North American press. He declared, 'The Cuban revolution has been the most important social movement in all Latin America. The defense of this revolution by Mexico is fundamental to the struggle against North American imperialism.' " It was the last time, so far as we know, that Sr. Siqueiros was seen publicly in company with President López Mateos. Two months later he was in the penitentiary on a charge of social dissolution, specifically of inciting to riot, and the arrest was made at the order of President López Mateos.

In some of the articles following the arrival story it was explained that the Mexican government was drastically tightening its security measures. The Cuban exiles were mentioned, and it was noted, "In the past four days these exiles have abandoned their almost daily visits to domestic newspapers and foreign newspaper bureaus. The telephones of these exiles have not been answered for several days. There are recurrent reports that some of the exiles are under temporary arrest or at least under surveillance, and others have been advised to remain out of Mexico City during the Dorticós visit."

The plot began to thicken in July of 1960. One dispatch noted, "A struggle appears in the making between Cuba and the United States over Mexican crude oil." All of this began shaping up less than a month after the Dorticós visit. The dispatch continued, "It is considered certain in well-informed quarters that Cuba has unofficially expressed a desire for a sizeable amount of Mexico's crude oil as complementary to the shipments it is receiving from the Soviet Union. This is a matter of conviction here despite official denials from Petróleos Mexicanos (PEMEX), the Mexican nationalized petroleum industry, that it has ever been approached with a formal offer by Cuban representatives.

"Again it is considered certain the United States is prepared to go to unusual lengths to discourage the sale of Mexican crude oil for refining in the British and American-owned plants newly seized in Cuba by the Castro regime. A Cuban commission has been in Mexico the past week inspecting the operations of PEMEX and interviewing Pascual Gutiérrez Roldán, director general of the petroleum organization. Robert C. Hill, the United States ambassador to Mexico, paid a surprise visit yesterday to Sr. Gutiérrez Roldán at PEMEX headquarters here. A spokesman for PEMEX explained the commission was comprised of petroleum engineering students studying Mexican refining methods."

The habitually ebullient and forthright Ambassador Hill described his visit to Sr. Gutiérrez as a purely personal one. The Ambassador explained he had just returned from vacation and decided to drop in on his old friend Pascual, a story nobody gave much credence. Sr. Gutiérrez Roldán was almost as coy, but he finally agreed that he and the Ambassador had had "some conversation over the fuel export situation."

The air of tension and mystery was growing rapidly at this time, quite possibly the most dramatic period in what might be called "act one" in the Cuban affair. The curtain line to that act came July 7, when in the Chamber of Deputies Representative Emilio Sánchez Piedras told a cheering audience that Mexico was definitely on the side of Cuba. Sr. Sánchez Piedras was president of the Permanent Committee of Congress, a body that sits while the regular Congress is in recess.

To bring the Sánchez Piedras remarks into perspective one had to go back five days to the incident which led up to this remarkable performance from the legislative representative of a country which ordinarily loses no possible opportunity to stress its tradition of neutrality. On July 1, 1960 in Guaymas, Sonora, President López Mateos set a news conference abuzz and electrified the nation when he defined for newspaper, radio, and television reporters the policy of his government as being of the extreme left, "within the Constitution."

My dispatch of July 2 in respect to President López Mateos' policy announcement noted, "The clarification of policy made at a news conference at Guaymas, Sonora last night follows a week of confusion in which the national policy was defined variously by top administration officials and by leaders of the administration's political organization, the Institutional Revolutionary Party. Last week the leader of the administration party, Alfonso Corona del Rosal, announced the administration's ideological position as being 'moderately left.' Since that time the debate has been carried on with rising heat by both the extreme left and the extreme right. More moderate authorities began advocating a clear-cut pronouncement of national policy by the president himself.

"In response to a direct question last night the president replied, 'The line of policy either right or left depends on the point of view of the center. In reality you know that our Constitution emanates from a typically popular revolution.' The president then went on to say, 'Our Constitution is derived from a popular left constitution in the sense we give the word 'left' in Mexico. Now my government is, within the Constitution, of the extreme left.' "

And so back to Sr. Sánchez Piedras. On the afternoon of July 7, 1960 he had called an extraordinary session of the Permanent Committee. The purpose of the meeting was to define the 'extreme left' statement of President López Mateos, or perhaps "discuss" the statement would be a better word because in Mexico the Congress accepts the presidential pronouncements with very little question. At any rate, word got around rapidly that afternoon that the committee president was going to drop a blockbuster, thus assuring a large audience. My account of it, sent that afternoon but unpublished, noted, "Mr. Sánchez Piedras told the committee, 'In the conflict confronting the United States and Cuba, which is each day becoming more tense, Mexico is with Cuba.' The committee president added, 'In this critical moment for our sister republic, when it seems our northern neighbor closes its doors to friendship and understanding in relation to Cuban desires to live in liberty and economic independence, we the representatives of the people of Mexico offer our friendship to the Cuban people. We are sympathetic to the Cuban people in their right to live, and we are certain their right to live in social justice and economic liberty will prevail on this continent.'

"This represents the most concise statement made publicly thus far of Mexican policy regarding Cuba. It is being taken here as an authorized statement of policy inasmuch as the Permanent Committee speaks with the voice of Congress and in a matter of this importance Congress would hardly speak without having advised the government and the political organization of the administration of its intentions."

A day later Manuel Moreno Sánchez, leader of the Senate and a party hack who rarely overlooks an opportunity to take off from a publicity springboard,[34] undertook to clarify further the administration's position vis-à-vis Cuba at a press conference. My story noted, "In so doing he declared bluntly that Mexico should give oil to Cuba. He declared that Cuba was undergoing a 'period of crisis, not political but social and human.' The senator added 'I do not believe any people of the Americas, including us Mexicans, can be indifferent to such a situation.' "

At that time Senator Moreno Sánchez dismissed the remarks of Deputy Sánchez Piedras as being his own views and not necessarily reflecting the official attitude. A story filed July 9 noted, "It has been learned from an authoritative source that this same view was expressed last night to United States Ambassador Robert C. Hill by the Mexican foreign minister, Manuel Tello." Before Ambassador Hill called on Foreign Minister Tello in Mexico, Ambassador Antonio Carrillo Flores in Washington had

[34] During the early summer of 1968, Sr. Moreno Sánchez, no longer a member of the Senate, published a series of articles in *Excélsior,* noteworthy for their informed and critical tone, about the operating political procedures of the PRI. This action suggests a person of greater substance and complexity than the Kennedy categorization would suggest. [Editor's Note]

been called to the Department of State to explain what the Sánchez Piedras remarks had amounted to officially. Ambassador Hill emerged from his hour-long meeting with Sr. Tello looking grimmer than I had ever seen him. We were nominally on quite friendly terms, but for the first and, so far as can be remembered, only time, he brushed aside questions with "no comment."

On July 11, I wrote, "Foreign Minister Manuel Tello reiterated today Mexico's sympathy for Cuba but suggested a solution should be sought in the inter-American system in Cuba's dispute with the United States. The foreign minister's statement issued this afternoon followed five days of confusion caused by a congressman's statement Thursday that Mexico was on the side of Cuba in its dispute with the United States.

"Sr. Tello made two additional points in his three-hundred-word statement. These were: that U.S. Ambassador Robert C. Hill was within his diplomatic rights calling on the foreign ministry as he did last Friday for an explanation of the statement of Deputy Emilio Sánchez Piedras and that the statement of the legislator did not compromise the Mexican administration and was not necessarily a reflection of the administration's viewpoint. There still remains a conviction among many observers here, however, that Sr. Sánchez Piedras could not have made his statement without prior knowledge of the administration's Institutional Revolutionary Party, of which he is a prominent member.

"Editorial comment has been critical here of the United States ambassador's request for an explanation of the remarks as an intrusion on Mexico's sovereignty. In his statement Foreign Minister Tello observed that during his ambassadorship in Washington he called on the State Department several times for clarification of remarks made in the United States Congress." There were continued mumblings of criticism in the press and radio, however, over the affair.[35] Throughout the turbulent days Foreign Minister Tello and Ambassador Hill remained on their usual friendly terms, and both Sr. Tello and Ambassador Carrillo Flores went to unusual lengths to calm the situation.

Senator Moreno Sánchez was later depicted in cartoons with a zipper on his lips. Deputy Sánchez Piedras caused another flurry three months

---

[35] The confusing series of events caught up the staid and conservative American Chamber of Commerce in Mexico as well as some assorted travel agents who foresaw a loss of revenue from the adverse effect of the news on tourism. Both groups were inclined to place the responsibility, not on those responsible for creating the farcical chain of events, but on the foreign correspondents for having reported the affair. As the indices for foreign investments began tobogganing, the indignation and criticism grew. One lesson that could have been learned from this entire affair was that foreign investors were not remotely concerned with the comments of legislators or others, but rather pinned their action in restricting the flow of investments solely to the few words of President López Mateos. [Author's Note]

after his original remarks when he spoke at a legislative session welcoming invited guests to the one-hundred-fiftieth anniversary of Mexico's independence. He told the assembled guests, among them three United States legislators, that the Cuban revolution had freed that country "from outside forces as sinister of those of Nazism, Fascism, and Francoism." The three legislators were Senators Kenneth B. Keating of New York and Thomas J. Dodd of Connecticut and Representative John J. Rhodes of Arizona. The three, along with Ambassador Hill, declined later to attend an official luncheon for foreign delegates. In a formal statement Ambassador Hill deplored the "unfriendliness and discourtesy" of the remarks. A representative of President López Mateos called on the United States delegation with personal apologies. Deputy Sánchez Piedras dropped completely out of the public eye.

In retrospect this entire series of events loses much of its starch and becomes what in reality it was, a diplomatic drawing room comedy. It is related here to demonstrate how wheels within wheels may be set in motion by the random remark of a chief of state.

It was not until 1961 that our file began reflecting what proved to be Mexico's permanent policy on Cuba, that of strict neutrality. In a dispatch of May 5 of that year it was noted, "This country appears to be making a fresh appraisal of its position vis-à-vis the Cuban-United States conflict. The indications are that the original official attitude of neutrality in principle is becoming more pronounced. There are signs too that the man in the street is re-examining his own attitude, which has rarely approached neutrality in principle. It has heretofore been largely in support of Cuba. The re-evaluation process appears to have begun with the anti-Castro invasion of Cuba in mid-April and been given distinct impetus by the May Day address of Prime Minister Fidel Castro four days ago.

"The attitude of strengthened neutrality was interpreted into the action of Congress this past Thursday in refusing permission to Mexican citizens to participate in Cuban military activities either for or against Castro. The action was taken by the Permanent Committee of Congress, which has full legislative authority in certain matters when Congress as a whole is not in session."

Later in this same article it was stated, "It is an open secret that a sizeable body of official opinion is convinced a show of hands among the hemisphere nations is becoming more imminent in the Cuban affair. In this official sector it is felt that Mexico will experience real difficulty in maintaining its distance in the United States-Cuban dispute. It is known that the United States embassy here has had conversations recently with the Foreign Office relative to the Mexican position. It appears that in these conversations the Mexican officials have indicated concern over some sort of a showdown on Cuba. The obvious explorations in this connection would be to sound out Mexico's position should the dispute be taken to the Organization of American States, a move gathering some support from the Latin American countries."

Certainly events were picking up speed, and looking back now with the advantage of hindsight these events appear to have all been building up toward the Organization of American States intervention. It developed there had been real reason for concern on the part of the United States. In December 1961, Mexico was the only other nation besides Cuba to vote at Punta del Este against holding a convocation of foreign ministers for consideration of the Cuban question. At that time Mexico specifically wanted to make clear that its position was based on juridical considerations.[36]

The Senate, with Manuel Moreno Sánchez leading the way, voted to approve the action of Vicente Sánchez Gavito, Mexican ambassador to the Organization of American States, in placing Mexico against the resolution. It was officially explained at the time that it had not been made certain that the resolution came within the mutual assistance article of the 1947 Rio Convention. The United States had been extremely anxious to get a unanimous vote, and Mexico's dissidence caused deep-rooted resentment. Senator Moreno Sánchez explained later, "any interpretation that this was an unfriendly act on the part of Mexico against anyone is in itself an unfriendly act against Mexico."

---

[36] One of the basic tenets of Mexican foreign policy has been nonintervention in the internal affairs of other states. This attitude was a natural response to the country's historical experiences before and during the Revolution, when military, political, and economic interventions on the part of the United States and European powers were endured. This principle, as well as related ones, was restated and to a degree systematized by the so-called Doctrina Carranza ("Carranza Doctrine") during the Revolution.

The Foreign Ministry follows, therefore, a very strict interpretation of Article 15 of the OAS Charter, which prohibits its members from intervening in the affairs of other states, including even discussing them at international conferences. When, in December 1961, the OAS discussed the calling of a Consultative Meeting of Foreign Ministers regarding the Cuban situation, six Latin American nations, including the three largest, demurred, but when the chips were down Mexico found herself alone in casting a negative vote along with the Cuban representatives. Mexico's dedication to principle, admirable as it was, resulted in her finding herself diplomatically isolated at Punta del Este, an unenviable and costly position for an emerging nation placed in geographic proximity and intimately tied economically to the most powerful nation in the hemisphere. Special effort was made by Mexico's leadership to avoid a repetition of this untenable situation at the ensuing Consultative Foreign Ministers Meeting in Punta del Este in January 1962 and subsequently at the Ninth Consultative Meeting of Foreign Ministers in 1964. At the latter meeting Uruguay, Chile, and Bolivia joined with Mexico in casting negative votes on a resolution related to Cuba. Since that time Mexico is the only country which has continued to maintain diplomatic relations with Cuba. [Editor's Note]

In April 1962, for reasons never made clear, José Antonio Portuondo, an intellectual follower of Castro and a probable militant Communist, was replaced as Cuban ambassador to Mexico by Carlos M. Lechuga, a political activist. Two months later, in June, Blas Roca (Francisco Calderío), secretary general of the Communist Party in Cuba entered Mexico (four days before the visit of President John F. Kennedy) and disappeared for four days. In October, the chain of events being dealt with here, that is the strengthening of forces leading up to a probable OAS meeting, was interrupted by the larger event of President Kennedy's television talk announcing Cuba's nuclear buildup. It made an enormous impression in Mexico.

The Mexican role in this revelation by the United States president was the dispatch of notes by President López Mateos to presidents Kennedy and Dorticós. In the notes, dispatched by the Mexican president while on a trip to the Near East, according to official Mexican report, the president "made a plea for peace and, with reference to the existence in Cuban territory of platforms for launching projectiles of medium and long range capable of nuclear cargoes, he expressed to President Dorticós his fervent desire that these projectiles should not be used in any manner and further that offensive arms should be retired from Cuba."

The simple notes failed to reflect the important fact that President López Mateos had been placed in quite a difficult spot. He had, on the one hand, indicated sympathy for certain Cuban aims and certainly had greeted President Dorticós warmly. On the other, however, he had adopted as one of the main pillars of the international policy of his administration complete hostility to the introduction of nuclear weaponry into Latin America. He had, long before the Cuban crisis, taken the lead in Latin America against development and testing of nuclear weapons in the area and, indeed, had been mentioned tentatively by the Mexican press as a Nobel peace prize candidate for his vigorous efforts in this direction.

Mexico appeared to take this dilemma in stride. In fact a number of prominent Mexicans we mentioned it to failed to understand the awkwardness of their president's position. A Mexican president on taking over his country's leadership inherits a set of contradictions he must live with over a six-year term. Basically, he is required to actively demonstrate his independence at all times from the United States, and yet while doing this he is expected to maintain at least the essentials of a working relationship with the northern neighbor. The time-worn phrase about Mexico being "so far from God and so near the United States" is at least partially true in respect to that country's position. Mexico appears to be closer to God than it was when the classic remark was uttered some four decades ago, but it must struggle to maintain a distance from the United States, in its own mind and in the mind of others, or suffer a serious sapping of strength.

In the spring of 1964 Venezuela became active throughout Latin America in promoting its resolution for an Organization of American States meeting of foreign ministers to consider diplomatic and economic sanctions against Cuba. The conference was finally held in Washington in August 1964, and something of a shock resulted when Mexico, along with Uruguay, Chile, and Bolivia voted negatively on Venezuela's resoluton to break diplomatic relations with Cuba.[37] The vote was 16 to 4.

There was no occasion for surprise in Mexico's action, however. Long before the conference took place, Foreign Minister José Gorostiza, who had earlier replaced Sr. Tello on an interim basis, had politely informed Marcos Falcón Briceño, Venezuelan foreign minister, that Mexico could not be counted on to vote against Cuba. The specific complaint against Cuba was that the Castro regime was responsible for having sent to Venezuela a quantity of arms which had been discovered buried the previous November. A news agency dispatch, according to Sr. Gorostiza, had speculated that Mexico would join in some form of censure against Cuba. The Mexican foreign minister informed Venezuela of its feeling in the matter, while formally denying the news dispatch.

As late, however, as three weeks before the meeting was to have been called there did not appear to be complete unanimity in the Mexican government about its position at the forthcoming meeting. Sr. Gorostiza, following a conference with President López Mateos July 1, told newsmen that Mexico did not have a "rigid position" on the Venezuelan proposal. At that time if Sr. Gorostiza knew he was to be passed over as head of the Mexican delegation to the forthcoming OAS conference he did not mention it. Two weeks later an announcement came from the National Palace that Vicente Sánchez Gavito, Mexico's ambassador to the OAS, was going to head the Mexican delegation at the conference.

Friends of Sr. Gorostiza reacted to this decision with profound sympathy for the foreign minister. He had served the government many years, and it was well known he was contemplating retirement. It was felt that

[37] Mexican recognition policy is based on the noninterventionist concept incorporated in the Estrada Doctrine, formulated by Mexico's foreign minister in 1929. That doctrine stipulates that recognition or nonrecognition of a foreign government should not be determined by the type of administration in control because this would constitute a moral judgment implying intervention; rather, recognition should be based solely on the regime's capacity to control the country. This doctrine was influenced to a considerable degree by the recognition policies of President Woodrow Wilson and his successors toward Mexican revolutionary governments in particular and toward Latin American governments in general. [Editor's Note]

the final honor of speaking for his country at an international conference, a highly important one, could have been awarded him without too much difficulty. The official explanation, which was not given much credence, was that duties concerning the coming change in administration required the presence of the foreign minister in the country.

The consensus among foreign diplomats and most foreign correspondents appeared to be that the failure to follow tradition was a form of protest on Mexico's part against the virtual certainty of a favorable vote on the Venezuela resolution. In any case, Sr. Gorostiza retired from the foreign service in 1965 when the Foreign Ministry was taken over by the former Mexican ambassador to Washington, Antonio Carrillo Flores.

Mexico's negative vote came through as expected, and a diplomatic chill set in between Mexico and the United States. Only some fast diplomatic footwork by Ambassador Sánchez Gavito brought about something of a thaw. He had arranged a luncheon for the Mexican newsmen covering the OAS conference in Washington, at which Thomas C. Mann, assistant secretary of state for inter-American affairs and a personal friend of Sr. Sánchez Gavito, gave the principal talk. Referring to the recent strain over the OAS vote, Mr. Mann commented, "Our differences, if such exist, are of such a nature that they can be arranged if not today, then tomorrow." I reported the following day, "The daily press here, representing all political shades from far left to far right, gave the most prominent display possible to the State Department official's remarks."

Immediately after the conference, on August 3, Sr. Gorostiza issued a statement from the Foreign Ministry declaring Mexico would not break relations. A week later Chile, one of the four countries that had voted against the resolution, changed its position and announced suspension of relations with Cuba. In turn Uruguay and Bolivia also announced suspension, thus leaving Mexico alone in its position. It was not an enviable position, but enviable or not it was the position inherited by Gustavo Díaz Ordaz when he took over leadership of the government in December 1964. It was insistently rumored the position was not particularly to the liking of the new president, but it had not been changed by late 1965 and there were no indications that it would be under present circumstances.

Relations between the United States and Mexico continued on an even course and in some instances even reached a degree of warmth as in the resolution of the ancient border dispute over the Chamizal district in El Paso, and in the at least partial solution to the Mexicali Valley saline water dispute. Whereas the Cuban problem was a latecomer in the century-old pageant of difficulties between the United States and Mexico, the Chamizal dispute was one of the oldest and most perplexing of the lot. It was hopefully written off once and for all in September 1964, when

Presidents López Mateos of Mexico and Lyndon B. Johnson of the United States gave one another a fraternal *abrazo,* or "hug," on the International Bridge between El Paso, Texas, and Ciudad Juárez, Mexico. Formal diplomatic and international legalistic niceties had been observed, and with this person-to-person act of friendship on the bridge the old and rancorous Chamizal dispute had been brought to an end.

Shortly after the ceremony on the bridge the two presidents went to the disputed area, gave brief speeches expressing mutual esteem, which gave every appearance of sincerity, and the disputed piece of land was in large part officially turned over to Mexico. Two things emerged with clarity in the settlement: first the disputed area was never worth the bitterness it created over the years between the two nations, and, secondly, the turning over of the property by the United States to Mexico was about the most meaningless, yet one of the most effective diplomatic gestures in our history.

Decade after decade since 1852 El Chamizal was intermittently brought out into the open like a tired, old horse, beaten thoroughly as the two nations glared at each other across the scrubby waste, and then allowed to go back to sleep until brought out the next time. At the bottom of the whole matter was the capricious old Rio Grande, or Río Bravo, as it is known south of the border. The river has shifted its banks so often that during the half-century before the settlement no less than two hundred tracts changed hands, quite peacefully and without benefit of fanfare, from Mexican to United States ownership or vice versa. The meandering river would cut off a piece of Mexico in one place and put it on the United States side, and at another place add a piece of United States to the Mexican side. The cut-out portions were called *bancos,* and under the treaty of 1905 many thousands of acres formerly on the United States side of the river passed to Mexican sovereignty and many other thousands formerly on the Mexican side passed to U.S. sovereignty. These shifts were arranged quietly and amicably. But the Chamizal was different; it became a cause.

A disproportionately large amount of space is devoted to the Chamizal here because for years on end it presented one of the most difficult problems in international relations. All-out Mexican nationalists and dedicated anti-gringoists never lacked for a call to common action as long as there was a Chamizal. The subject of the ancient quarrel is a 600-acre tract just south of the rapidly growing city of El Paso, Texas, which is contained to the north by mountains and to the south by the Mexican border. A vagary of the Rio Grande placed the area in Mexico in 1852, but the United States maintained it had never left the United States. An arbitration commission in 1911 awarded most of the disputed area to Mexico, but the United States, after having agreed to the arbitration, de-

David Alfaro Siqueiros in his studio, holding up one of hundreds of paintings he did while in jail, says "They didn't let me see the real flowers, so I painted them." (Basil Williams/Camera Press-Pix)

The section of Diego Rivera's mural in the Hotel del Prado in Mexico City which caused a furor when unveiled in 1948 because of the words "God does not exist." The mural was boarded over until 1956, when Rivera painted over the offending legend. (Wide World Photos)

Facing page: Dr. Atl in 1951. (Abitia Photos)

Paul Kennedy at Teotihuacán with archeologists from the
National Institute of Anthropology and History. (Photo by
Tor Eigeland)

clared it would not accept the commission's decision. Meanwhile El Paso was not only clamoring for title to the property but was actually building on it. The nominal value of the disputed area was $20 million more or less, and was increasing as downtown El Paso began edging into it. But that price tag was not the point at all.

Time after time since the arbitration award, in totally unrelated disputes with Mexico, the United States asked for international arbitration, but Mexico fell back on the old Chamizal award and declined to enter into further arbitration agreements, arguing with validity that it saw no future in another "heads I win, tails you lose" proposition. Finally, in his visit to Mexico in 1962, President John F. Kennedy agreed that the dispute had gone on long enough. He and President López Mateos issued a joint communiqué, which stated, "The two presidents discussed the problem of the Chamizal. They agreed to instruct their executive agencies to recommend a complete solution to this problem which, without prejudice to their judicial positions, takes into account the entire history of this tract."

With that, the matter was placed in the hands of Thomas C. Mann, at that time United States ambassador to Mexico. Mr. Mann, a thoroughgoing professional in the diplomatic field, had three problems facing him, each of them serious: First he had to deal with the Mexican government, which over the years had become case-hardened to the Chamizal as an issue; secondly, he had to fight his way through a ton of documentation in our State Department archives, documentation proving or supposedly proving the purity of the United States' purpose in Chamizal. And finally, the most important of all so far as Ambassador Mann was concerned, he himself was not only a Texan but also a member of an old El Paso family. His people had had a law firm in El Paso for many years, Mr. Mann himself having hereditary rights in it. There probably was not an El Paso family involved in the Chamizal that was not known to him or perhaps even represented in one way or another by the law firm of Mann and Mann.

Mr. Mann, noted for the "soft sell" in diplomatic dealings and with a number of tough assignments behind him, began making small dents and finally larger ones in the problem. For the record, it seemed to many of us observers at the time that he was having as much difficulty with his own State Department and his own El Paso as he was having with Mexico. In February 1963 I noted in a story, "Thomas C. Mann, United States ambassador to Mexico, left the capital last night for four days of negotiations with Texas authorities over the Chamizal area. Before departure he expressed hope for an agreement over the disputed area soon. His trip at this time has added to recent optimism that the 112-year-old quarrel over the highly-complicated El Chamizal is nearer to solution now than at any time since it began in 1852." This assessment was not as prophetic as many, including myself, would have liked it to be. Mr. Mann's office in the embassy had passed out the word that the boss appeared on the verge of closing the decisive deal, but we were not to attribute it to the embassy for fear of a backfire.

A number of snags were forthwith encountered, followed by a number of frustrations. But on July 18, 1963 simultaneous announcements were made by Presidents Kennedy in Washington and López Mateos in Mexico that a settlement had been agreed on through which a major part of the disputed area would be returned to Mexico. Mexico's attitude over the years might be gauged in a single headline appearing in one of the Mexico City papers that morning. It read, "We get it back and we pay nothing for it because it was always ours."

The last I heard about El Chamizal in the Mexican capital was a report that a commission had been appointed to oversee the beautification and utilization of the land. By the time the settlement was reached several Mexicans, some of them government officials, had bought up property on the edges and saw it jump in value overnight. It is planned now to present the Chamizal area as a showcase of Mexico to North Americans as they enter, and above all to prevent it from becoming what Ciudad Juárez already is, a center of vice for North American amusement.[38]

Another perennial basis for bitterness between Mexico and the United States has been the deep-rooted system of *bracerismo*. *Braceros* (from the Spanish word for "arm") are Mexican farm laborers who, until midnight on December 31, 1964, were brought by the hundreds of thousands into the United States to harvest crops, mostly in the rich valleys along the border from California to Texas. But this labor was not confined to the border area. It was used effectively as far north as the state of Washington on the West Coast, Colorado in the Rocky Mountain area, and Michigan in the Midwest.

To get into the highly complex problem even superficially one has to unravel some of the paradoxes involved. Highly-placed Mexicans often refer to the bracero system as "our shame." Various state governments, in an orgy of ambivalence, have attempted to make the bracero candidate work on Mexican farms for certain periods as a condition for receiving permission to go to the United States. But at the same time the bracero

---

[38] In December 1968, the two presidents participated in a joint ceremony to divert the Rio Grande at El Paso and Ciudad Juárez back to its original course. Mexico gained possession of 630 acres, while 193 were assigned to the United States. In the minds of Mexicans, the event had far greater psychological impact than its physical dimensions might suggest. For them, it meant that they had gained diplomatically a portion of land, albeit miniscule, from the "Colossus of the North," which had taken so much from them in the past. [Editor's Note]

has been warmly encouraged to take off for the states as quickly as possible so as to begin sending back remittances to his home.

Learned professors of sociology and anthropology over the years have talked and written at length about the dislocation involved in this mass population shift each year. As the migration began, wives and sweethearts in the *poblaciones* mourned, as New England women mourned when their men went down to the sea, and children wept. Publicly the national government managed a stern, no-nonsense attitude toward Mexicans leaving their native land, but privately the procedure was approved because of the boost to the national economy and the highly useful factor of helping to overcome Mexico's perennial trade imbalance.[39]

From the first the leftist factions never ceased opposing the system and went so far as to issue a propaganda film, *Espaldas Mojadas* ("Wetbacks"), which was distributed widely in Mexico and in many countries of Latin America. The film was a bitter one, unabashedly an attack on the United States rather than a documentary treatment of the early braceros. It strengthened arguments in the diatribe against conscienceless United States employers who hired illegally-entered Mexicans under slavelike conditions. Yet even a documentary treatment could have presented an effective case against the employers, for many wetbacks, so-called because they waded or swam across the Rio Grande to enter the United States surreptitiously, actually worked until they were apprehended for little or no take-home pay.

When the treaty finally ran out and the door was closed, at least temporarily, to braceros, *Siempre,* a moderately left magazine which had been vigorous in its attacks on the entire system, did something of a turnabout in its first issue following termination of the treaty. A cartoon was published depicting farm laborers facing a closed door marked "USA—No More Braceros Wanted." One of the laborers was shown walking away muttering, "All right, we will go back to our own national prosperity."

There is no precise history of how Mexican labor came to be utilized in the United States. Certainly the procedure began under conditions of concealment and did not come fully into the open until 1942, when the first formal agreement was executed between the two countries as a result of labor needs for the war effort. Executive agreements of one kind or another existed between the two countries from that time until the beginning of 1965. At first these agreements meant little. They established

[39] The remittances of the braceros during peak years have been estimated to amount to $100 million annually. In addition, the movement of labor northward helped to resolve some of the population excesses in rural areas and in depressed mining zones. [Editor's Note]

certain rules under which Mexican nationals could be hired through a system of certification. But this over-the-table hiring of legally imported Mexican labor did not prevent the wholesale under-the-table employment of illegally imported wetback labor.

In 1952 the National Farm Labor Union of the United States submitted a memorandum to the House Subcommittee on Labor and Labor Management Relations declaring that for some crops in the Imperial Valley of California 60 per cent of the total work force was illegally imported Mexican labor, with about 25 per cent legally imported labor and the remaining 15 per cent United States nationals. Also included were statistics indicating that in one year, 1951, 40,000 illegal entries, wetbacks, were employed in California alone, with probably many times that number hired totally in Arizona, New Mexico, Texas, and Florida. Richard H. Hancock, in *The Role of the Bracero in the Economic and Cultural Dynamics of Mexico,* published by the Hispanic American Society of Stanford University, offered statistics to show that 1,000,000 wetbacks were apprehended by the United States Immigration Service in both 1953 and 1954. The data, the source of which was the House Committee on Agriculture, showed that in 1953 a total of 198,424 Mexican farm laborers were admitted legally and in 1954, 310,476 were.

More than five years before the bracero program was brought to a showdown resulting in termination of the public law, Gladwin Hill, the *New York Times* correspondent in Los Angeles, began calling the turn. Mr. Hill, interested for years in the migratory labor problem, filed in April 1959 from Los Angeles a story which began:

"What are those people doing?" asked Alice, surveying a vast fertile southwestern valley.

"They're cultivating surplus cotton and lettuce," replied the Red Queen.

"Who are they?" asked Alice, tactfully ignoring the matter of why anyone should produce surplus crops.

"They are Mexicans imported because of the labor shortage," explained the Red Queen.

"Labor shortage?" asked Alice, "I thought we had 3,000,000 unemployed and a million or so migrant farm laborers who need work."

"Obviously," retorted the Red Queen testily, "you don't understand the American agricultural system."

Mr. Hill went on to explain that the paradoxes in this apocryphal episode from "Alice's Adventures in Wonderland" were a source of growing perplexity to economists, legislators, farmers, and farm leaders.

Shortly after Mr. Hill's article appeared a conference of a joint United States-Mexico Trade Union Committee was held in Mexico City. It adopted a resolution declaring, "The employer shall not pay the Mexican workers less than the prevailing wage rate paid to domestic workers" and so on.

The treaty which expired at the end of 1964 was promulgated under Public Law No. 78, which since 1944 had governed the hiring of Mexican labor. The Eighty-eighth Congress adjourned in October 1964 without renewing the law, which expired at the end of that year, and along with it the current treaty. The impact of the failure of Congress to renew the law was felt long before the treaty expired. In October 1964 I sent an article stating, "It is expected that the bracero employment this year will fall considerably below that of the nearly 200,000 in 1963. The number has been declining steadily since the 1956–1959 period in which upwards of 400,000 Mexicans were imported annually for seasonal labor. In 1960 the number had declined to 318,000; 1961, 300,000; 1962, 275,000; and last year slightly under 200,000."

If Alice was perplexed over the paradoxes in 1959, she would have had a surfeit of perplexity in the first months of 1965 after the braceros were cut off. The unemployed laborers of California, estimated at around 400,000 failed to show up for the available farm work primarily because the going rate of $1.05 to $1.10 per hour established for bracero labor and kept in force after the treaty expired was not considered sufficient. But to heighten the paradox these domestic workers were demanding at least a part of the privileges and guarantees which had been assured the Mexican bracero under terms of the treaty when it was in force. These privileges included specified types of housing, transportation, sickness and health insurance, and other benefits which the domestic laborer was not getting after the treaty expired.

Still another paradox: Mexicans bearing a special green card giving them immigrant status to the United States evolved almost overnight into the elite of the Mexican working force. What with braceros cut off and with United States labor hard to get at the relatively low current rate, the green-card-holders, numbering into the thousands along the border, suddenly became the prize laborer for the planters in the various valleys.

The green-card-holder was glad to work for the going wage because he was able to live at home on the Mexico side much cheaper than he could live in the United States. Secondly, at the going wage rate he could make in an hour about as much as he could make in a full day in his own area in Mexico. Finally, he had no problem at all with the arduous field labor at which he had worked all his life. The American unemployed for the most part had grown away from so-called stoop labor and detested it. The planters in turn detested them and sent up special prayers each night for a return to bracero labor. Secretary of Labor Willard M. Wirtz was unmoved in late 1964 and early 1965 by the pleas of the planters. He suggested that if they offered $1.40 an hour they could get sufficient labor in the United States.

Early in 1965 while shuttling back and forth between Mexicali on the Mexican side and the Imperial Valley in the United States, we were being told constantly by the planters that they were firm in their declarations that they would abandon vegetable and tree crops in the United States unless they were given relief in the labor situation. They said they would turn their land into row crops, such as cotton, which could be harvested mechanically and invest in produce farming in Mexico.

Federal and state employment authorities on the United States side maintained these threats were a bluff on the part of the planters. On the surface that appeared to be reasonable. Investigation, however, revealed that large syndicates of United States planters actually were discussing contracts for Mexican land, particularly in the state of Sinaloa. An American-educated Mexican tourist official in Tijuana explained that he was giving up his fairly high-level job with the Mexican government to settle in Culiacán, the capital of Sinaloa, to establish an advisory service for American planters preparing to establish themselves in Mexico.

Under growing pressure from the planters, the Department of Labor eventually relented somewhat in its attitude. A formula was being worked out under which a certain number of foreign laborers could be imported under government auspices The formula was to specify that the imported laborers must be protected by all the rules of the former bracero treaty. At the time, however, the Department of Labor reiterated its overall policy of eliminating foreign farm labor in favor of domestic.[40]

---

[40] The intricate problem of the legal and civil status of the Mexican farm immigrant had not moved much closer to solution by the end of 1969. The 44,000 to 150,000 braceros who were being admitted each year by the Immigration and Naturalization Service—not to mention some of the approximately 3.5 million Mexican-Americans—still were working for less than the minimum wage and living in substandard conditions. Senator John Williams' Subcommittee investigating these problems recommended the inclusion of farm labor under the Labor Relations Board Act, but opposition from strong private interests continues to block enactment of this legislation. A refusal to work by grape pickers denied the right to organize in California, which attracted national attention and some support in the form of a boycott against employers' wine products, continued, with neither side showing signs of weakening. However, late in July 1970, 26 grape growers (representing 65 per cent of the grape industry) signed a union contract with César Chávez and the United Farm Workers Organizing Committee. Meanwhile, AFL-CIO officials have reiterated over and over again their opposition to the entry of Mexican labor while unemployment exists. This has not deterred the migration, which continues to provide the Mexicans with a steady source of capital and the fruit farmers with the cheap labor they claim is necessary for their survival. [Editor's Note]

Four Artists

At the end of 1964 there were about fifteen thousand artists in Mexico, and the number was increasing daily. Yet age and the ravages of hard living in youth, have thinned the ranks of Mexico's great painters of the past. Of Mexico's "Big Three" artists, the trio whose works were blazing across the world shortly after the turn of the century, only one remains, David Alfaro Siqueiros. Diego Rivera, the political termagant, and José Clemente Orozco, ranking with the greatest muralists of all time, have gone. The field is left to Siqueiros, a leader of Mexican Communism and an indomitable political agitator who has survived imprisonments, attempts on his life, and an endless series of brawls and street fights. He has through it all remained extremely active as a painter, and is now approaching seventy, is finishing murals left undone because of his last imprisonment, traveling between Mexico and Europe, preaching death and destruction to the United States, and haranguing radical meetings. In his spare time he is still organizing leftist movements against the government. This remarkable person—"remarkable" in virtually any way one might want to apply the term—is so deeply steeped in controversy it is unlikely that he will be brought into clear focus for several generations.

Though an artist, he has seen more violence and bloodshed, and often contributed to it, than most men dedicated to violence. His elaborate attempt on the life of Leon Trotsky was as carefully planned as it was comically aborted. In the years I knew him he was as rabidly anti-American as he was fond of publicity in the North American press and as disdainful of United States capitalism as he was fond of the stiff fees his works brought in the United States. He was extraordinarily fond of *The New York Times,* which he grandly denounced as the paragon of Yankee reaction.

My first contact with the maestro was about a year after arrival in Mexico, in December 1955. He had just returned from a trip to Russia, Poland, and several Western European countries. He was in a fine, fighting mood when I finally got him on the telephone to learn his latest impressions of the Soviet Union. I asked him about an interview he had given on his arrival in Mexico in which he denounced Mexican art, including that of his friend Diego Rivera: "I say we have had enough of pretty pictures of grinning peons in traditional dress and carrying baskets of flowers on their backs." My story reported, "Getting warmed up to his subject the painter declared, 'I say to hell with oxcarts—let's see more tractors and bulldozers.'"

To fail to give attention to Siqueiros would be tantamount to failing to cover an explosion of Popocatépetl should that majestic old fellow go on another rampage. The volcano does not explode these days, thank Heaven, but Siqueiros does, on the slightest provocation, and at times with no provocation at all, and he will most likely continue to explode until all the explosion is gone from him.

His public appearances were as tempestuous as his interviews in the quiet elegance of his home were subdued and thoughtful. My clearest memory of one of these interviews is of a warm afternoon, when we sat in his cool drawing room sipping imported French cognac, and I glanced occasionally at the gleaming new Mercedes-Benz in the porte cochere. The painter talked gravely about the sins of the bourgeoisie of my country and about the irresponsibility of wealth. The object of that interview was to learn about a mural for the Motion Picture Actors Association. He had been happily working away at his mural when association directors came by to investigate. There had been reports that the mural was far different from the sketch on which the contract had been granted, and the reports were completely accurate.

The artist worked imperturbably on after a fiery scene, but that evening after finishing the day's work he boarded up the mural and did not return. The motion picture people were suing him in every possible court. The difference of opinion, he explained, arose over a matter of viewpoint. He was painting the struggle of humanity, the iniquities of the imperialists, and the final victory of social justice instead of a history of the motion picture industry in Mexico as had been contracted for. "Just a difference of opinion is all," he explained quietly. "They wanted a history of motion pictures and I felt that all of life went into the history of motion pictures."

Siqueiros was in and out of jail many times; the only imprisonment from which it was feared throughout the world he would not return began in August 1960. He had been arrested in connection with a series of student demonstrations which the government insisted he had instigated. He pleaded not guilty, but was sentenced to eight years' imprisonment on a formal charge of social dissolution. An appellate court upheld the sentence after a scene in which the prisoner at the bar grandly denounced the entire judicial system, the Mexican government, and the non-socialist world as a whole. His wife, who visited him daily in prison, relayed information regularly about his physical and mental condition and his work. He painted incessantly in his cell until he became ill. It was feared he might not come out alive, but he maintained his painting pace as long as he could, and a profitable pace it was too. His pictures from the penitentiary cell were selling for as much as $4,000 each, and he turned out many of them from month to month.

In July 1964 a call came to the office from an American friend whose apartment overlooked the Siqueiros home. He reported that some sort of a fiesta was going on over there and he was almost certain he saw the bushy-haired artist living it up with a throng crowding the patio. There had been rumors for a week that the artist was about to be released from prison, and apparently this was it. At his home, when we got there, the rum was flowing profusely and the mariachi bands had assembled. A roaring fiesta was in motion, and the maestro was in the center of it all, roaring, shouting, and hoisting toasts to one and all.

So far as I could see, I was the only gringo in the place. Artists, leftist and Communist personalities, and old friends were there for the welcoming party, and they were regarding me for just what I was, an interloper, until the maestro and his wife took me in tow. One thing which struck me was the coldness with which I was greeted by leftist editors and commentators such as Manuel Marcué Pardiñas, editor of the radical left magazine *Política,* and José Pagés Llergo, editor of the moderately left *Siempre.* I called on them regularly from week to week to discuss leftist and Communist viewpoints, and the relationship had been invariably cordial. But the painter and his wife were extremely warm and friendly. He introduced me around as his "imperialist" friend, and the señora told of the events of the morning when the artist was freed.

The artist himself was laughing and joking until we asked what his plans for the future were. "Work," he answered soberly, "work and get back to my party activities. My art is my life but my party is my duty." He could be critical, brutally so, of Soviet art, but not of Communism. His duty to party ran so deep that when his old friend and colleague Diego Rivera was expelled from the Communist Party Siqueiros abruptly cut off the friendship and did not renew it until the older artist, following considerable humiliation and apologizing, was finally readmitted. Friends of Rivera said later that the coldness of Siqueiros was the cruelest cut of all in the former's losing fight to maintain good standing in the party.

Rivera was totally different from the ebullient Siqueiros, at least in the final years of his life when I knew him. Whereas Siqueiros joined in a little joking over his anti-Americanism, with Rivera it was no joking matter. He despised all Americans and all things American in those years. He allowed some of us to come to his frequent news conferences, which were usually taken up with ideological matters rather than art. But even after having invited us he would perceptibly scowl as we entered. He abruptly commanded one American woman correspondent to leave the studio after she had asked what seemed to us a perfectly innocuous question, so innocuous in fact that none of us could correctly remember what it was.

Quite possibly his animosity was a device he had invented in late years to protect himself from new attacks in the party, or perhaps it was something that came naturally with his increasing conviction of the necessity of total war on the Western world, and of the necessity of carrying Mexico right along with it. But whereas Siqueiros could cheerfully slice up the gringos verbally one moment and then look appreciatively over the sales slips of his paintings the next to see how the North American market was holding up, Rivera preferred that his paintings not fall into American hands. But again it should be stressed that this assessment of the man was based on the time I knew him in the closing years of his life. He never failed in those days to dwell at length on the inferiority of America as a nation and of North Americans as a people.

Sr. Rivera was particularly bitter in his denunciation of the United States following his return from Russia, where he had been treated for cancer. He insisted that he had been completely cured and maintained that the Soviet Union was further advanced than the United States in medicine. He subsequently died of cancer.

But injured nationalism would be misplaced and petty before the magnificent things this man accomplished at the height of his powers. There was none in Mexico, friend or otherwise, who would deny Don Diego was the maestro of maestros in Mexican painting at the beginning of its renaissance. John Canaday, art critic for *The New York Times,* observed from Mexico City, "Diego Rivera deserves the position generally accorded him as the father of Mexican painting, no matter how badly his own painting deteriorated and no matter how badly even the best of it has worn."

Rivera shared much with his sometime friend, Siqueiros. Although they were born ten years apart, Rivera in 1886, their stars were ascending simultaneously. They shared originally and finally the same political views, and the life of Rivera was, just as that of Siqueiros continues to be, one of continuous controversy. Rivera's works were reviled and praised just as were those of Siqueiros, and each would, except in the years of separation, come to the other's assistance with fire and brimstone. Even in death controversy dogged Rivera; at his funeral a full-fledged quarrel erupted between relatives over to what extent the Communist Party was to be allowed to participate in the ceremonies.[41]

And thus his political attachments had followed him literally to the grave. His path in Communism had been a rocky one despite his slavish obedience to it. He was expelled in 1929 from the party for which he had done so much and for which he was to do much more before his death. Ostensibly his expulsion was caused by his early Trotskyist sympathies, which he tried in every way to expunge from his record. He was instrumental in bringing the Russian revolutionary to Mexico, the latter landing at Tampico January 9, 1937 with full assurances of safe conduct from President Lázaro Cárdenas. The Russian was brought immediately to the home of Rivera and his wife, Frida Kahlo. What happened between them was never made clear, but the quarrel must have been extraordinarily bitter because Trotsky moved out and never saw the Riveras again.

Trotsky was the object of an unsuccessful assassination plot hatched in May of that year by Siqueiros. The assassination was finally accomplished by a Spanish Communist named Ramón Mercader del Río, who had entered Trotsky's household as a Belgian named Jacques Monard. He was arrested and sentenced to twenty years imprisonment in 1943. He was last heard of in Prague following his release. The charge that the attack had come from Stalin's private police was never conclusively proved, but Rivera, when asked to comment on the assassination the day after the attack, said cryptically, "The happiest day of my life was when I sketched Stalin."

There was hardly a time when Rivera's murals were not under fire from one source or another. None of his works, however, was attacked with the same fervor and over such a prolonged period as his famous "Sunday in the Alameda". The mural, in dream sequence, consisted of the heroes and the villains of Mexican history for centuries past on a Sunday stroll through the jewel-like Alameda park in the heart of Mexico City. It was painted for the Hotel del Prado, a government-owned operation which was directly across from the park. When the mural was unveiled in 1948 it created a furor.

The principal attack came from religious groups, almost wholly Catholic, which objected to the legend on a scroll held by the famous states-

[41] Previously, the death of Rivera's artist wife Frida Kahlo had led to a political tempest. As a recognition of her established place as a Mexican artist, it was arranged for her body to lie in state in the Palacio de Bellas Artes. Diego himself stirred the controversy, which was to cost the Fine Arts Palace Director Andrés Iduarte his post, by insisting on draping the coffin with a flag bearing the hammer and sickle. [Editor's Note]

man, reformer, and atheist Ignacio Ramírez: "God does not exist."
Religiously inclined viewers, particularly prominent Mexican Catholics,
insisted that the government, which owned the hotel, board up the entire
mural. This, however, was far from the unanimous reaction of the church
membership. Many powerful Catholics, including the late Denis Cardinal
Daugherty, archbishop of Philadelphia, defended the painting as a whole,
including the controversial inscription, as being historically accurate.[42]

In any case the disturbance became so heated that the government
was seriously considering painting over the entire mural. It was brought
out, however, that under Mexican law the artist has control over his
work even though it has been sold. Finally, to put an end to the controversy the government boarded over the offending mural, and thus it
remained until 1956. The argument, however, was anything but boarded
over, and it continued to rage through the years. Art lovers in Mexico
and throughout the world, urged on by friends of the artist, continually
launched campaigns to make the work available to the public, either in
the hotel or in a museum.

One of the leaders of these campaigns was Carlos Pellicer, a prominent Mexican poet and museum authority, who was a close friend of the
Riveras. To make his role of conciliator still more impressive, he was a
militant lay Catholic. Rivera, who had early been inclined to erase the offending legend, had become obdurate and bitter about it all. Thus he was
adamant in his refusal to alter the picture, and the government was just
as adamant in refusing to go through another donnybrook such as the
one that followed the original unveiling.

Finally, in January 1956 Pellicer received a letter from the artist, who
was at that time in Russia undergoing the cancer treatment, agreeing to
an erasure of the legend and the substitution of another, but with the

---

[42] During the height of the controversy, students would enter the hotel and
scratch out the Ramírez words, and Rivera, with considerable enthusiasm, would
paint them in again. He facetiously suggested that the archbishop bless the
hotel while condemning his mural or, alternatively, that a Catholic artist be commissioned to paint a mural "proving that God exists" on the opposite wall.
Newspapers published caricatures of the artist exaggerating his natural ugliness and
showing him eating human flesh. When the controversy had run its course and
the full publicity had been squeezed from the trumped-up issue, Diego calmly
painted out the offending phrase and substituted an innocuous one as Kennedy
notes below. A similar uproar arose regarding Rivera's painting the image of
the Virgin of Guadalupe on the "gabardeen" of the superb Mexican comic
Cantinflas, who was depicted taking from the rich to give to the poor in the
mural on the marquee of the Teatro de los Insurgentes. Cantinflas himself cut
much of the ground from under the controversy when he commented that he had
always carried the Virgin in his heart and therefore saw no objection to carrying
her on his sleeve. When the hue and cry had died, Diego mounted the scaffolding
to paint out the image of the Virgin. [Editor's Note]

proviso that in the new legend "history be respected." Sr. Pellicer praised the artist's attitude and, emphasizing that he was speaking as an ardent Catholic, characterized the entire wrangle as "stupid," a condemnation in which large numbers of totally uncommitted persons in Mexico and throughout the world joined.

The artist returned to Mexico in April, but in the meantime the job of painting over the legend had been assigned to Guillermo Sánchez Lemus, director of the Institute of Fine Arts team charged with restoring Mexico's art treasures. Rivera would have none of that. Ill or not, he insisted on doing the work himself.

So on April 13, at 6:30 in the morning, the seventy-year-old artist ascended the high scaffolding and worked for two hours without stop. In place of the offending legend he painted an inoffensive reminder of a historically significant conference held in Mexico in 1836. While at work on the scaffolding, the artist touched up the portrait of himself as a boy of ten (with a frog in one pocket and a snake in the other), which, incidentally, is the central portrait in the sixty-foot mural. He said he had chosen the early hour for the work so that he could be alone. As it turned out, he could not have been less alone. At the bottom of the scaffolding were foreign and domestic newsmen, photographers, hotel personnel, and early-rising breakfasters, no doubt mystified by the strange customs of Mexican artists who began work at daybreak. Also in the throng was Sr. Sánchez Lemus, the nation's outstanding art restorer, who was standing by in case his services were called for, which they were not.

The artist, lumbering and still far from being a well man, crawled down off the scaffolding and, true to form, startled one and all by announcing, "I am a Catholic." Again true to form, he took advantage of the throng gathered for the occasion and launched into a glowing account of his stay in Moscow and the glories of Soviet art, medicine, and life in general. After this, the mural was again on public view and was out of the news and into history, except for some stories at the time of its transfer from one part of the lobby to another. The moving of an entire wall in order to resettle the mural was considered a noteworthy engineering feat.

Mexico's art history is as brilliantly kaleidoscopic and as controversial as the artists themselves. No matter what was thought of the artistic durability of their work, and serious questions have been raised in this respect, there were giants in those days, and some of them are still around. Aside from Siqueiros, the age of the heroic muralists is being carried on by Juan O'Gorman, muralist and architect extraordinary. The major monument of this gifted Irish-Mexican artist is the mosaic-mural complex forming the walls of the library of the National University. The mosaic murals of the great building depict the history of Mexico and are formed of stones of natural color gathered from the regions of Mexico. In size, color, and design it must be classed among the most imposing buildings of its kind in the world, and, as O'Gorman himself remarked, it certainly is the greatest postal card attraction anywhere. Someone else, a visiting librarian, remarked of the giant building almost without windows, "It's as big as a barn and about as empty."

Another of the fine O'Gorman works is in the Castle of Chapultepec, where he and Siqueiros, of whom he is not overly fond, exhibit neighboring murals. In the opinion of many, the two murals display the temperamental differences between the two outstanding artists as graphically as they display differences in technique. That of O'Gorman depicts the great figures of Mexican history against a sweeping background of Mexican landscapes. The Siqueiros mural depicts scenes of violence in Mexican history.

When Sr. O'Gorman begins a mural he is to all intents removed from the society of friends and family and from everything except the work at hand, which he remains at from early dawn until the late hours of the night. He loses weight and appetite. His wife, Helen, an American-born botanist and authoress, becomes worried, and the famous O'Gorman house, built into volcanic stone and one of the showplaces of Mexico, becomes a subdued place indeed. When the work is finished, life returns and the O'Gormans show up once again in society, with Juan the charming conversationalist as ever.

The mild, soft-spoken O'Gorman, like his colleagues, has had his share of controversy. This did not reach the worldwide stage, however, until 1963 when the American embassy in Mexico City denied him a visa to visit the United States, where he was invited to speak at a number of universities. The artist was on one of his periodic South American tours at the time, but his wife was extremely bitter over the way things were going. My story noted, "Invitations from several universities and museums to Juan O'Gorman, Mexican artist and architect, to lecture in the United States have been cancelled because of his inability to obtain a visa to the United States. Helen Fowler O'Gorman, American-born wife of the famous Mexican muralist, architect, and mosaic artist, said today that the University of California at Berkeley, among others, had withdrawn its invitation to the artist because of uncertainty over his visa. The Mexican-born artist of Irish parentage was not immediately available for comment.

"The artist's wife, an authoress and one of Mexico's best known authorities on Western Hemisphere plants and flowers, said the various lecture invitations had been issued her English-speaking husband because of an exhibit of his works currently traveling in the United States. She said the universities and museums desiring his appearance had been insisting several weeks for an answer to their invitations. When his attempts to obtain information on his visa application from the United States embassy here failed, Mrs. O'Gorman said, the institutions notified the artist they were reluctantly withdrawing the invitations.

"An embassy spokesman here dictated a brief statement stating, 'Spokesmen for the embassy explained that the application for a visa is being processed in the normal way for visas of this type and that as soon as the decision has been reached the applicant will be informed.' "

Sr. O'Gorman, who had in the past expressed leftist leanings as a matter of course, as indeed have a majority of Mexican artists, steadfastly denied any Communist connections (about a year later he joined the PRI). Nevertheless, day after day he visited the consulate and waited two hours for his visa. Finally he addressed a letter to Ambassador Thomas C. Mann, enclosing copies of urgent telegrams from museums and universities demanding information on his engagements.

He received no answer, and indeed it appeared to be a hopeless cause until an editorial appeared in *The New York Times* simultaneously with a letter-to-the-editor from Frank Tannenbaum, professor emeritus of Latin American history at Columbia University. Professor Tannenbaum charged that the McCarran-Walter Act, under which Sr. O'Gorman was being denied his visa, was "at present the single greatest obstacle to the flourishing of goodwill and friendship between ourselves and our neighbors to the south." The teacher and historian added, "Someone ought to call the attention of the Congress and the President to the fact that the millions of dollars we pour into Latin America will go down the drain and the high purpose of the present administration [that of John F. Kennedy] will be defeated if the respected and often beloved leaders of Latin-American cultural life are degraded and insulted by obscure administrative officers insensitive to the values represented by people such as Juan O'Gorman and who are so unaware politically as not to realize the harm they are doing to their country."

The editorial stated, "Juan O'Gorman is a leftist who the State Department feels needs to go through what might be called the 'McCarran-Walter wringer.' If his trip is seen to be purely cultural, the visa should be granted. Delaying or withholding visas to artists, writers, musicians, scientists, teachers, and the like is not only humiliating to them; it is humiliating to Americans. The premise is that Americans must be protected from ideas that differ from theirs."

The aftermath of it all was that Robert F. Kennedy, then attorney general of the United States, ordered an investigation, and the visa was granted on a qualified basis. The first visit was such an artistic success that Sr. O'Gorman was invited back for another and finally for a third, the last time to give a series of lectures on architecture at Yale University.[43]

Undoubtedly one of the greatest characters of all time in Mexico's art world was Gerardo Murillo. He loathed this name and was known in the world of art and volcanology as Dr. Atl, a name he fashioned for himself meaning "water" in the Nahuatl language, the tongue of the Aztecs. A diminutive man with a stump of a leg, he gave the impression on first meeting of a towering prophet with a wild beard and flashing eyes. Like the volcanoes he loved so much, he was eternally in a state of eruption and being swept along on the river of his own words.

A drive through the Mexican countryside with this authentic genius was an extraordinary experience filled with excitement and wonder. It appeared there was not a single hill or valley of his beloved country the history of which he did not know, and not just the political and economic history but the geologic origins as well. I heard him discourse for an hour about an obscure foothill. He could carry on light conversations in French, English, and Italian, but when he got down to business, namely art, volcanoes, or women, he instinctively went into his native Spanish.

His enormous interest in all phases of living, loving, and dying fascinated all who came in contact with him. He walked, or rather hobbled, along with ministers, savants, and presidents, many of whom were occasionally exasperated with him but all of whom either loved him or at least had unbounded respect for him. He was an internationally recognized volcanologist and one of the world's outstanding writers in this field, in addition to being one of the world's prominent painters of volcanoes. He died in 1964 at age eighty-nine. One of his last visitors before he lapsed into a coma from which he never emerged was President Adolfo López Mateos, a friend of many years. He was also a friend of President John F. Kennedy, who had one of his volcano paintings hanging in the White House. An obituary I wrote at the time of his death stated he was one of Mexico's most "bizarre and beloved characters." That appeared extravagant at the time, but in retrospect it seems almost an understatement. He was as unpredictable as one of his volcanoes. He never married, explaining, "I have never understood marriage. I believe

[43] As Paul Kennedy noted, considerable damage has been done to the image of the United States by incidents of the type experienced by O'Gorman. An awareness of this fact has brought a much more sensible approach by the Department of State on the handling of cultural exchange visas. However, this has not prevented consular officials and immigration officers from side-stepping the problem on so-called controversial personalities, and incidents of downright discourtesy unfortunately are not unknown, as is attested by the recent episode in Puerto Rico in which the outstanding Mexican novelist Carlos Fuentes was refused entry into the United States. [Editor's Note]

two people should meet, fall in love, and separate in twenty-four hours, or if they are deeply in love, maybe forty-eight hours." His love affairs, and the famous ones numbered in the dozens, lasted about that long, but most of his old loves appeared to have remembered him with fondness.

One day when he was in his mid-eighties I accompanied him to Cuernavaca, where he was executing what proved to be his last mural. He was called down from a swinging scaffolding which he had devised to compensate for his missing limb, and two frail old ladies went into deep conversation with him. "Two of my old sweethearts," he said afterwards as he swung himself up and away across the mural of fiery volcanoes.

Dr. Atl despised smallness, whether in people, painting, or any aspect of life. He took life in great, happy gulps and regarded both his greatest successes and the loss of several fortunes with the same equanimity. He once explained, "I attribute my happiness to my terribly disordered life and the pleasure I get from giving away everything I have." For a reason no one was able to understand, he was inordinately proud of the name "Atl." At the death of José Clemente Orozco, Dr. Atl was offered the coveted seat left vacant in the National College of Art. The offer was addressed to Sr. Gerardo Murillo. The painter replied indignantly, "Do not address me as Gerardo Murillo. My name is Doctor Atl, and Dr. Atl does not accept vacant seats offered to Gerardo Murillo."

He was born into a Spanish colonial family in Guadalajara in October 1875. His family claimed relationship to the Spanish painter Murillo, but Dr. Atl, an ardent Mexican nationalist and anti-Spanish, refused to discuss the matter. He was educated in Rome and Paris, and his name was early connected with outlandish pranks and awesome scandals in both cities. He made some sort of history early in his student days in Rome by stripping and bathing one afternoon in a fountain in front of Saint Peter's. To furious police he explained, "It was hot and I felt like a swim."

He founded the intellectual magazine *Action d'Art* in Paris in 1913 and edited it for three years. Then he grew tired of it and returned to Mexico where he founded and edited *Acción Mundial*. In 1923 he was made head of the Department of Archeological Monuments. Later he was made director of the entire Department of Fine Arts. Early in his career he became fascinated with Mexico's volcanoes and painted them continuously and wrote numerous books about them with equal facility. His fascination nearly cost him his life on several occasions. The last time was on the hemisphere's newest volcano, Paracutín, where he had an accident which cost him his leg.

His flair for doing things in the grand manner led to his buying the newly-active Paracutín outright before the Mexican government realized what was happening. "The campesino who owned the land did not want it with all that fire flying around, so I bought it," he explained. He established himself in a hut on the edge of the boiling, exploding volcano and recorded in words and sketches the day-by-day developments. An accident to which he at first paid no attention led eventually to amputation of his leg, but until he was rescued he remained in the hut painting and making notes day and night. When rescued he was delirious with pain and on the point of starvation, but he had some remarkable sketches and notes presently being used by volcanologists the world over.

These notes and sketches and the books and paintings of Paracutín that he eventually produced, worth a fortune, were turned over outright to the National Institute of Fine Arts. His ownership of the volcano, which Mexican authorities challenged menacingly as soon as they had recovered from their astonishment, was turned over with a grand gesture to the Ministry of the Interior.

Stories of Dr. Atl's younger years became so embellished it was difficult to distinguish between fact and legend. He cheerfully agreed with everything said about him, good or bad. His affairs with the beauties of Mexico, France, and Italy have provided parlor conversation for years, and occasionally Sunday supplements still come out with full-page spreads about his prowess in romance.

Despite his size and apparent frailty, his record as a revolutionary fighter is also colorful. He fought under some of the great leaders of the Mexican Revolution, and there were times when the revolutionaries of the day were apparently not quite certain whether Atl was fighting under them or giving the orders. There was, for instance, the story about him, which he readily confirmed to me, that during one of the engagements he rode into Mexico City with one of the revolutionary generals and personally ordered the national treasury to be opened and $3,000,000 in gold pesos to be distributed to the capital's needy. In confirming the story to me he explained it was the only humane thing to do. But the population was so starved, he added, that the $3,000,000 were not enough, so he ordered grocery stores to begin distributing their stocks free. When asked on whose authority he was making the order, he replied, "On my own authority, of course." He later explained that the project had been so grandiose it never occurred to anyone to question him. He told me once that he had learned early in life that the wilder and more improbable his schemes were the more readily people were convinced by him. His gifts to his nation were of such magnitude that he was branded an idiot, but with his usual luck he found he could not give away quickly enough. The more he gave, the greater his prestige, and his works became collector's items.

At the height of his popularity he went to Europe for the dual purpose of purchasing a new type of artificial limb he had heard was being manufactured in Germany and of organizing another expedition to search for the lost continent of Atlantis. He fancied himself an authority on Atlantis and had written a book and several scientific papers on the subject. The artificial limb did not come up to his expectations. The "new data" on Atlantis on which he had intended to base his expedition turned out to be material he himself had written long ago and discarded.

By the time he returned, however, he had learned to handle himself so expertly with the aid of crutches that he gave up the idea of an artificial limb. He was soon hopping about volcanoes, and at age eighty-one he again climbed his favorite, the rugged Popocatépetl. His method at that time was to drive as far as he could in his battered pickup truck and then continue on burro until the beast could go no farther, and there Atl took over with his crutches.

In his last years, after eighty-five, he found climbing volcanoes with crutches too arduous and perfected a method of observing the volcanoes from a helicopter especially fitted so that he could see and sketch while the pilot hovered above the craters.

His final project was the establishment of a Temple of Man in an abandoned monastery near Tepoztlán in the state of Morelos. He wanted to build a colony where, he explained, the great brains and moving spirits of the world could gather and discuss problems of the universe. As the need grew for more money, he painted faster and faster, and with his usual good fortune the sales kept pace with his endless expenditures. At his death he, inexplicably, had about one million pesos unspent, which he left to his maid, his nurse, and his chauffeur, who he had constantly complained was systematically robbing him.

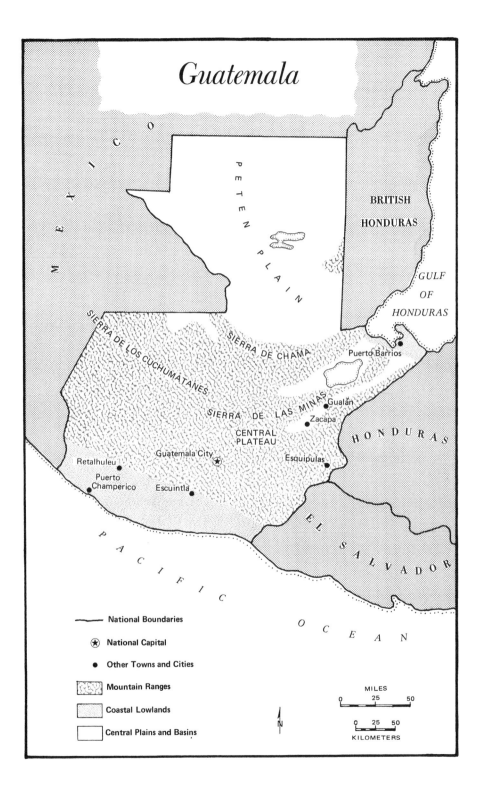

Guatemala

MEXICO

PETEN PLAIN

BRITISH
HONDURAS

GULF

OF

HONDURAS

SIERRA DE LOS CUCHUMATANES

SIERRA DE CHAMA

Puerto Barrios

SIERRA DE LAS MINAS

Gualán

Zacapa

CENTRAL
PLATEAU

HONDURAS

Retalhuleu

Guatemala City

Esquipulas

Puerto
Champerico

Escuintla

EL SALVADOR

PACIFIC

OCEAN

National Boundaries

⊛ National Capital

● Other Towns and Cities

Mountain Ranges

Coastal Lowlands

Central Plains and Basins

N

MILES
0   25   50

0   25   50
KILOMETERS

Guatemala

It was a soft, sunny day in Central Plaza, as all days are soft and most days are sunny in the City of Guatemala.

The month was June and the year 1954 and a giant Yankee-go-home rally was in progress in the plaza. The fifty thousand or more attendants were being addressed by Manuel Pellicer, one of the more rabid of the pro-Communist, anti-American leaders of the Jacobo Arbenz Guzmán regime. The speaker was standing before the National Palace haranguing the crowd to greater heat.

It was only another in a long line of somewhat similar affairs, and the only distinguishing feature of this particular one was that it was the first such experience for some of us. There were only a few foreign correspondents in Guatemala up to that time. Two had already been expelled. They came later in droves, but on this day the late Lisa Larsen, photographer for *Life,* and myself were watching the show when suddenly we were swept into the throng. When we finally scrambled out of the mob, Lisa, who had been wearing a wide patent-leather belt with some sort of hook arrangement to hold up her skirt, had been frisked of her belt, and I had been frisked too.

"I've lost my pocketbook," I yelled to her over the noise.

"Pocketbook hell, I'm losing my clothes," she screamed back.

With inexplicable naiveté we explained the loss to police in the square and they patiently took down our names, addresses, and pertinent details. One of them finally looked up and asked, "Are you Catholic?"

"What has that got to do with my pocketbook?" I demanded.

"Well you could pray to St. Anthony to return it," the policeman replied in complete seriousness.

That was my introduction to Guatemala. Misfortune served up with a laugh! Since then Guatemala has become better known, and thousands of writers, including the great nostalgic poet, Padre Rafael de Landívar, have repainted the perennial blue of her skies and the ever-brilliant flowers. But for me there remained the first impression, the nagging suspicion that when things get too difficult to cope with St. Anthony or some equivalent will finally have to be brought in to assist in getting things straightened out. It would be difficult to point to a country more favored by nature and with a people with a greater gift for enjoying life. Natural beauty, rich earth, one of the finest climates in the world, and a people gifted with natural gaiety. And along with it all eternal political unrest, revolts, violence. Tragedy done to the music of pipes!

In land area Guatemala is fourth among the Middle American countries under consideration, after Mexico, Nicaragua, and Honduras. It has a total area of 42,040 square miles and in 1964 a population of 4,200,000, with an estimated population by 1970 of 5,700,000. Its population is presently the largest of the five Central American countries, with El Salvador, Honduras, Nicaragua, and Costa Rica following in the order named.[1]

Geographically, the country shares with the other Central American states the flat Caribbean lowlands, particularly in the northeast, and the Pacific slopes. Like all the other Middle American countries except El Salvador, it bridges an area from the Pacific to the Caribbean. The distance is about two hundred miles from Puerto Barrios on the Gulf of Honduras in the Caribbean to Puerto Champerico on the Pacific. This distance is heavier going than it would seem in the mere telling. There are lonely and, at times, terrifying valleys off the Caribbean where in the early 1960's guerrillas came out of the hills to question motorists, occasionally taking a few quetzals, which are on a par with the United States dollar. The highway thence proceeds to the Central Plateau, which comprises roughly a tenth of Guatemala's land area and where about one-third of its population lives. From the plateau there is a descent into the piedmont region leading to the Pacific lowlands, and, finally, into the steamy lowlands themselves. Along the excellent highway of this coastal

---

[1] The population in 1967 was estimated at 4,717,000. Population density was 110 persons per square mile, except in the central plateau region where it averaged 870. With the annual rate of population growth at 3.3 per cent and with 56 per cent of the nation's population under twenty, the problems of illiteracy loom large. Nevertheless, in 1966, when illiteracy in the rural areas was 78.8 per cent, the government allocated only 15 per cent of its budget to education. [Editor's Note]

strip a major portion of the country's population is encountered, which in turn makes up between 30 and 40 per cent of the total population between Mexico's southern border and the northern border of Colombia. Rising from the coastal strip into the foothills is the area where most of Guatemala's coffee is produced. It is some of the world's finest, which like that of the other Central American countries is so valuable that small quantities of it are used in flavoring the blends of the heavier producing countries.

Cattle, cotton, and sugarcane also are grown in the western part of the country, but the principal cotton and banana production is in the eastern area, which in the lowlands is tropical in foliage and temperature. The banana, over which revolutions have been fought in Guatemala, appears to be slowly giving way as an economic mainstay while cotton is gaining in importance. At least that has been the story in recent years.

Economically, Guatemala could and probably eventually will be one of the richest countries in Middle America. It contains great plains like the Petén, which can become great farming areas. There have been significant petroleum explorations in the Petén and much mysterious talk about unspecified results. The blatant and somewhat comic-opera claims advanced by President Miguel Ydígoras Fuentes concerning Guatemalan ownership of British Honduras probably had to do with the need for a direct passageway for petroleum transport from the Petén to deep water should oil be discovered. At any rate, his loudest claims were being advanced at the time of greatest likelihood of oil strikes in the Petén area. Of course it is possible that he was simply using the claim to divert attention from the domestic problems of his administration.

In the decade from 1954 to 1964 most of the revolutionary activity in Guatemala, and there was lots of it, concentrated in the area south of the Petén leading to Puerto Barrios. That was along the railway and highway route from the capital and the Central Plateau to the Caribbean. In November 1960 Puerto Barrios was actually seized by rebel bands. The rebels had cut communications with the barracks city of Zacapa and appeared to be in a position to take over the entire eastern portion of the country. I went to Guatemala from Mexico to cover the story.

While awaiting transportation from Guatemala City to the areas of action, I dropped in on Dr. Mariano López Herrarte, a Harvard-trained physician and surgeon who was minister of health and an old friend. His offices were in the National Palace. He was out when I arrived, so I left a calling card. According to the story as I heard it later reconstructed, after he returned he found my card on his desk about the time someone called his office complaining bitterly about a notorious bordello in the capital. He absently wrote the name and address of the place on the back of my card and left again. While all this was going on President Ydígoras de-

cided to fly into Puerto Barrios, rebels or no rebels. Having learned I was
in the capital and assuming I would call on Dr. López, he had an aide
call the minister's office to learn whether I would like to accompany him.
The doctor's secretary read off the address on the back of my card and
the aide explained to the president something about that address. "Well if
he is enjoying himself," the President decided, "let's leave him here."
And that was how I missed the liberation of Puerto Barrios.

The name López Herrarte will appear a number of times in this work
because of his ubiquity. In the 1954 upheaval he was physician for the
Mexican embassy, where several hundred exiles from the Arbenz regime
took refuge, and he passed along the story of a disastrous typhoid epi-
demic shaping up in the embassy. A near-revolt by the wealthy landowners against the Castillo Armas regime? The doctor was squarely in the
middle, with many of the landowners as clients. A medical student uprising? He operated his own hospital and lectured at the National University medical school. What a news source! Additionally, as happens with
medics, he always had a good Rabelaisian story on tap.

Guatemala was well advanced toward a showdown long before we got
there in June 1954. The background was clear, remarkably simple, in
fact, in the context of the usually complex politics of Guatemala. Another period that was not so complex was from 1931 to 1944, the era of
the dictator Jorge Ubico Castañeda. He was a ruthless, thoroughly dissolute, and extremely intelligent man, and in the end he was betrayed by
his own intelligence and was forced to resign. Ubico turned power over
to a military triumvirate nominally headed by General Federico Ponce
Vaidés, who, soon after being installed as provisional president, was
overturned by the same forces which had rebelled against Ubico.

Before General Ponce's government fell in a welter of student strikes
and demonstrations, the groundwork for Communist infiltration had been
laid. In a brief time the names which were to dominate the Guatemalan
scene for many years began to appear. Víctor Manuel Gutiérrez, later to
become one of the most militant exponents of the Moscow line, was one
of the leaders of the group which in 1945 captured the teachers' union,
the most influential trade union within the Confederation of Guatemalan
Workers. Sydney Gruson, my predecessor on the Middle American run
and presently foreign editor of *The New York Times,* wrote in a magazine article in January 1954: "All this time the Communists were operating in the colors of the non-Communist revolutionary parties, principally
within the Partido Acción Revolucionario (PAR), the leading government political organization. It was not until September 1947 that the
Communists founded within the PAR a cell known as Vanguardia
Democrática. The leader, José Manuel Fortuny, claimed later this was

the first successful founding of a Communist party in Latin America."

After General Ponce's overthrow, Juan José Arévalo was elected president. He was a fine figure of a man, a liberal, and a dupe for the Communists who infiltrated his regime. He was succeeded in 1950 by Colonel Jacobo Arbenz Guzmán, whose appearance on the scene was clouded by the murder of Colonel Francisco Xavier Arana, who most likely would have been president had he lived. The finger of guilt seemed to point at some of the supporters of Colonel Arbenz.

Hubert Herring, in his authoritative book, *A History of Latin America,* commented on the attempts of the Arévalo and later the Arbenz regimes to deal with abuses in land ownership and labor exploitation: "The new leaders of the country addressed themselves to the correction of these abuses with much energy. A new constitution was adopted in 1945, its provisions resembling those of the Mexican instrument of 1917, with generous guarantees for all the basic rights of labor and free institutions and including authorization for land reform. Up to this point the course of events seemed reasonable, but in 1950 the Communist party injected the slogans and the tactics which have proved so disruptive elsewhere. In many ways the scene resembled that of Mexico in the 1920's and 1930's but with one important difference: Mexico's revolutionists had been purely Mexican; Guatemala's bore the markings of Moscow."

Expropriations were carried out by the Arbenz regime under the 1952 Agrarian Reform Act. About 234,000 acres were expropriated from the United Fruit Company's Tiquisate property on the west coast. The government allotted less than $600,000 as compensation for property valued at over $4,000,000. The United States Department of State handed the Guatemalan government a note of protest in March 1953 asking early compensation for the fruit company. The note was rejected. In April 1953 the State Department asked $15,854,849 for the expropriated acreage, but Guillermo Toriello, the Guatemalan foreign minister, refused even to accept the note.

That was about the position of the two countries when the Tenth Inter-American Conference convened in Caracas in the spring of 1954. Sr. Toriello and his delegation pulled out all the stops at that meeting, and the attacks on the United States delegation, headed by Secretary of State John Foster Dulles, were prolonged and vicious. There were indications that although Mr. Dulles and his delegation had been fully aware of what the general program of the Guatemalan delegation would be, they were somewhat taken aback by its unabashedly vitriolic tone.

Possibly the tone was accentuated somewhat by the almost-certain knowledge of Toriello and his people that even then United States agents had been having conversations with Colonel Carlos Castillo Armas in San

Salvador about organizing a rebel force with which to launch an invasion on Guatemala from neighboring Honduras. Sr. Toriello, whose proletarian role was somewhat vitiated in the light of his position as a member of an aristocratic family with large land holdings, tore into the "big stick" policy of the United States. He was the hero of the conference by day, where virtually all hands were getting huge enjoyment from the abuse being heaped on the United States. He was also the glamor boy of the social set by night, with an easy grace, proficiency with the guitar, and a repertoire of songs heard rarely in diplomatic circles. Aside from these and assorted other antics, the Caracas conference seemed to change the course of hemisphere affairs very little.

The various delegations listened with sympathy to the Guatemalan diatribe, but when the chips went down they voted 17 to 1 with the United States for the Caracas Declaration on Communist threat in the hemisphere. Mexico and Argentina abstained.[2]

Events were running inexorably into a clash in Guatemala. The United States delegaton, while listening to the fulminations of Sr. Toriello and his delegation, knew that the delegation and the government it represented were headed on a collision course with other forces and that the result would be far more telling than the Caracas conference. The Guatemalan delegation probably realized the same thing. The difference, of course, was in the assessment of the end result.

In any case, after the party had broken up and all hands, including the correspondents, had gone their way, Latin America was electrified by the news that the freighter Alfhem, after changing its course several times from its point of departure at Stettin, Poland, was heading toward Guatemala loaded with Czechoslovakian munitions. At that moment I was in Honduras covering a banana workers strike which later was discovered to have been fomented and fostered by the Arbenz government. It was

---

[2] The one-sided vote for the Caracas Resolution is deceptive as an indicator of Latin American attitudes. Secretary of State Dulles went to the Caracas meeting with the almost exclusive intention of obtaining American solidarity against intervention by international Communism. Professor Robert J. Alexander described the impact of Mr. Dulles' single-mindedness in his book entitled *Communism in Latin America* (Rutgers University Press, 1957): "Dulles seemed to the Latin Americans indifferent to their feelings, their fears of 'Yankee Intervention', and the concentration of their interest in entirely different problems. He stayed at the Conference only long enough to see the adoption of the Resolution. . ." (p. 400).

Subsequent events merely tended to confirm Latin American fears. Many viewed the events in Guatemala in 1954 with dismay and considered the developments as a renewal of the tradition of United States intervention. There can be no doubt that inter-American amity was injured by the policy and action of the United States in the Guatemalan situation. [Editor's Note]

never convincingly established how deeply the Arbenz administration itself was involved, but it appears quite clear that Arbenz knew about the subversive elements working in Honduras. Further, it would have been to his great advantage to have brought down the Honduran government, which at that moment was antipathetic to his administration, and he almost succeeded in doing so.

There were scores of estimates at that time, and there have been many more since, on the size of the Communist movement in Guatemala in those days, but none, so far as I could tell, are solidly-enough based. It was certain, or at least the Communist leaders such as Fortuny, Gutiérrez, and Pellicer boasted it was certain, that trusted party members were installed strategically in the larger unions, on agricultural boards, in state education, and, of course, at international policy levels of the government. The Communists at that time had only four seats in the fifty-six-seat Congress, and President Arbenz and Foreign Minister Toriello used this as an argument against the growing conviction that the party was on the verge of taking over.

My first story out of Guatemala was an interview with the late Right Reverend Mariano Rossell y Arellano, archbishop primate of Guatemala. The story noted, "In private audience the archbishop conceded that Communism had made significant inroads in the country, but he said he felt that Roman Catholics, which make up about 95 per cent of the entire population, are 'awakened to the danger and are now ready to combat it.'

"Monsignor Rossell y Arellano aroused the Guatemalan nation last week with a pastoral letter which called the attention of all Catholics to the presence of Communism here and demanded that 'people of Guatemala must rise as a single man against this enemy of God and country.' "

The next day the story dealt with the recall of Ambassador John E. Peurifoy to Washington. It said, "There was no doubt here that the primary purpose of Peurifoy's Washington visit will be to exchange ideas at the State Department about the United States' next move on the anti-Communist resolution adopted at the Tenth Inter-American Conference last month at Caracas. The resolution, sponsored and pushed by the United States, scored international Communism as a threat to hemispheric peace. It passed with only Guatemala voting negatively and with Mexico and Argentina abstaining. The vote was considered something of a victory for the United States, which until almost time for the final voting had been afraid the vote would be cut down to a bare majority or might even fail in passage, thus resulting in a serious diplomatic defeat.

"The resolution was passed in essentially the form the United States desired, and now the time has come to see how it can be implemented. While our delegation at Caracas was extremely careful not to name names while fighting for the resolution, it went without saying either by ourselves or by Guatemala and her friends that the resolution was leveled at this nation.

"It has been known for some time that Ambassador Peurifoy has submitted to Washington a series of recommendations for dealing with the Guatemalan situation. The government here, while not Communist in itself, is infiltrated by acknowledged Communists at high official levels and in strategic places in the government machinery. While the Peurifoy recommendations have been kept in closest secrecy there has been considerable speculation here that other Central American countries, fearing Communist infiltration from Guatemala, might be prompted into taking some sort of multilateral action, either under the Caracas resolution or outside it.

"In this connection El Salvador and Honduras have been particularly restive recently over the violation of their borders by persons they claim to be Guatemalan Communists. Michael J. McDermott, former State Department press officer and now United States ambassador to El Salvador, left suddenly last week for Washington. It was explained at his office that the visit was largely a personal one, but it is known he will spend most of his time in Washington in State Department consultations.

"There is general agreement here that the recent abortive revolt in Nicaragua, during which an attempt was made on the life of General Anastasio Somoza, the president, was in some way connected with a growing distrust in Guatemala of Somoza's dictatorial regime and with Guatemala's fear of multinational action by some of its neighbors.

"As against these possible threats to its security, however, Guatemala has fast friends in almost any sort of an argument. Of these Mexico and Costa Rica are in the forefront, with Bolivia and Chile not far behind. Thus while unilateral action of any kind by the United States against Guatemala would appear to be far-fetched at the moment, multilateral action by the United States and others would harbor distinct possibilities of spreading."

A few days later Nicaragua broke relations with Guatemala, and Somoza took the initiative in sounding out other Latin American republics on the possibility of calling a consultative meeting of the Organization of American States to discuss the advance of Communism in Guatemala. By this time I was back in Honduras, where the formation of a Guatemalan army in exile was underway. It was headed by Colonel Carlos Castillo Armas, who was being supported in funds and supplies by United States agencies.

At about this time Mr. Gruson wrote from Guatemala that that country had proposed a treaty of friendship and non-aggression with Honduras. He cabled, "The proposal apparently was aimed at countering increased fear in the hemisphere that Guatemala's recent purchase of about 2,000 tons of arms from Czechoslovakia had created a Communist menace to the safety of the Americas and particularly the safety of Guatemala's neighbors. Indications were that the Guatemalan government, for the first time since the present crisis developed with the arrival of the arms May 15, was seriously concerned that what it had always considered a war of nerves against it might turn into a shooting war."

Thus the situation was becoming more bizarre by the minute. Arbenz was trying to organize a friendship pact with a government he had almost certainly helped plot against a few weeks before, and the Honduran government was completely convinced that Arbenz had been directing the attempt at overthrow. Moreover, Arbenz had positive proof that the government with which he was trying to work out an entente was giving assistance and protection to an armed force rapidly preparing to invade his own country.

Meanwhile Ambassador Peurifoy had returned to Guatamala and had an interview with Foreign Minister Toriello. Neither of the two commented at any length on what was discussed, but whatever the subjects were their talk failed to ease the tension, and it was becoming increasingly evident to even the most hopeful that there was to be no turning aside now. The four principal actors in the drama were President Arbenz, Sr. Toriello, Colonel Castillo Armas, and Ambassador Peurifoy. Each was immersed in his own role and each appeared to be getting a certain amount of enjoyment out of the growing tension. Each, that is, with the possible exception of President Arbenz, who as a professional soldier must by this time have begun having doubts about the outcome.

Of the four principal actors the United States ambassador was far and away the most colorful and, apparently, the most entertained by the goings-on. The ambassador had been sent in fresh from a successful assignment in Greece to shore up the American position. Whether he knew the depth of our commitment at the time of his assignment is a matter of some debate. General Miguel Ydígoras Fuentes, later to become president of Guatemala and at that time in contact with both Colonel Castillo Armas and Ambassador Peurifoy, maintains in his book *My War with Communism,* that the ambassador had no part in the early planning. Most of the evidence, however, would appear to be against General Ydígoras. The only matter apparently in question was one of timing, that is, when Ambassador Peurifoy was given full details of the U.S. agency commitments and when he was given instructions to abandon cajolery of Toriello and Arbenz and let strong-arm persuasion take over for a while.

The ambassador was constantly being accused of protecting the United Fruit Company. The line of claiming that the fruit company was at the bottom of the whole thing was palpably followed for propaganda purposes, but the agitators and Communist powers behind the government must have known, as the government itself must have, that Peurifoy's sole assignment at this time was to make way for another government in Guatemala. When this eventuality became certain, and, as was indicated, it apparently had become a certainty even while the Guatemalan and the United States delegations were fuming at each other across the conference table in Caracas, it was the ambassador's job to see to the installation of a regime not only anti-Communist but also pro-American.

There appeared to be some question at the outset whether Colonel Castillo Armas would head that government. He was to run the show so far as the revolt was concerned, with, of course, the assistance of the United States. Yet even when he came into Guatemala a victor, he had not received the mandate. It was only after the junta had been winnowed out, with Ambassador Peurifoy supervising the winnowing process, that Castillo Armas emerged on top.

Ambassador Peurifoy, who later died in an automobile accident, was a handsome, strong-willed extrovert, who made enemies far easier than friends, at least on his assignments. His gay sports jackets, slacks, and sporty borsalino with a feather stuck jauntily in the band set him apart from the run of the mill anywhere, but particularly in Latin America. An Eric Ambler type almost too true—and to set the type still faster, under his sports jacket he carried a snub-nosed 38-caliber pistol slung in a holster. Here was an ambassador the news people could get their teeth into for good copy, the only difficulty being that only a very few could learn what he was up to, and those few, not very often.

In May both Ambassador Peurifoy and Ambassador Michael Mc-Dermott of El Salvador were called to Washington for consultations, as mentioned previously. The object of these consultations was to coordinate action between El Salvador, Guatemala, and Honduras in the forthcoming push on the Arbenz regime. In this the president of El Salvador, Oscar Osorio, was counted on heavily, and President Juan Manuel Gálvez of Honduras had already opened his borders for the invasion of neighboring Guatemala, needing only an incident to make it legal. The late Ambassador Whiting Willauer had things so well under control in Honduras there was no need for him to go to Washington.

Colonel Castillo Armas, at the head of a ragtag but moderately well-trained and equipped force of five hundred, more or less, invaded Guatemala from Honduras on June 17, 1954. As revolutions go, this one would have been in the nature of an *opéra bouffe* had it not been for the brutalities inflicted by the Arbenz government when desperation set in. Later retaliation came about by the Castillo Armas followers. Planes of the United States P–47 Thunderbolt type swept the capital occasionally, inflicting minor damages with the exception of blowing up an arsenal.

Colonel Carlos Castillo Armas during the ten-day rebellion in June 1954 which overthrew the regime of Jacobo Arbenz Guzmán. He once remarked that his .45 caliber automatic, nicknamed "Chalelita," was his best friend during the rebellion. (Wide World Photos)

Colonel Carlos Castillo Armas embraces Colonel Elfigio Monzón after signing the Pact of San Salvador, July 2, 1954. (Wide World Photos)

President Ydígoras, shouldering an automatic weapon, visits air force barracks after a short-lived revolt in late November 1962. With him are Defense Minister Enrique Peralta Azurdia, left, and Hernando Morales, center, president of the Guatemalan Supreme Court. (Wide World Photos)

José María Lemus, ousted president of El Salvador, arriving in San José, Costa Rica, October 29, 1960. (Wide World Photos)

Joseph Silverthorne, an American bush pilot who was operating cargo and troop planes in the revolution on a United States agency contract, used to tell some hilarious tales of the affair. One of these involved the "incident" for which Honduras was looking so that it could claim its borders had been violated by the Arbenz regime. It, like all of Joe's stories of Central America, was long, involved, and spellbinding, but the gist of it was that he flew from Honduras with a low-powered bomb, crossed into Guatemala, flew back over a Honduran airstrip, and kicked the bomb out, and the "incident" was duly put into the record book.

The rebel forces had been keeping up a barrage of propaganda by long-wave radio. This, combined with the sporadic and generally ineffective bombings of the capital, and combined too with the further fact that the Guatemalan armed forces had little heart for the Arbenz regime, led to complete apathy in the face of the invading forces. Esquipulas, the shrine city of the famous Black Christ, was the first objective of the Castillo Armas forces. After considerable wavering Arbenz sent troops out to oppose the rebels on June 20, but there was never a major engagement. In the entire conflict, there were something like 120 wounded on the government side and 18 dead and 30 wounded on the rebel side. There were probably far more civilians killed and mutilated throughout the country in government reprisals for the invasion. Indians down from the highlands in the pajama-colored native dress were armed, and patrolled the blacked-out streets of the capital. The doors along the streets of the commerical section are set flush with the sidewalk, and thus it was a simple matter for the Indians to clear the streets simply by standing at one intersection and spraying machine-gun fire down the entire block.

In the light of later developments, it appeared Castillo Armas could easily have marched into the capital, but by this time the war had turned toward talk and away from whatever action there had been. President Arbenz threw in the sponge early, turning over the power of office to his loyal Chief of the Armed Forces Colonel Carlos Enrique Díaz on June 27. Eventually the power shifted to Colonel Elfigio H. Monzón as head of the military junta. Díaz and Monzón came together in El Salvador, but failed to reach agreement. It was at this point Ambassador Peurifoy, jaunty hat and gay jacket, took off for San Salvador, thirty minutes away. "I'm going to bump some heads together," he muttered at the airport before taking off. An agreement was signed two days later in the Pact of San Salvador. Some say "Smiling Jack," as the ambassador was called, was responsible. Others, that it was President Osorio. Whoever was responsible, a sort of peace came to Guatemala.

On July 3 Colonel Castillo Armas came to the capital and received a hero's welcome in the same Central Plaza in which I had lost my pocketbook two months earlier. The colonel's speech from the National Palace balcony promised fair but stern treatment of those found guilty of abuses. The National Palace was just around the corner from the Mexican embassy, where President Arbenz and several hundred of his regime had obtained asylum. Colonel Castillo Armas was installed as chief of state on July 3, and on July 4 Ambassador Peurifoy gave a grand party for him, for the junta, for the correspondents, and for those of the American colony who had not fled the city.

An aftermath to the whole affair came years later when Senator Thruston Morton, Republican of Kentucky, gave a more or less official version of what happened in Washington. In a speech given in February of 1963 at a GOP dinner in Baltimore, Senator Morton said the plans to overthrow the Guatemalan government had been spread out before President Dwight D. Eisenhower, who asked if it were certain the plan would succeed. He was assured it was, and then said, according to Senator Morton, "I am prepared to take any steps that are necessary to see that it succeeds."

Parenthetically, following the fall of the Arbenz regime a group of foreign correspondents accompanied officers of the victorious Castillo Armas forces into the Casa Presidencial behind the National Palace. There we discovered rooms filled with school textbooks, and some of us took samples. Several of the textbooks we took were, according to the imprint, published in the Soviet Union. There was considerable speculation later, however, that the books had been planted in the Casa Presidencial for the special benefit of the correspondents. At any rate, the incident was suspicious enough that some of us held off on the story.

After the overthrow, the United States began sending in funds to bolster the new regime. The early effort was a pump-priming operation of nearly $4 million and was badly needed because of the dismal state the national economy had fallen into. More came shortly afterward. Even then it came late. A story cabled in December 1954 noted, "The present assistance comes almost six months after the revolution in which Castillo Armas took over the government. It also comes at a time when popularity of the administration is extremely low and the country is abounding with rumors of plots to overthrow the government." The story also pointed to serious dissatisfaction among the wealthy and professional classes, which had been alienated from Castillo Armas through his attempts at tax reform, which were aimed directly at those classes. A friend came to my hotel room late one night to tell about a plot he had stumbled onto to assassinate Castillo Armas. That plot was squashed.

Certainly, it was a nerve-wracking time for the landowners. My friend Dr. López Herrarte was telling me one day about his troubles arising from the dreary economic atmosphere. The campesinos on Guatemalan fincas record their debts in a *libretto* or "little book." They are almost never out of debt, what with borrowing from time to time as much as the landowner will permit, and thus they are bound to their plantation almost as irrevocably as if they were indentured servants. At that particular time, Dr. López was experiencing some severe financial difficulties as a result of taxes, poor exports, and a half-dozen other drains, and was faced with debts running probably into the thousands. He happened to mention his difficulties to one of his old plantation workers one day, and the aged campesino suggested gently, "Never mind, Señor Doctor, you can put it in my libretto."

The workers on that plantation, incidentally, never got a rest from the physician's experiments. He was eternally examining them and prescribing for their ailments. One time he ran an extensive examination resulting in the discovery that virtually all his workers were suffering from varying degrees of anemia. He immediately ordered a five-gallon drum of elixer and directed the workers to line up twice daily for a tablespoon of the vile-tasting stuff. The campesinos quite naturally hated it, but it worked. Production on the finca zoomed.

This particular anecdote came to light because it later figured slightly in international policy. Dr. López was drafted to be an interpreter at a breakfast attended by Guatemalan officials and President Eisenhower and Secretary of State Dulles. During the conversation Mr. Dulles commented that perhaps Latin America would advance faster if more work were produced, a remark to which Dr. López responded, "Mr. Secretary, I respectfully submit that if you had the anemia of most of our Latin American workers you wouldn't even be at breakfast this morning."

The honeymoon period of the Castillo Armas administration definitely began fading by early 1955. In January of that year I wrote from Guatemala City describing a plot which had to be quelled with machine-gun fire. The rivalry between Colonel Castillo Armas and Colonel Monzón broke out into the open, and the latter was sent into exile. The assistance from the United States was too little and too late to shore up the sagging economy. Unemployment was mounting, as were complaints from all sectors. At this particular juncture, the new chief of state seemed to be deriving the waning support he still had from the middle and upper-middle classes, with none from the higher or lower classes.

Colonel Castillo Armas, while more adept as a political theoretician than most of his military colleagues, was still clearly ill at ease in his role as chief of the Guatemalan state. In innumerable interviews it was apparent that he was almost completely without the saving grace of a sense of humor, and as he progressed in office even his usually abundant supply of philosophic patience rapidly began playing out. An appealing, soft-voiced man, he had known more violence and physical danger at thirty-nine than most men see in a lifetime. He had been imprisoned, sentenced to be shot, beaten, and starved, and had gone through endless privations and suffering before finally emerging victorious. His daring and near-miraculous escapes from prison showed plainly his steel nerves. And yet occasionally during an interview a quick expression seemed to appear as if he were mutely asking, "What am I doing here?"

Colonel Castillo Armas had ordered a plebiscite, either at the suggestion or with the full acquiescence of the United States, and on October 10, 1954 he had been elected president of Guatemala. It was a "yes" or "no" affair and quite naturally aroused a storm of criticism and increased appreciably the opposition to his administration. Yet the new chief of state referred to the plebiscite in his first anniversary speech in July 1955 and maintained that in it the people of Guatemala had shown their support for his government.

The administration of Castillo Armas was an uneven one and gave the impression of going downhill until his assassination in 1957. Two groups wanted to have Colonel Castillo Armas out of the way, but it would be invalid to conclude on the evidence available that either group would have resorted to assassination to accomplish this. It would probably be fairer to say that both groups would have preferred to see him alive and in some position other than in the presidency. It is certain that one group, the extreme left, was beginning to make itself felt again in 1957. It is equally certain that the other group, the wealthy and the political right-wingers, were fully aware of this and were apprehensive.

Labor was one of the principal factors involved in the growing opposition to Castillo Armas. The regime had early applied a stranglehold to organized labor. The movement had come severely under the influence of the extreme left, including Communist organizations, in the preceding regime, and now it got little encouragement from the Castillo Armas administration in its struggle to regain democratic processes.

The plots grew more frequent as the Castillo Armas regime progressed. There was hardly a week in which the secret service did not uncover one or more. In June 1956 the president declared a state of siege. He noted in his decree that investigations "have brought to the government's knowledge that Communist agitators have prepared a conspiracy and it has become indispensable to adopt severe and drastic means of repressing it." The decree gave the government the right to "impede, suppress, or suspend strikes of any nature which might alter public order." The decree also prohibited the carrying of personal papers or printed matter considered damaging by the authorities. It also gave authorities, of course, the right to search the person, the automobile, or the home.

The attitude of the president seemed clearly expressed in an interview with him in respect to his new electoral law, which at that time was coming under increasing criticism.[3] The interview as filed began, "President Carlos Castillo Armas had shrugged aside criticism of Guatemala's new electoral law as being unimportant in comparison to security and political processes which he declared the new law would afford. In an interview shortly before the Constituent Assembly approved *in toto* the controversial law, the president declared, 'My historic promise to the Guatemalan people was to exterminate Communism and I would rather have criticism than to betray this trust.' "

In July 1956 the university students went on a rampage, a sure sign of grave difficulty in Guatemala. The government exiled thirty of the young demonstrators, putting them across the Honduran border. This developed into a doubly-embarrassing situation, for while the repercussions were acute in Guatemala, they were even more so in Honduras. President Julio Lozano was at that moment having his own difficulties with students, and the addition of thirty incensed Guatemalan student leaders, all of them militantly left, put the old Honduran president on the spot. He got rid of the visitors in a hurry despite his great friendship for Castillo Armas and his sympathetic view of the latter's predicament.

In December 1956 I filed a story stating, "An apparent plan to keep the administration of President Carlos Castillo Armas off balance by recurrent plots is unfolding here. This plan apparently has been progessing since November 1. It was finally brought into the open this week when Ismael Ortiz Orellana, director general of security, issued a statement that his government was informed of a plot hatching in Mexico to overthrow the government. His statement followed publication in the semi-official paper *Nuestro Diario* of a detailed outline of such a plot in Mexico coordinated with one in San Salvador.

"*Diario's* account charged that the Mexican portion of the plot was being led by former Foreign Minister Guillermo Toriello and the former Minister of the Interior Augusto Charnaud MacDonald. Both have been in Mexico since the overthrow of the regime of Colonel Jacobo Arbenz Guzmán in July 1954.

"Competent observers here both in and out of the National Palace appear not to attach so much importance to the plotting as to the internal attempts at causing uneasiness and dissension within the armed forces. At

---

[3] In February 1956 a Constituent Assembly adopted a new constitution which was criticized both for its restrictive electoral provisions and for permitting the suspension of civil rights in an emergency by presidential decree. In the ensuing congressional elections, Castillo Armas's party ran unopposed. By June, as noted, the president declared a state of siege, arrested leftist agitators, and censored domestic and foreign press notices, which resulted in considerable criticism and unrest. [Editor's Note]

least one potentially embarrassing international incident occurred in early November as a result of recurring plot rumors. This took place when a squadron of Guatemalan air force fighters swept over the Mexican border penetrating as far as Tapachula and swerving down to the Pacific coast.

"The incident, which brought an immediate protest from the Mexican government, was officially closed when Guatemala explained in a diplomatic note that the flight had been due to the oversight of green pilots. It is general knowledge in diplomatic circles here and in Mexico, however, the the planes were actually on a reconnoitering mission as a result of reports of an invasion buildup taking place in the vicinity."

There were certainly many straws of trouble in the wind, but there were also factors in the regime's favor to make the difficulties seem not too insurmountable. Julio Vielman, the resident Guatemalan correspondent at that time for *The New York Times,* wrote in an economic survey, "Despite a number of agricultural problems Guatemala appears to face a year of strong economic activity in 1956. United States economic development aid, foreign loans, and the return of economic confidence of native businessmen here were contributing factors."

On the positive side, the administration had in its favor:

1. Increasing assistance from the United States, a returning confidence among domestic and foreign investors, and increased foreign loans.

2. The support of the large and powerful middle and lower-middle classes.

3. The support of the Roman Catholic Church, which before the Castillo Armas regime and after it was having its own difficulties, but during that regime was a powerful force indeed.

Another sector, the agricultural one, was an unknown quantity. The Castillo Armas regime made tentative and almost-timorous explorations in the area of agrarian reform and agricultural development. Yet the best hope of the country at that particular time was the reasonably rapid and substantial economic progress that might be brought about by improving agricultural productivity. The important manufacturing industries in Guatemala were still some years away.

The administration had begun a program of improving the basic transportation and communications systems. But the surest way of raising the standard of living, a system, that is, of diversification of agriculture for domestic use and for export, persistently eluded the Castillo Armas regime, just as it did the succeeding regime of General Ydígoras Fuentes. President Ydígoras was immersed deeply in land problems, but his interest was focused largely on the highly productive and valuable properties of German nationals which had been expropriated during World War II and which were the subject of great speculation and graft during the Ydígoras Fuentes regime.

There were then and still remain extensive plains on the Pacific and the Caribbean and, of course, the great Petén plain. These are only sparsely settled and contain great tracts of arable land, most of which belongs to the nation. Notwithstanding the extensive arable land not under cultivation Guatemala has the highest rural population density of all the Middle American states under consideration, with 1,389 persons to every 1,000 hectares (2,470 acres) in crops and pasture. In 1950, according to a United Nations survey, 69.2 per cent of the entire population was rural, with the remaining 30.8 per cent urban. At that time 39 per cent of the urban population over 10 years old was illiterate, and 81.5 per cent of the rural population was illiterate.

In connection with agriculture a cable I sent from Guatemala in April 1957 noted, "Guatemala's current boom is presenting enough contradictory factors to perplex the most enlightened economists." It will be recalled that at that time the impact of United States spending was beginning to be felt. I continued, "Millions of dollars are being poured into public works and many more millions are on the way. This has created an extraordinarily strong labor market. And yet wages appear generally to be decreasing in the greatest labor area of all, agriculture.

"More money is getting into circulation than at any time in recent years. Yet merchants here in the capital are complaining that retail business has reached a plateau in some instances and in others is actually falling behind that of last year. Hotels are running generally at over 90 per cent capacity. Yet there are complaints that the clientele comprises mostly serious workaday commercial travelers who are keeping out the free-spending tourist trade.

"Despite the complaints, however, an observer just coming onto the scene sees in Guatemala a picture of intense economic activity. The usually spick-and-span capital is coated with dust from old business buildings being torn down to give way to new ones; streets throughout the city are being torn up for improvements or for the installing of new telephone lines. Private building permits for the capital in January totaled this year over $1,700,000, as against $700,000 for the same month in 1956. Private building in the capital for 1956 totaled $10,217,441, nearly double the figure of 1953, which was the last full year of the Arbenz regime.

"The story behind all this activity, of course, is the great amount of new money being pumped into the country's economic stream plus an accelerated amount of United States money in one form or another. The estimated expenditure on public works projects for fiscal 1957 is about $63,217,000. Of this the United States will put up an estimated $23,217,000. Guatemala has budgeted $22,000,000 but probably will increase that to $40,000,000 with new appropriations.

"Additional new money has been brought into the country by oil interests preparing to explore nearly half the entire country. Twenty companies including some of the largest in the United States have acquired drilling rights in Guatemala, and it was announced officially this week that these companies have invested a total of $2,500,000 in calendar 1956."

A subsidiary of the Signal Oil and Gas Company of Los Angeles was awarded the first of the Castillo Armas big oil concessions, with drilling rights to something over 600,000 acres. Under a new petroleum code drawn up by the administration, the right to grant petroleum concessions was the prerogative of the chief executive.

On March 1, 1957 the president gave his last major speech and the last of his annual messages to Congress. He declared, "We have freed Guatemalans from the political drawbacks that have weighted them down and can therefore not conceive of any factions in opposition to the work we are carrying out."

On the night of July 27, accompanied by his wife he was walking down a corridor in the Casa Presidencial, located behind the National Palace, when a member of the palace guard shot him at close range with a rifle. The assassin committed suicide immediately. It was later announced that investigation revealed him to be a half-crazed political fanatic. There were a multitude of questions concerning his past and his placement in such a sensitive position as palace guard. At any rate, from that date until March 1958, when General Ydígoras Fuentes was sworn in, Guatemala was held together by a succession of governments. That it held together at all was something of a miracle. General Ydígoras had considerable support from the landowners and the professional classes, who publicly praised him for his efficiency but secretly were hoping for some sort of return to the old dictatorial days of General Ubico. There was a solid basis for hope on the part of these classes that General Ydígoras would indeed bring back what to them were the "good old days." Years before he had been a disciple of the redoubtable Ubico, and in some ways, though not many, emulated his former chief.

General Ydígoras was far and away the most unpredictable and, from a newsman's point of view, the most fascinating president known in ten years on the Middle American beat. He had, so far as could be discerned, no set rules governing the conduct of his office. Or perhaps it would be better to say he made up the rules as he went along. He had a multiplicity of eccentricities, but they were his own and few of them were traceable to the flamboyant group of Central American rulers to which he belonged.

He was, to begin with, a model family man and that in itself placed him somewhere in outer space as regards the general run of the Central

American presidential club. The president was utterly devoted to his gentle, unassuming wife and fiercely loyal to his family. This loyalty drew him into strange byways and contributed to the stain on his administration. He was consistently sold out by members of his family, and while at times plainly vexed, he nevertheless invariably came back for more of the same treatment. This disadvantageous attachment extended even beyond his family to various persons who had no possible reason to wield the power they did, many of them flashy sycophants who fattened their wallets without contributing anything but confusion to his program.

The president's enemies, who proliferated rapidly toward the closing days of his regime, insisted that some of the machinations and corruption of the palace pack had reached into the president's own office. Others were equally insistent that while the administration was undoubtedly tainted, the president himself had remained consistently aloof. To be coldly realistic, there was no reason for the president to participate in the backstairs chicanery, even if he had been receptive to the idea. He could, and did, retire a wealthy man from the normal returns of office. The Guatemalan president receives $12,000 a month plus basic living and entertainment expenses, which, along with a privy purse not accounted for, ran to nearly $2,000,000 annually.

Our first acquaintance with General Ydígoras was during his campaign for the presidency. He was then in his sixties, perhaps in his late sixties. No one knew. He never revealed his true age. He gave various years of birth, sometimes obviously in a spirit of good, clean fun, and at other times in stern warning not to pry too closely. But whatever his age, he was a towering campaigner and two or three days in the provinces with him was all the average correspondent could, or at least wanted to, take. He was not the flaming orator he fancied himself to be, but he swayed crowds, probably with the sincerity and the appearance of logic he employed so effectively. He was a trained engineer and a self-trained agronomist, and by the time of beginning his political career he acquired a smattering of economics. He had enough of all these to confound his listeners in the Guatemalan hustings.

In his book *Central America,* Harold Lavine came up with an apt French expression, *un original,* to describe General Ydígoras. On looking back over those years, the two of his characteristics that remain most vivid were his enormous personal courage and his overwhelming compulsion for intrigue. Regarding the former, some insisted it was not courage at all but rather a complete absence or an ignorance of fear. It never occurred to him that from time to time his life might have been in danger. Once a young fanatic was disarmed while preparing to shoot him. The president gave him a dressing down, admonished him against entertaining such low thoughts as the assassination of a president, and sent him home.

One of the great mysteries of the Ydígoras administration was how the president found enough time in the midst of his administrative duties to work out the highly involved intrigues he was forever immersed in. He had an apparent Machiavellian disdain and distrust for any strategy that called for moving from one point to another in a straight line. He wanted to see alps behind alps and have great numbers of people involved. And the wonder was that some of his most intricate schemes actually worked, the most notable failure being the last one, which pulled him and his government down.

Along with these two characteristics was his unquenchable optimism. The last interview I had with him was in a shabby hotel room. He was in exile with his political career junked. But despite everything he had a sprightly hope that somehow, sometime his star would break out again.

In office his military aides and his staff despaired of his work habits. Periodically he would resolve to establish some sort of a work schedule and would actually follow it for a few hours, but by mid-morning the entire thing evaporated. He would suddenly become bored with work and summon all hands to take off, perhaps for a walk through the city or a drive in the country, or on an aimless expedition to see what might turn up. His walks through the city caused great worry among traffic police and astonishment among bystanders. He would be at the head of an unwieldy procession beginning with his military guard, who were followed by close advisers, and then by palace hangers-on hoping for a chance at his ear. The rag-tag procession would move along the narrow sidewalks of Guatemala City's principal streets while traffic became snarled. To complicate matters further the president would invariably spot either a friend or a political enemy he had been considering talking to for some time and would have one of his staff fetch him. Long, animated conversations would take place in the street, with the crowd growing larger by the minute.

In his office his schedule would be still more chaotic. On occasion I went into his office with the stern admonishment by his military staff that the interview was to last ten minutes and no more. After half an hour the staff would come in to haul me away, but they would be grandly waved aside by the president while the anteroom began overflowing with applicants being kept waiting for their appointments.

He would alternate in dress between Savile Row tailored clothes, which he had come to appreciate while ambassador to the Court of St. James, and an old field outfit in which he campaigned for office. If his attire did not please him for some reason he would slip off for home and a quick change. He was an erect, well-preserved man and wore his clothes well. He looked the part of a president, or at the very least a senator.

His ambivalent attitude toward newspapermen was a matter for wonderment. One day he actually took a kick at *The New York Times* Guatemalan correspondent Vielman for something Julio had written about the national economy. Later, after Julio had left the newspaper business to become a bank manager, the president called him personally for advice on national financial matters.

On another occasion, after he had had a foreign correspondent arrested for something he had written, I was walking along a street when he was taking one of his walks on the opposite side. He sent an aide over to summon me and spent at least fifteen minutes explaining why he had not really been angry with the writer, who by this time had been released. He asked me to bear a message to the chastised correspondent saying the president wanted to see him at the National Palace.

President Ydígoras was a product of Guatemala's national military academy and rose to a generalship and to near-ministerial rank under the dictator Jorge Ubico. In later life he had difficulty living down his Ubico connections. His enemies were convinced he would bring Guatemala back to those dreaded days, and his supporters were hoping he would do just that. In point of fact he did neither. He denied any attachment to the Ubico philosophy of government and termed himself, of all things, a "progressive conservative."

He was in exile from 1950 to 1954 and was chairman of an organization known as the Council of Guatemalan Anti-Communists in Exile. At one time or another he was military attaché in Washington and Paris, and later ambassador to London and to Bogotá, Colombia. From time to time he made a point of his admiration for Great Britain and things British, even while he was blasting the English over British Honduras, which he insisted Guatemala was going to annex and toward which end he broke off relations with England. He decreed that the British possession be called forevermore "Belice" rather than British Honduras and banned maps in Guatemala that did not designate the possession as disputed territory. The entire Western Hemisphere was bemused for a time over the possibility that General Ydígoras might actually declare war on England.

The president spoke English adequately but demanded insistently that correspondents should interview him in Spanish. In the many interviews I had with him, he would invariably begin, "Well, how is your Spanish now? You must at least be bright enough by this time to carry on a conversation in my language, so let's talk in Spanish." Then before the first question could be put, he would launch into a long soliloquy, always in English.

Ydígoras had a number of counts against him when he went into office. His flamboyant, even rabble-rousing tactics had caused considerable concern. His early public background as an official who had been delegated a lot of responsibility under Ubico aroused the suspicion he would, if allowed to, follow a dictatorial course. This suspicion became still stronger when he threatened to bring thousands of campesinos into the capital to see that he got a "fair" election. Actually he did not get a fair trial in his first attempt at the presidency but neither did he summon in the campesinos.

A confidential memo, not directly from a United States government source, came our way before the 1958 elections. It said in part, "U.S. officials are deeply concerned over Ydígoras. They are convinced he is getting support from Trujillo [Rafael Leonidas Trujillo, dictator of the Dominican Republic]. And they hear that he is insinuating in places where it will help him that he has United States backing. This, they fear, could seriously damage U.S. prestige."

This appears to have been a poor bit of political reporting from our embassy in Guatemala. If Ydígoras ever mentioned purported United States support, he did so in complete privacy. In fact he voiced on occasion his suspicion that the United States was opposing rather than supporting him. He certainly received no encouragement from John Foster Dulles, then secretary of state, nor from Roy Rubottom, then assistant secretary of state for inter-American affairs. He made no attempt to conceal his chagrin and disappointment both before and after the election.

He received a plurality in the 1958 election but not the majority required under the constitution. The election was thrown into Congress, where after some of his sharpest horse-swapping, he was able to gain the victory and to be inaugurated into office in March. Incidentally, because his rank of general had been questioned, in pique he wore his cadet regimental sergeant's stripes at the inauguration ceremony.

From the moment of taking over the presidency until long afterwards he fought off the "dictator" charge. In February 1960 he said in an interview, "Dictatorships are obsolete forms of government and the dictator is living politically beyond his time." Then in one of his typically graphic expressions he added, "Why should I become a dictator and erase with my elbow all I have written with my hand?"

Possibly his deep earnestness during that interview was prompted in part by the knowledge that at that particular moment he might well have been on his way toward dictatorship had he so desired. Before the December elections of that year he had a minority of twenty-five members of the sixty-six-member Congress, but in the elections he had picked up thirty-three new members, with twelve additional pledges, thus giving him a comfortable working majority.

The supreme and appellate courts were elected by Congress, and thus General Ydígoras was given effective control over all branches of the Guatemalan government. The president's efforts from the time of his inauguration until the December elections had been spent largely in consolidating his power and in endeavoring to shore up the shaky economy. He might have gone considerably further than he did, but at about that time the corruption which was to haunt his administration began to take shape.

Whether as a cause or an effect of this he began encountering serious political opposition. The first big crisis came in November 1960, when an armed rebellion against the government broke out. The uprising, beginning with the taking over of a barracks in Guatemala City had centered on the Caribbean coast at Puerto Barrios, where the rebel forces had actually taken and held the city. In telephonic communication with the National Palace the rebel leaders gave a list of demands, all of which were, characteristically, turned down by President Ydígoras. His one demand was that the rebels clear out of Puerto Barrios immediately. On November 14, I cabled that the city had been given up by the rebel forces and that President Ydígoras had flown to inspect the damage. That was the flight I missed because of confusion over the calling card address. Zacapa and Gualan, both barracks towns, had already been retaken by government forces and the president had won his first big contest.

A member of the Ydígoras government later related to me that much of the matériel the president had used in reducing the garrisons of Zacapa and Gualan and in winning back Puerto Barrios had been furnished by the United States. The planes and some of the personnel, this informant reported, came from the area around Retalhuleu where forces were being secretly trained for the invasion of Cuba. The ferrying-in of personnel and equipment, it was explained, was the first opportunity to test the newly-built airfield and the maneuverability of the air assignment at Retalhuleu.

The uprisings brought on the inevitable reprisals, newspapermen being counted among the victims. A search order was issued by the National Palace for Ramón Blanco, managing editor of *El Imparcial.* That paper was suspended from publication because of a first-person story written by Sr. Blanco about the siege. He had been trying unsuccessfully to inform the Palace from his place of hiding that he had been in Puerto Barrios on a social visit when the rebels took over. Later the president ordered the arrest of Robert W. Rosenhouse, correspondent for *Time-Life,* and still later he spent a quarter hour explaining to me that he had nothing against Mr. Rosenhouse. These were the first of a series of impulsive acts by the president from which he subsequently backed down, but only after sacrificing some of the prestige of his office.

Many of us were convinced then that the hasty action by Ydígoras was precipitated by a firm belief that a push on his government from Castro's Cuba was underway. He had, in fact, some basis for this conviction.

Arbenz had gone to Havana and was thundering away at the Ydígoras regime by shortwave radio, which was easily received throughout Guatemala. Shortly after the Puerto Barrios affair I wrote, "The Caribbean, perennial spawning ground for meteorological and political storms, appears to be outdoing itself in the multiplicity and intensity of the latter. And there appears little peace in prospect. Throughout the area washed by the Caribbean Sea this is a period of revolutionary thought and activity. Sporadic upheavals, as those of the past days in Nicaragua, Costa Rica, and Guatemala, have been to a great extent snuffed out in their infancy, but there are few knowledgeable observers who see an immediate end to widespread unrest and incipient revolution sweeping the entire area."

The story continued, "There is disagreement over the extent of physical contribution on the part of Premier Fidel Castro's Cuba to the state of affairs. There is little disagreement, however, over the psychological impact of 'Castrismo' or the concept of revolt against social and political forms in the Caribbean region. The inclination, especially among the intellectuals, is to strip Castrismo of its symbols and its exterior ideology and adopt it as a type of supraregional political doctrine.

"This revolution of ideas, which has manifested itself physically in sporadic outbursts, has two salient features common to virtually all affected countries of the Caribbean: it is leftist ranging from moderate to extreme and, secondly, it has a definite anti-American strain." The story went on to state that the extent of Castro's contribution was difficult to assess because of the increasing tendency of chiefs of state to attribute even minor disturbances to Castro's agents. Whatever validity this type of thinking had, it certainly colored the thought processes of Ydígoras for the remainder of his regime. There was never a time after the Puerto Barrios incident that Guatemala was not either preparing to defend against a Cuban-inspired assault or preparing its own assault on Cuba.

In fact it appears the president had been preoccupied in this direction long before the Puerto Barrios affair. In May 1960, for instance, I filed a story from Guatemala based on an interview with Ydígoras. It began, "Guatemalan armed forces will until further notice conduct continuous guerrilla warfare training maneuvers, President Miguel Ydígoras Fuentes said today. General Ydígoras himself observed maneuvers along the Caribbean coast yesterday. The plan is for half of the armed forces to undergo a period of maneuvers, alternating with the other half after determined periods, the president said. Last week defensive maneuvers against sea landings were held in Amatique Bay on the Caribbean. Land and air forces successfully repelled simulated enemy landings.

"The president, in an interview this afternoon, reflected the recent state of nerves in official circles here as a result of rumored invasion attempts. The president said he had received in recent days definite information that guerrilla bands were occupying training camps in Honduras near the Guatemalan border as well as in the mountain areas on the Nicaraguan border. He said these bands were being trained by Cuban revolutionary personnel.

"Guatemala suspended relations with Cuba last month after having declared the Cuban ambassador, Antonio Rodríguez Echizábal, *persona non grata*. It was claimed then that the Cuban embassy was interfering in Guatemalan political affairs. Foreign Minister Jesús Unda Murillo later amplified the causes of diplomatic suspension. He said that the ambassador's private secretary, Víctor Mirabel Acebal, had been discovered attending political meetings and disbursing election funds. When the ambassador had been asked to dismiss the private secretary, he declined, according to Unda. With that the secretary was forcibly ejected from Guatemala under arrest."

Just what the alleged disbursement of election funds amounted to I never learned, but it was about this time that Francisco Villagrán Kramer, leader of the leftist wing in Congress, told me the leftist group had been visited by an unidentified Cuban embassy official. The official had outlined a long list of instructions from Ernesto "Che" Guevara, at that time minister of industries in Havana. Sr. Villagrán Kramer said the instructions had to do mainly with the circumstances under which the Cuban government would contribute funds to the leftist candidates in Guatemalan elections. It was not brought out at that time whether funds actually were forthcoming, but Sr. Guevara's interest in Guatemala was keen, since he had served there under Arbenz as advisor to Fortuny and Gutiérrez.

In the light of later events it is easy to understand the president's preoccupation with Cuban intervention. It developed that at that time he was in the early stages of conversations with the United States about establishing a training base in Guatemala for some type of Cuban offensive. He was laying the groundwork for the explanation of his future actions. In November the president told me that the military training program for virtually all of Guatemala was being oriented to guerrilla tactics.

The November interview continued, "The president's comments [about guerrilla training] were made in answer to a question concerning the establishment of a large and heavily guarded military base on a coffee plantation near Retalhuleu. There have been repeated reports that a base was being established there with United States assistance as a training ground for military action against Cuba.[4]

"The president branded these reports, 'a lot of lies.' He said the base on the Helvetia estate near Retalhuleu, about ninety miles west of Guate-

[4] See the appendix, "The Base at Retalhuleu." [Editor's Note]

mala City, was one of several on which Guatemalan army personnel were being trained in guerilla warfare. The object of this training, he said, was to combat the type of invasions occurring recently in Honduras, Nicaragua, and Panama. The president said that modern United States weapons were being used and United States military personnel were being consulted.

"Opposition deputies in the Guatemalan Congress last month asked for an investigation of the Helvetia base. The request was voted down by administration forces in the House on grounds that the debate would bring out military information. Later President Ydígoras invited Congress to appoint a commission to go to Helvetia to conduct its own investigation. The opposition declined the invitation, maintaining it was too late in coming. The president said there were several installations throughout the country where Guatemalan military personnel were being trained in guerrilla warfare, but that Helvetia, with a barracks and landing field, was the largest. Referring to rumors concerning the Retalhuleu project, the president said, 'You must remember the world is full of rumors and Guatemala is a rumor paradise.' "

The invitation to the obstinate congressmen to visit Helvetia was, it developed, an enormous bluff by President Ydígoras, leaving room for speculation about what the wily chief of state would have done had Congress accepted the invitation. Some of the opposition members of Congress, such as Sr. Villagrán Kramer, were trained attorneys and clever investigators and it is difficult to imagine that they would have fallen for a spoon-feeding tour of the Retalhuleu foothills, as did a group of newspapermen later.

Early in January 1961, I was in Guatemala and called first at the office of Auguste Mulet Deschamps, information officer for the National Palace. We had been friends for a number of years, and mainly to observe his reaction I asked him, "Just what are you people up to in Retalhuleu?" Ordinarily a jovial type, Auguste became utterly serious and replied, "You stay away from there. I am warning you for your own good, you will get into trouble mixing in that."

A lead that broad could not be passed up, so the next day I hired a car and went up to Retalhuleu. The story published two days later stated, "This rich Pacific slope area is the focal point of Guatemala's new land and air military preparation effort for what is being considered in Guatemala an almost inevitable clash with Castro's Cuba. There is intensive daily air training here from a partially hidden airfield. In the cordillera foothills a few miles back from the Pacific, commando-type forces are being drilled in guerrilla warfare tactics by foreign personnel, mostly from the United States." The United States, the story continued, "is assisting in this effort not only with personnel but with matériel and in the construction of ground and air facilities."

Apparently the paragraph which later caused greatest annoyance among United States authorities was, "Although the air operation is about ten miles from the commando-training area, the two are geared for quick cooperative action. This was tested in early November during an abortive barracks revolt in which three important garrison cities fell to the rebels before they were defeated.

"The rebels were defeated by a combination of air power and ground troops. The commando groups were flown immediately to their respective military zone units where they were immediately integrated. They were sent into action, which, with the exception of Jalapa, was limited. They were returned to the Helvetia training center after limited combat."

It was not until some days later that I discovered that President Ydígoras himself had been at Helvetia on the day I was there and almost certainly knew of my presence there. For security reasons I did not use sizable portions of the material gathered.

I was denounced a few days later in the official administration paper edited by Sr. Mulet Deschamps, who was reported to have said in an interview that the whole story was a hoax fabricated by me to justify an extraordinarily large expense account. That ended my involvement in the Retalhuleu affair. The Cuban invasion was, of course, launched from there through Puerto Cabezas in Nicaragua.

In April I returned to Guatemala and did a story saying that Communists of the Arbenz regime were returning to the country. It was noted, "A five-year decree ordered by the late President Carlos Castillo Armas enabled the government to prevent the return of Communists who fled or who were forced into exile when Castillo Armas overthrew the regime of Colonel Jacobo Arbenz in 1954. That decree expired March 1 of this year, and the government at present appears helpless to prevent the returns. At least nothing has been done thus far in the case of Carlos Manuel Pellicer, one of the most fiery Communists in the infiltrated Arbenz regime," the story said and continued "Pellicer not only returned but immediately on his return entered a newspaper controversy with rightist members of the National Liberation Movement. This movement is formed with Castillo Armas followers."

The story was published April 10, and the following morning I was informed in my hotel room that two special police were awaiting me in the hotel lobby. They informed me the district chief of police wanted to see me immediately, and a few minutes later I was informed that the president had ordered me to leave Guatemala at the earliest convenience. The conversation as written in my notes later went like this:

Colonel Francisco Ardón: "President Ydígoras has always been your friend and he still likes you, but you have written something and he wants you to leave the country."

Myself: "What did I write that he objected to?"

The Colonel: "I don't know. You can send him a telegram and ask him for particulars, but he said you were to go as soon as you could arrange your affairs. He did not set a time limit, but you are to go voluntarily as quickly as possible or other means will be used."

Myself: "You mean force will be used?"

The Colonel: "You are to go as quickly as possible."

From there on out the story degenerated into pure O'Henry Central American horse opera. After trying to get the president, who was on one of his up-country trips, I finally took a plane for El Salvador (where General Ydígoras went when exiled the first time), and the morning paper *Prensa Libre* took a picture of me waving farewell from the plane ramp.

The next morning I received a cable from the presidency in Guatemala asking me to return and call on the president. When I appeared at immigration in Guatemala the day after I had left, the immigration officer looked up from the paper he was reading to examine my visa, took one startled look at me, and then shouted for the chief of immigration. The entire front page of the tabloid paper was filled with my picture waving farewell the day before. By this time the entire terminal was more or less in an uproar, and I was hustled off to the immigration chief's office while he telephoned the president's residence, Casa Crema. After the telephone conversation, I was instructed to wait in the chief's office until the president sent for me. Then, bag and baggage, I was taken to the Casa Crema, where the president was having lunch with his family.

After lunch we had a long interview which began, of course, with, "Well, how is your Spanish? etc." My story that day, slugged "Reconciliation," began, "Forces now training in Guatemala are not going to invade Cuba unless there is an attack on Guatemala, President Miguel Ydígoras Fuentes said today.

" 'If Castro ever should make a strike at us, however, we would hit something in Havana in hours,' the president said in an interview. He defended Guatemala's right to have foreign troops training on its territory. 'We are doing all right with our own troops, but if we needed outsiders I do not see why we should not have them,' the president said."

The story went on and on and on and in the final paragraph it noted, "The interview was something of a reconciliation meeting between the president and this reporter. The writer was expelled from Guatemala yesterday but was invited back today."

The interview concluded, the president ordered a car to take me and my luggage to a hotel. At the doorway I remarked, "Thank you, your Excellency, for inviting me back to Guatemala, but if I am not too impertinent, why did you expel me in the first place?"

"You made a lot of trouble for us before and I thought maybe you were going to make some more," he replied with a smile.

All of that was well and good, except the president had been misleading in his interview. At the moment of the interview, it developed, things were getting into motion for the Retalhuleu troops to invade Cuba at the Bay of Pigs. On April 14 my story began, "Guatemala is presently undergoing one of its periodic spells of political and economic nerves. There is widespread apprehension over the country's possible involvement in the Cuban situation." The story continued, "The national economy, while statistically favorable, is being confronted with dubious symptoms. Political momentum has come almost to a standstill, with the executive branch engaged in a slugging match with the legislature, and the country's political parties are plagued with internal eruptions.

"In the economic area, valid statistics to the contrary, the economic rhythm of the country has slowed down in past months. In this even the sternest critics of President Miguel Ydígoras Fuentes, and there are many such here, are reluctant to place the blame on the administration. There are numerous contributory causes. There is, primarily, a faltering coffee market. There is a hesitancy on the part of business in the face of uncertainty over the government's attitude in the Cuban matter."

The story said in respect to Cuba, "The Cuban situation revolves around repeated reports that an expeditionary force is being trained in this country for an attack on Castro. Authorities here have just as repeatedly denied there are invasion units training in this country, asserting that the troops in training here are purely for defensive purposes."

On the day of the Bay of Pigs invasion, April 17, the president issued a denial that Guatemala had participated in the invasion, but the denial was aimed at what it claimed had been a report, which I had never heard, that part of the invasion had been launched from Guatemalan territory. The official statement declared, "Anyone interested in proving the inaccuracy of those accusations may inspect the seventy kilometers of the Guatemalan Atlantic coastline and the cities of this littoral." The government was eminently correct in this. The troops, as has been noted, were flown from Retalhuleu to Puerto Cabezas and thence to Cuba. Our story noted, however, "The Association of Engineering Students at the Guatemala National University issued a statement last night criticizing the government for allegedly allowing foreign military bases on Guatemalan territory. The statement declared that the association was 'greatly preoccupied by the gravity of the existence of foreign military contingents on our soil.' "

On April 19 my story dealt with growing concern in Guatemala that there would be retaliatory measures from Cuba. The legislature passed a couple of resolutions asking the executive branch to intercede with the Security Council of the United Nations to prevent the conflict. For some reason even at this late date the government in Guatemala continued denying our story about the Retalhuleu training camp.

President Ydígoras, in his book *My War with Communism,* said in regard to this matter, "Representatives of the United States came to see me about training the Cuban anti-Castro forces, and we came to a spoken agreement. My government granted permission for the training of Cuban contingents and for the massing of arms and planes on Guatemalan soil. The entire training program was in the hands of American officers assigned to the task, and the troops were entirely Cuban patriots."

The president later noted, "If the United States press had maintained patriotic discretion, perhaps certain decisions taken by the White House in the most crucial moments of the attack on Cuba could have been different, and today Cuba would be free and America would breathe easier." This ingenuous viewpoint, of course, lends itself to endless debate, but suffice it to say the legislative branch of President Ydígoras' administration failed to appreciate fully his own "patriotic discretion."

The storms which were eventually to sweep President Ydígoras from office began gathering as early as midwinter 1961. The economy by that time was definitely faltering. Julio Vielman, an astute Harvard-trained economic observer, wrote to *The New York Times* in December 1961, "This country heads into 1962 fighting what at best is a holding action against depressive economic forces. Because of various stringent measures adopted, monetary authorities had hoped that dollar reserves at the end of 1961 would be $44,700,000, but they barely reached $40,000,000. The Guatemalan quetzal is on a par with the dollar.

"Government economists are of the opinion that the deficits in the country's balance of payments in 1958 and 1959 (and presumably in 1961) reflect structural deficiencies in the economy that are being difficult to correct." In a later paragraph the writer observed, "Banco de Guatemala (the national bank) economists have warned the monetary authorities that the deficits in the balance of payments will continue in spite of foreign investment and the United States aid, because the flaw is of a 'structural nature.' "

That was the economic cloud on the horizon. The political cloud was more ominous still. Late in December of 1961 a copy of a letter sent from Juan José Arévalo to Guillermo Palmieri came to us. Palmieri and his friends had been extremely active in endeavoring to bring back Dr. Arévalo from political exile and place him in the 1963 presidential elections. As it developed, the gigantic, handsome political figure of years past had not the slightest chance of gaining the presidency. But he proved the final undoing of President Ydígoras and came near to setting off a revolution.

My story of December 22, 1961 was based on the letter sent to Palmieri and noted, "Recent political developments here indicate that Guatemala's next government will inevitably be leftist and quite possibly radically so. The probability has been highlighted recently with the announced intention of Dr. Juan José Arévalo to return from exile to enter the 1963 presidential race.

"In a letter to supporters here Dr. Arévalo agreed to a proposed common effort on his behalf by left-wing parties which had supported his administration as president from 1945 to 1951. The letter, which has not yet been made public, expressed pessimism over the proposal to form a left-wing block with these parties. The former president suggested instead forming a loose federation of leftist groups, including student and labor organizations, which were instrumental in 1944 in overthrowing the thirteen-year dictatorship of Jorge Ubico.

"Dr. Arévalo was a self-proclaimed socialist and during his regime steadfastly turned back attempts of Communists to become a legally recognized force here. His regime did, however, witness a strong infiltration of Communism, and his administration was followed by that of Colonel Jacobo Arbenz Guzmán, which was largely directed by Communists who had originally gained influence under Arévalo."

The article went on to state that with the victory of Colonel Carlos Castillo Armas in 1954 indictments were handed down *in absentia* against both Arévalo and Arbenz charging them with complicity in the assassination of Colonel Francisco J. Arana, chief of the Guatemalan armed forces in July 1949. Colonel Arana was a candidate against Arbenz to succeed Arévalo in the presidency.

Then came a paragraph in the story that foreshadowed to some extent the events which finally took place: "President Miguel Ydígoras Fuentes has let it be known he would not hinder the return of Dr. Arévalo. At times there have been indications he would even welcome the return so as possibly to offset the growing influence of Mario Méndez Montenegro." Sr. Méndez Montenegro was head of the mildly left Revolutionary Party and a personal as well as political enemy of both President Ydígoras and Dr. Arévalo.

Juan José Arévalo was born into a farming family in the department of Santa Rosa on September 10, 1904. He finished normal school in Guatemala and on an Argentine fellowship received a doctorate in philosophy at the University of La Plata in 1934. He returned to Guatemala to enter the Ministry of Education and almost immediately ran into difficulty with the dictator Ubico. As a result he left to study in Europe. He later returned to Argentina, where he taught and from that distance helped to direct the rising tide against General Ubico. He participated in the junta which drew up the provisional constitution of 1945 and in that year became president. He tolerated Communists as individuals but resisted their attempts to establish a formal Communist party in Guatemala.

His following in Guatemala in later years was formidable. A certain mystique had grown around him, and his image was that of an incorruptible administrator and a champion of far-reaching reforms. The height of his popularity, interestingly enough, was during the latter days of the Ydígoras regime, when because of his long exile, most young Guatemalans had never seen him. The dream of an efficient and corruption-free government had a certain hypnotic effect, even among the hundreds of thousands who were not at all in sympathy with his liberal leanings.

Dr. Arévalo's detractors, and they also came by the thousands, discredited this image, especially Arévalo's much discussed administrative ability. They argued he was a self-propelled educator who came into office at a time any normally endowed person could not have helped but make a spectacular showing. He followed, his detractors explained, thirteen years of dictatorship, with all its sins, and the nation was with him wholeheartedly at the outset. Thus he had it made, even before he drew up his chair to the presidential desk.

Dr. Arévalo, incidentally, was extremely bitter toward the United States. His views on North American economics and economic policy were advanced in his book *The Shark and the Sardines*. His observations in this book comprised a litany of crimes of Wall Street, the State Department, and the United Fruit Company.

The unrest grew as the year 1962 advanced. In mid-March of that year there were days on end on which police had to quell disturbances, none of them too serious, but in the aggregate troublesome enough to preoccupy the administration. On the morning of March 17 the police raided a rightist opposition meeting and arrested several leaders of the group. One of those arrested had been a minister in the Castillo Armas cabinet, another was a prominent Catholic lay leader, and a third was one of the most respected physicians in Guatemala.

Difficulties continued to mount. On March 20, 1962 I wrote: "The fourth major attack on the administration of President Miguel Ydígoras Fuentes since he took office in March 1958 appears to have been suffocated. The capital was tranquil today with no new outbreaks reported. The known deaths here in Guatemala City rose to twenty-two last night with the shooting of a student by troops. The wounded in clashes during the eleven-day period of crisis stood at somewhere between 300 and 500, the wide difference in estimate attributable to the various sources of information and to the fact that many wounded were taken to private homes.

"There is general agreement," the story continued, "that while the government has won in this instance, heavy pressure has been built up. It is also generally agreed that unless President Ydígoras can find a way to release this pressure, other attempts against his regime will be made. With the exception of the June 1956 affray in the regime of the late Carlos Castillo Armas, when police killed five demonstrating students, this is the first time in recent years police and troops have shot into crowds of demonstrating citizens with intent to kill.

"Why President Ydígoras abruptly changed his policy and ordered such drastic means of stopping the demonstrations is a matter for widespread speculation. It is certain now that the students were taken by surprise, as were the spectators, many of whom were accidental victims. It is considered certain too that the far left and the Communist sectors, who have been enthusiastically fanning the flames, were surprised at the turn of things too, pleasantly so.

"The immediate cause of this latest attack on the Ydígoras administration was a student protest over the December 3 congressional elections. The government won 25 of the 33 seats at stake in this election and there were immediate charges of fraud. There were demonstrations by students and the defeated parties in late December, but these demonstrations were suspended for the Christmas holidays.

"Further demonstrations were planned for January, but a state of siege was imposed with the assassination of Ranulfo González Ovalle, chief of the secret police, on January 24. The state of siege was renewed for thirty days in February, and it was renewed for still another thirty days last night."

Less than a month after this dispatch was filed, there were insistent demands that President Ydígoras resign from office. It was during this time that the president made a significant remark. "Before I become a fugitive president," he said, "I will become a dead president." It was an impressive declaration but hardly a prophetic one.

There were more demonstrations and more wounded during April 1962. There was also increased guerrilla activity in the eastern part of the country. During this period I asked President Ydígoras in an interview why, if he had things as well under control as he said he had, were the guerrilla forces in Isabal department able to continue their activities unabated? They had been having signal successes under Antonio Yon Sosa, a defected lieutenant of the regular army. The president replied, "The trouble is they know the same things on both sides. Officers on both sides were trained by your people at Fort Gulick." Authorities in the Canal Zone, where Fort Gulick is located, said they had no record of Yon Sosa's having trained there.

The president also said during that interview that Dr. Arévalo could return to Guatemala if he wanted, but that he would not stand a chance in the presidential race. "The anti-Communists are too strong," he said. According to my notes on that interview, President Ydígoras made one further interesting observation: "There are no liberals," he said, "there are only rightists and leftists, and the leftists are all Communists."

Toward the end of April, the president, who up to that time had supported his friends, abandoned a large part of his cabinet in the face of demands from irate students and enemies of his regime. One of those let out was his friend and his physician, Dr. López Herrarte, the minister of health. The latter did not seem to mind much and continued as physician and medical consultant to Casa Crema.

My story on April 26, 1962 said, "Some resolution of Guatemala's political crisis may be expected today or tomorrow, President Miguel Ydígoras Fuentes said this morning. The President said the 12-day struggle to form a new government possibly will end today or tomorrow and he thought it probable a new cabinet would be announced within the next twenty-four hours. He was considering several possibilities but would retain some of the old cabinet, including the ministers of defense, foreign relations, and communications, he said.

"The nation has been in political upheaval since January," the story noted and continued. "The situation has been increasingly tense, however, the past two weeks, with demands from several quarters that the president resign. It appeared yesterday that General Ydígoras was getting the upper hand in the situation and that he was so confident of this that he ordered all political demonstrations broken up. One of these, scheduled to be one of the most intensive demonstrations of the entire series thus far, was scattered within a matter of two hours by massive police action in which tear gas and riot clubs were used."

The president, in an interview on which the preceding story was based, said he had not even considered the demands that he resign. He blamed the crisis on a combination of economic and political factors, particularly soft spots in the coffee market and the relentless pressures of Castro against his regime. He said over thirty persons had been killed and three hundred wounded in the demonstrations which had taken place since January. David L. Graham, later to become a representative in the Maine legislature, wrote in the June 1962 *Nation:* "And so Guatemala's tragic history grinds on—a tragedy flecked with farce. The aging and bizarre president has clung to his lucrative post with a tenacity and cunning that would be comic were it not for the disaster being inflicted on the nation."

There were further demonstrations throughout the year, and it was now becoming increasingly evident that the president's fast political footwork was wearing out. Added to his other problems, the economy was getting into deeper trouble. Julio Vielman filed a story announcing that the quetzal, which had been freely convertible since 1925, had been placed under the exchange controls. The gold and dollar reserves had reached a low of $30,000,000 after steadily declining from a high of $72,000,000 in 1957. That meant that importers had to obtain permission to get the foreign exchange necessary for their purchases.

In the latter part of November, units of the air force rebelled and attacked the president's residence and the nearby Military Academy with bombs and machine guns. In the light of subsequent information, it appeared that the government would have been overthrown then except for the failure of the infantry to join the attack. There were wholesale arrests following this abortive attack, both in the military and civilian ranks. Among the latter, the puzzling feature was that the arrests extended from the extreme right to the moderate left but not to the extreme left.

It was at this time that Carlos Manuel Pellicer, one of the most militant of the radical leftists in Guatemala, broke with the Communist Party, or so at least he announced. In identical letters to Nikita Khrushchev, Mao Tse-tung, and Fidel Castro, the defecting leftist listed the causes of his decision. They were numerous and were printed at length in the afternoon paper *El Imparcial*. He was living in Mexico at the time of the purported renunciation, and what his action meant was difficult to fathom. To President Ydígoras it meant quite a bit because it was the only letup at that time in the harrassment from the radical and moderate left.

The same *El Imparcial,* nominally an extremely conservative afternoon paper, created a stir November 26 when it published on its front page a photograph showing four alleged leaders of the air force uprising as guests of officers of the United States Air Force a few days before the attack. They were shown with Major General Perry B. Griffith, sub-inspector general of security at Norton Air Force Base. Guillermo Palmieri, broadcasting in his campaign to bring back Dr. Arévalo, noted that President Ydígoras had charged the air force plot was attributable to pro-Castro influences. The broadcaster then inquired, "What were those four pro-Castro air force colonels doing as guests of the United States?"

By mid-March 1963 it was so evident that something was imminent in Guatemala that correspondents began drifting in. On March 27 I filed a story stating, "Political activity is building up here rapidly as the country goes into the third day of a state of siege. Scattered bomb explosions yesterday and last night marked the first stages of the state of siege decree. There were no casualties reported in the four relatively light explosions last night. One bomb exploded in the neighborhood of Casa Crema, the presidential palace."

My story on March 29 stated, "The leftist parties supporting the candidacy of Dr. Juan José Arévalo voted last night to cancel a massive political demonstration originally scheduled for Sunday. The decision, voted after vigorous and sometimes bitter debate, was taken, according to one party officer present, because of a fear of violence and of widespread retaliation by the army. According to the state of siege order under which Guatemala has been operating since Monday all political activity is forbidden as is the right of assembly abrogated."

The story continued, "There is a growing impression here that presently at least the national direction has come under the domination of the armed forces and that President Miguel Ydígoras Fuentes is playing a conciliatory but secondary role. There is a further impression that the administration's presidential candidate, Roberto Alejos, is taking a significant role in the current events despite the fact he has no office in the administration. The president has lately told intimates he has been under great pressure and the impression is that the pressure is mainly coming from the armed forces and Sr. Alejos."

On March 30, I "pigeoned" (had a traveler deliver) a cable out to El Salvador. This is a crude but sometimes successful method of getting past a tight censorship and is most effective when the government is in such confusion that few of the censorship precautions are observed. That story, with a San Salvador dateline, said, "Guatemala is in a state of mounting tension. Travelers to El Salvador from the neighboring country are reporting that while President Miguel Ydígoras Fuentes remained in the office of chief of state the country was coming increasingly under the domination of the armed forces. Predictions were being freely made that a military coup was inevitable and only the timing was in doubt.

"The catalyst in the turbulent state of affairs is Dr. Juan José Arévalo. The former president galvanized Guatemala today when it was learned he had slipped into the country last night. His appearance before a few representatives of the foreign press and television was made under dramatic circumstances which have made an enormous impression on the Guatemalan capital, according to traveler accounts."

What actually happened on the night of March 29 was along the lines of a classic Central American plot. A few correspondents of press, television, and radio were alerted in the afternoon. My own instructions were to be standing on an isolated street corner at a certain hour, holding, as I recall, a package of cigarettes. At the appointed time a car drew up, and the driver, a stranger, inquired if I were waiting for someone. I was taken to another site, and another car took me to the rendezvous.

There was a group waiting in the living room. The television cameras had been set up and drinks had been served. We were sipping highballs when the door leading from the kitchen opened and Arévalo, the most hunted man in Guatemala at that moment, walked in wearing sports clothes and, as I recall, a long-billed fisherman's cap. The news conference was somewhat routine, but all of us were charged up because the implications were clear. Arévalo's presence in Guatemala was certain to lead to political chaos and quite possibly to violence or even civil war.

Considering the risks he had already taken in getting there and the further great physical danger ahead, he was remarkably relaxed that night, or at least gave an excellent imitation of being relaxed. My own role in the performance was something less than dramatic. Our paper in New York was on strike and our West Coast edition had already gone to bed, so I was sitting on a fine story with no place to send it.

The following day there were wholesale arrests in an effort to learn how Arévalo had gotten into Guatemala and where he was hiding at that moment. Events moved rapidly, and early the next morning the army rose. President Ydígoras was arrested, and he and Señora Ydígoras were shipped off to Nicaragua in an air force plane. With characteristic refusal to consider defeat, the president had ordered the tiny palace guard to resist the entire Guatemalan armed forces. A light tank battered open the Casa Crema gates, and by the time I got out to the presidential residence trucks had been backed up to the main entrance and workmen were casually, routinely loading files and documents.

My personal luck improved. *The New York Times* started publication on April 1 after 114 days of strike shutdown, and I was on page one with the Guatemalan overthrow. Further, there was an interview with Colonel Enrique Peralta Azurdia, the fifty-five-year-old minister of defense in the Ydígoras cabinet, who had been made chief of state. He assured me at the time he wanted nothing more than to clean up the mess and to get back to the barracks. Two years later when I interviewed him he repeated this wish. He appeared totally sincere both times.

The tightest of newspaper censorship was immediately put into effect with the overthrow. That morning I put in a call to a blind number in New York explaining I wanted to speak to my wife. The call went through and I began dictating at top speed when I was suddenly cut off. "But you can't stop me from talking to my wife," I shouted. The censor calmly replied in English, "One does not say 'stop,' 'quote,' 'unquote,' and 'paragraph' to one's wife." Colonel Peralta himself had to give the order to let the copy pass.

President Ydígoras, recounting the overthrow in his book *My War with Communism,* said he had withstood seventeen national strikes, 685 terrorist bombs in the capital, two military rebellions, seven attacks on his life, and massive acts of terrorism. He added, "But on the night of March 30, 1963 I was defeated by the enemy within, my own Minister of Defense, Colonel Enrique Peralta Azurdia." The president understandably was bitter, but the accuracy of his statement is debatable. It is known that Colonel Peralta repeatedly resisted the demands of his military colleagues to strike against the administration, and according to his friends, he acquiesced only when he was convinced it was either that or unmanageable chaos.

The divisive tactics of General Ydígoras to destroy opposing forces, most of them democratic, in honest opposition to his regime tended to jell the scattered strength of the leftist groups. The uncontrolled, and quite likely uncontrollable, creeping of corruption into high levels abetted the decay of an administration that at the outset promised much.

With the left becoming stronger by the hour, the president bent further and further to their will because the army was at that moment placing great pressures on the administration and the president apparently felt the left could give him substantial support. President Ydígoras was never able to fully convince the armed forces that he had not in some way abetted the entry into Guatemala of Dr. Arévalo.

These then were the three decisive factors that brought about the president's downfall: his failure to recognize in the beginning the depth and strength of the moderate left, and his overevaluation of it later; rampant corruption in his administration; and, finally, his apparent failure to assess correctly the seriousness of the abortive November air force revolt. The army had obviously been more deeply involved in that plot than the president realized, or admitted realizing.

Our next meeting with General Ydígoras was a pathetic aftermath. The caravan of big, black automobiles was missing. The dozens of neatly uniformed palace guardsmen who scurried about when he gave the slightest command were for the most part in prison for having obeyed his last command, to defend the Casa Crema. The former president was in a shabby hotel room in Managua, Nicaragua, and his patient wife was sitting on a twin bed darning one of his socks. She was sitting on the bed because the general and I were occupying the only two chairs in the room.

He appeared a bit sadder, somewhat subdued, and perhaps disillusioned, but his great optimism still had not deserted him. He insisted he had not completely lost power, despite assurances of those around him that he had indeed. One thing was certain, he remained a wealthy man. He had no worries on that score because the million or so dollars he had picked up from his salary and allowances were prudently put away in the United States and elsewhere.

Our last word from him up to the time of this writing was a Christmas card in December 1964. It was a color photograph of him and some members of his family, his happily-smiling señora included, in a field of chin-high cotton, and the inscription was "Don Pablo—I am now a planter and am prospering." He was in exile in Costa Rica at the time.

El Salvador

El Salvador is the little fellow in the drama who persistently wanders in out of character. A model of peaceful charm while its neighbors are glaring and scratching at each other, it suddenly takes a notion to do a bit of brawling on its own just as the others have settled down to a peaceful interlude. I once characterized the country in a dispatch as "an oasis in an angry desert" or some such, and within a short time it came so close to a violent revolution that citizens would not walk the streets at night.

It has been seen what happened when the big neighbor Guatemala decided in 1821 to drag little El Salvador into the Mexican empire. A perfect storm was raised. The smaller nation not only applied to the United States for annexation but it became so obstreperous that Augustín I had to send down troops to restore order by occupying the country.

In this connection El Salvador has throughout its recorded history resisted the many Guatemalan efforts to dominate it either morally or physically. In El Salvador the domination technique is called, always with a touch of disdain, *el capitán generalismo,* or "captain generalism," from the days when Guatemala was the Captaincy General for all of Central America. Many of the later rulers of Guatemala, notably Rafael Carrera and General Rufino Barrios, attempted to hold the smaller nation physically and Carrera effectively did so for a time.

El Salvador's soft, green hills and quiet valleys have seen some of the bloodiest fighting in the Middle American region, with Salvadoran peasants killing landowners and the landowners killing thousands of peasants. The estimates of the dead have been as high as twelve thousand. Additionally the country has been plagued with corrupt politics, some of the shenanigans being weird enough to make an old-time Tammany Hall alderman blush.

The country has some of the wealthiest people and some of the most poverty-stricken in all of Latin America. It has some of the most luxurious homes and in the past has had some of the meanest and most uninhabitable hotels. Recently the leading citizens, out of sheer embarrassment, subscribed to a new hotel, one of the finest in the region. The great majority of Salvadorans have suffered for centuries from diet deficiency diseases, and yet San Salvador has probably the finest restaurant between Mexico City and Bogotá.

That then is El Salvador, the little fellow, the smallest republic of Middle America, who refuses to stay in character, disdains being typed.

El Salvador came under the captaincy general of Guatemala as established by Pedro de Alvarado, a lieutenant of Hernán Cortés. Typically it was the first of the Central American countries to revolt against Spain, in 1811. It had been settled by the Spanish in 1523 and its early settlers did quite well, having set up their establishments along the highway laid out by the Spanish from Guatemala through Honduras and Nicaragua. The same general route is followed today in the Pan American Highway.

In 1821 El Salvador joined the other Central American states in declaring independence from Spain, and in 1823 it joined the others in the Provincias Unidas del Centro América. Aside from a disastrous civil war, the political highlight of the twentieth century was the fourteen-year dictatorship of General Maximiliano Hernández Martínez. He was overthrown in 1944. With but one brief interlude, there have been military governments since 1930. In 1965 the incumbent president, former Colonel Julio Adalberto Rivera, made the somewhat remarkable statement that should a civilian be elected president in 1967 he himself would recognize the new president. He added he thought the armed forces "would do likewise."[1]

Major Oscar Osorio, later to be a colonel, began a six-year term in 1950, and my introduction to the country was during his administration. The economy was booming. The coffee planters were sending their families to Europe and they themselves were buying Cadillacs like Texans. It was around this time the description of El Salvador as "the world's smallest Texas" began making the rounds. This little joke was a source of irritation to the "haves," but the "have nots" were not interested, never having heard of Texas.

On my first visit I was amazed to find a smooth-functioning economy

---

[1] For the actual course of more recent political events in El Salvador, see the Afterword. [Editor's Note]

in a country surrounded by bickering and bad business in its neighbors. My first story from San Salvador, the capital, noted, "This nation, coming into what might well be its biggest dollar-earning coffee crop, appears to be the only Central American republic without immediate problems, either political or economic." The story, with its somewhat staggering statistics, continued, "This year's crop is estimated to reach between 1,200,000 and 1,250,000 bags of 132 pounds. The biggest crop thus far quantitively was that of 1952–1953, with 1,283,000 bags, but expected higher prices this year would make the present crop a better dollar-earner. Last year's crop of 920,000 bags earned $80,000,000 of which the government got $15,000,000 in taxes. It is thought this year's crop could bring as high as $100,000,000 with the government's share $25,000,000."

The more sombre note entered a few paragraphs later: "There is only one serious shadow in the picture and that is labor, which does not feel its benefits and pay are in stride with the higher profits." The story added, "There is little doubt the administration would strengthen its position with labor by enacting stronger legislation if it dared. Coffee planters, however, have such power that the administration hesitates to enact legislation which would stir them up."

Had I had more background on El Salvadoran affairs when that was written, I would have been aware that at that time it was fanciful to think of labor expressing itself. The administration was holding office with the advice and consent of the oligarchic group which, at that time, represented about nine-tenths of all management. Further, had I had sufficient prescience I would have seen clearly that out of the imbalance between rosy prosperity and grinding poverty of those days there would evolve deeply significant reforms.

A majority of the most far-reaching of those reforms, when they finally came, affected the rural areas where most of the nation's problems are centered. In late 1964 and early 1965 the administration of President Rivera was still pushing through some of these reforms. His Ministry of Labor released figures at that time to show there were 88,105 farms in the republic. There were 54,776 families renting on a sharecrop basis and something like 440,000 unlanded farm laborers, of whom 55,000 were under fifteen years of age. There were 36,035 coffee plantations, of which 11,987 were of less than 2.5 acres. The remaining plantations ranged to over 6,000 acres each. In 1961 fourteen of these plantations, or fincas, of over 6,000 acres belonged to fourteen individual families or interlocking families.

There are dozens of explanations for the difficulties, past, present, and future, of El Salvador, but most of the explanations are buried in these and related statistics. In 1961 there were 3,295,670 acres of land under cultivation in El Salvador, of which it would be fair to estimate about 10 per cent was in coffee. Of this approximately 329,000 acres, 84,000 acres, or about 26 per cent, were owned by fourteen families or interlocking families.

In a previous chapter figures of the Inter-American Committee on Agricultural Development were quoted to show that in 1950 there were 201,900 agricultural families in El Salvador, of which nearly 10 per cent were low-income, landless workers. The figures have not changed much in the intervening years. When the current situation is analyzed, it appears that the 3,295,670 acres of cultivated land are worked on the basis of a 7.5-acre average per person contributing to production, one of the lowest averages in Latin America.

The overriding problem here is that not much can be done about it, barring violent social and political upheavals. At least there appears no peaceful solution in sight. El Salvador is one of the very few countries in Latin America, and the only one in Middle America, with little or no public land for further settlement. Land is obtained by the state on the rare occasions when it can be had, and is distributed forthwith. But even with the best of intentions on the part of both the government and the social, political, and financial leaders of the nation, land cannot be squeezed into the public domain when there is none available, short of, as we said, great upheavals. This brings into perspective the real significance of the freedom-of-movement concept within the Central American Common Market. Under this plan excess rural population would be free to travel into member countries which have great undeveloped or underdeveloped land resources.

The ruling families in the Salvadoran feudal system have become so sensitive about their position that they have abandoned to some extent their traditional aloofness before criticism. They write letters to the editor of a paper in which some dispatch or news item is considered objectionable. Or they invite an offending correspondent out for a neighborly drink, and in the flow of good scotch whisky they let him have their criticism broadside.

One of the constant complaints is that none of the newspapers or news magazines can make up their minds whether El Salvador is ruled by five, fourteen, or forty families. Some years ago Ricardo Quiñonez, a blunt and voluble member of an old and wealthy Salvadoran family, wrote a letter to our editor complaining precisely about this. He noted that in an editorial our paper had referred to the "thirty families" and that a weekly magazine just a short time before that had referred to the "Fourteen Families." Sr. Quiñonez wrote, "In my circle of friends we think the number should be closer to 500 typical Latin American families." No one seems to know the origin of the term "Fourteen Families" or *Cartorce Grande* ("Big Fourteen") unless, of course, it originated, as would seem probable, from those fourteen coffee fincas of over 6,000 acres each. Actually the ownership of those large fincas would involve from as many as twenty-five to forty or more families.

The families are so interlocking that, as Harold Lavine observed, "only a matriarch or so" remain who could untangle them. The line of the aristocracy is so thin in Central America and particularly in El Salvador and the discouragement of marriages of unequal social strata so obdurate that the aristocratic eligibles have to either marry among themselves or marry Europeans or North Americans. Thus when a young man of a great coffee family marries into a coffee-beer-banking family in El Salvador nothing much is changed in the overall scheme of things because the first family has married into the second family most likely a half dozen or more times in past years.

But there are subtle changes noticeable in El Salvador as well as other nations in the Middle American region. Sr. Quiñonez, for instance, in his letter to the editor first was fretful over "unrestricted liberty of press" and then commented, "We in El Salvador certainly are not blind, and we are very much aware that a tremendous difference exists between the very rich and the very poor. We are well aware that most of our inhabitants are poor and misery is rampant."

On one of my earlier trips to El Salvador, before the matter of the letter, a member of one of the country's more progressive and influential families explained to me privately that some of his colleagues had joined with him in attacking the agrarian reform problem. The need for action in the face of growing danger was fully recognized, he explained, but it was also recognized there was active opposition and even antagonism from other sectors of the oligarchy.

The same Sr. Quiñonez, in an interview a month after his letter to the editor, said concerning the aristocracy, "We have been negligent. We have been afraid to take part in the life of the country. We have been too busy making money to get into politics." He concluded in that interview in November 1960, "Finally we are being forced to enter the government and we are planning to do so. This is not a trouble we made, but we have to help supply the solutions." The speaker and his colleagues were to get their chance to become immersed in administrative affairs, which would be something of a departure from their traditional role of directing activities from barely visible vantage points. No one could have foreseen how or when this was to come about, but the signs were already there.

In 1954 President Osorio, a product of the military, was at the head of a mild dictatorship. He had been installed as the outgrowth of another overthrow of a chief of state[2] and, on the whole, he conducted a creditable administration, even if he did not appear to particular advantage in later developments. He worked in harmony with the oligarchy, in harmony, that is, to the extent of preserving the status quo. He pushed for Central American integration. At the time of the Guatemalan revolt he assisted, as far as El Salvador's surface neutrality would permit, the revolutionary plans against President Arbenz.

President Osorio proceeded on an amicable and cooperative basis with the United States ambassador at the time, the late Michael J. McDermott. It will be recalled that at the time there was a synchronization of action between Ambassador McDermott and ambassadors John E. Peurifoy of Guatemala and Whiting W. Willauer of Honduras. Ambassador McDermott, working with President Osorio, helped set up the final conference from which came the Guatemalan junta, with Colonel Castillo Armas as a member. At the time there was much speculation that President Osorio was more influential in bringing about the arrangement than was the late Ambassador Peurifoy.

As mentioned earlier, there was an economic upturn at this time. The country had passed through some bad years but now appeared to be in a robust period. The growth of industries was beginning. Politically, things were still quiet but the beginnings of things not-so-quiet were being noted as early as mid-1955. Long before the actual campaigning began for the 1956 elections, and that was fully a year before the change in administration, the various interest groups and prospective candidates began jockeying for position.

This premature activity could have been absorbed without too much difficulty, and, in fact, President Osorio was even then preparing for any untoward trends, but the major preoccupation just then was evidence of a split developing within the armed forces. That was always a bad sign in El Salvador, the system being what it was. Entrenched colonels were being jostled by cliques of majors and captains who had caught a distant scent of power. Added to this was the clear indication that for the first time since 1931 a civilian was preparing to run for the presidency. This was Roberto Canessa, a brilliant young statesman and member of a wealthy coffee family. For a brief time there were five contestants, and then four, three of them military or military-diplomatic, and finally there was only one, after possibly the bitterest campaign in the country's history. Sr. Canessa, in addition to having been constantly harassed by attempts to disqualify him, was physically attacked by an obviously

---

[2] Osorio had been installed provisionally by a group of military officers following a coup. Two years later, in 1950, he was elected president backed by a party of his own creation. [Editor's Note]

officially-inspired mob. Another candidate, Colonel José Alberto Funes, at the time an ambassador for his country, was charged with irregularities in the conduct of his office. And so it went.

Had it not been for the violence and the openly corrupt election practices, the campaign would have provided some humorous relief. Colonel José María Lemus, candidate of the administration's Partido Revolucionario Unión Democrático (PRUD), was challenged on the grounds that he was not born of Salvadoran parents, and his party forthwith displayed documents to show he was the illegitimate son of a Salvadoran schoolteacher and a Honduran woman. Sr. Canessa was challenged for allegedly falsifying his age on a birth certificate, and he produced his mother and father and the delivering physician to verify it. He was declared ineligible anyway. One of the more obscure candidates campaigned on a promise of an ox and six acres of land for every farmer. He was immediately denounced as a Communist. He escaped being jailed but lapsed into obscurity without a whimper.

Colonel Lemus, who in order to campaign had resigned his post as head of the Ministry of the Interior, which includes the national police, clearly had the advantage. To overcome this advantage the remaining candidates made a listless attempt at coalition, a classical gang-up strategy in Latin America which nearly always fails. The attempt to form an effective coalition failed for a number of reasons, including the fact that in the process some of the most promising of the eligible candidates were cancelled out.

Tension grew rapidly as the public learned that a blatant political fraud was underway. A virtual state of siege was invoked by President Osorio and along with it foreign press censorship, the latter being totally ineffective except for slowing down traffic while the correspondents found ways of getting copy out. Troops patrolled the streets throughout the nights and the rumors of revolt against Osorio and his disciple Lemus (whom Colonel Osorio was later instrumental in overthrowing) continued to proliferate so rapidly that very few persons left their homes at night.

The election, when it finally took place, was wholly farcical. Crowds of paid voters were openly hauled from one voting booth to another in government trucks. There was little or no control attempted at the various polling places. Foreign correspondents visiting the outlying voting stations were given ballots and told, amidst great jollity, to go ahead and vote. I kept mine for years as a souvenir.

Considering all that had gone before, the public had not expected much of Colonel Lemus and his government. Thus there was considerable surprise when he began his administration with a series of moves that melted away much of the opposition. The new president reached into parties other than his own for his cabinet, which was generally considered an excellent one. Further, he quickly nullified the widely-detested Defense of Democracy Law put through under the Osorio administration. This law was a piece of "shotgun" legislation which provided heavy penalties for dozens of offenses. Foremost among the punishable offenses was writing or speaking disparagingly of the president, members of the cabinet, or legislators.

Later President Lemus further endeared himself by ordering top officials, beginning with himself, to declare all their personal holdings before the Supreme Court. Simultaneously he set in motion a campaign to do away with bribes and tips to government officers and to cancel subsidies paid to the daily newspapers, which had enjoyed particular tax exemption privileges, and still do. This latter action, which had threatened to cut into the incomes of the leading newspapers, served to bring down fire on the administration. Surprisingly, however, when the administration later began coming under heavy attack from the foreign press, the San Salvador papers went vigorously to the defense of Lemus. This was in spite of what seemed a deliberate attempt by the president to antagonize the local press.

He angered the press the second time in one year by pushing through the "gag law," a notably obtuse piece of legislation. Under this law a publisher was not only forced to publish a reply from a person who considered himself to have been injured in the paper but was also forbidden then or afterwards to add an editor's note explaining the newspaper's point of view. While the controversy over this was going on, the president brought suit against a daily paper for an article he considered harmful to himself personally and to his office.

In other areas the new president was more tractable. He took up the amicable relations with the oligarchy where President Osorio, his predecessor, had left off. The political area, however, was the only possible one in which the new president could arrange a rapprochement with the wealthy ruling class. He himself had the humblest of origins, having had no established home from infancy until fortune brought him a scholarship to the National Military Academy. He had been born, it seemed, for the military life and, strangely enough was well suited to the scholarly life as well. The difficult regime of the academy was to him sheer luxury after the things he had gone through, and as a result he mowed down the competition, easily graduating first in his class. He caused considerable head-scratching among the old-line career officers by advocating more humanities courses at the academy.

Meanwhile Lemus himself had become something of a classicist in addition to becoming a good soldier and administrator. His special pursuits were the life histories of José Martí, the Cuban patriot, and Father Miguel

Hidalgo, the Mexican revolutionary. He published several works on these two. He prized his membership in the classical Atheneum Club almost as much as his colonelcy. He had to resign his army rank before announcing for the presidency but was allowed to resume it for pension purposes when he was overthrown and exiled to Costa Rica.

Incidentally, at the time of President Lemus' overthrow he became the fourth president in exile in San José, Costa Rica. An enterprising photographer conceived the idea of taking their picture as a group. The story, possibly apocryphal, goes that General Ydígoras, formerly of Guatemala and easily the most bizarre and colorful of them all, turned down the idea, saying, "I do not want to have my picture taken with those clowns."

President Lemus had served out nearly four years of his six-year term when storm clouds began gathering. In February 1960 I sent a story from San Salvador stating, "This smallest of Latin American republics appears rapidly approaching a period of serious political and social stress. In recent years while other Central American and Caribbean countries were undergoing political and social convulsions, El Salvador was an oasis of peace and stability. It appears now, however, that a deteriorating economy, with rising unemployment, and the culmination of twenty-nine years of almost uninterrupted military rule have finally caught up with the country."

The story went on to say that there was deep-seated restlessness and discontent among the lower and middle classes concerning national elections scheduled for April, two months from then. Opposition parties maintained they had no chance of putting up candidates in the election, and even if their candidates were inscribed they would likely be declared ineligible by the electoral board. "President José María Lemus in recent weeks has been outspoken in his conviction that Communists have infiltrated the political opposition," the story continued. An editorial apparently based on this story appeared in *The New York Times* three days later, and that, in turn, prompted the already-mentioned letter from Ricardo Quiñonez.

The blow fell nine months later. President Lemus was arrested and deported to Costa Rica and a mixed junta, three armed forces officers and three civilians, took over the government.[3] That was October 26, 1960. On November 8 I had an interview with the full junta, one of the strangest interviews in my experience. I had submitted a list of ten questions in writing and at the appointed time sat with the full junta, repeating each question. As a question was asked, the six members would whisper together before one took over the responsibility of answering. Either that,

---

[3] The coup deposing Lemus was engineered by leftist army officers and civilians on the grounds of his disregard for the constitution and his curtailment of freedom of expression and peaceful assembly. [Editor's Note]

or one of the six would answer immediately, at which the others would glare at him as if he had been talking out of turn.

From my notes of that interview, it appeared the sixth question was the one which created the greatest commotion. The question was: "There are reports that known Communists have been placed in relatively minor and, in some instances, major positions in the new government. Any comments?" There was a flurry of whispering and occasional loud protests of "false" and "absolutely untrue." Finally, Dr. Fabio Castillo, apparently the junta spokesman, declared as emphatically as a heavy head cold would permit, "Your answer is the junta said the reports are false and ill-intentioned."

Dr. Castillo, a physician who had taken postgraduate courses on various fellowships in the United States, was by far the most intellectual member of the junta and probably the most deeply anti-American. After the next overthrow he was offered a position in the cabinet of the junta which overthrew the original one, but he refused the job. He later emerged as rector of the National University and sometime still later was the center of a nationwide controversy when he invited some professors from the Soviet Union to lecture at the university.

The interview that day brought out an interesting note. One of the questions referred to rumors that former President Osorio had been instrumental in the overthrow of President Lemus. It will be recalled that Osorio, when president, had been a sponsor and supporter of Colonel Lemus and had probably been the principal instrument in his election. The answer from the junta members was that representatives of all groups in opposition to President Lemus had assisted in the latter's overthrow. The junta spokesman added, "it is naturally certain that Colonel Osorio was among them." The junta was emphatic, however, in stating that no commitments had been made to Colonel Osorio or to anyone else. That question was never to be definitively answered since not so long afterwards Osorio himself was sent into exile with the junta members, a very angry and, for some reason, disillusioned ex-president. The new junta, ideologically considerably to the left, never had a chance. In addition to its indigenous political coloration, it was predominantly pro-Castro and anti-American. As a consequence, recognition by the United States was held up until the junta was groggy from lack of support.

A story I filed on November 11 noted, "The new military-civilian junta governing this smallest of Central American republics is being given only an outside possibility of surviving until scheduled elections take place two years hence. Leaders of the revolutionary groups which brought off the coup maintain that without United States recognition soon it will inevitably fall. The State Department, according to reports here, is holding off recognition pending further clarification of the political leanings of the new junta, particularly of its civilian members.

"As seen here, the State Department assessment is that the civilian sector of the junta and a large part of the cabinet are anti-United States and are suspect of Castro leanings and/or Communism. There generally is little disagreement over the first supposition, namely the anti-United States attitude. Resentment toward the United States arises partially from the conviction that the North American diplomatic representation here was not unaware of the early activities in opposition to the Lemus administration but had not taken the trouble to inform itself of its true causes.

"The junta members as well as individual members of the new junta cabinet are particulary resentful that their political leanings are being questioned without having had a chance to expound them. None of the junta nor members of the cabinet questioned had ever met a United States ambassador, and most had never met any of the United States embassy personnel, they maintained."

The junta was eventually given recognition, but nonetheless was overthrown by another junta in January. Five members of the original junta were placed under arrest, and Colonel Osorio, as mentioned, was sent into exile.

The new group was far to the right of the overthrown junta. There was considerable shooting during the takeover, although there was never any doubt of the outcome once the plans for a coup became certain. The only man doing any talking in this junta was a relatively unknown lieutenant colonel, Julio Adalberto Rivera. His first statement to the press, or at least his first to me when I found him virtually asleep on his feet the afternoon of the overthrow, was that he was anti-Communist and anti-Castro and that the Cuban government would never be recognized by the new junta. Colonel Rivera continued to do most of the talking as the junta advanced in its administrative work, and, of course, he was finally elected president of the country in a perfectly legal but nonetheless extraordinary election.

Dr. Castillo of the former junta had been held under house arrest but finally was released and offered the post of minister of culture in the new cabinet. He declined with the explanation that some of his colleagues were being held under arrest. The former junta members were eventually all restored to freedom and, as noted, Dr. Castillo became the rector of the university. The new junta was comprised of three civilians and two military men. The sub-secretary of public security was Major Oscar Alfonso Rodríguez Simo, of whom more will be heard later.

At about this time the denouement of the Roberto Canessa story came about. The former presidential candidate was found dead in a New Orleans hotel room. Still in his forties at the time of his death, Sr. Canessa had come close to reaching the political heights in his country, as well as the political depths. His was the tragic story of a man who had had everything but ended with less than nothing. He was a handsome, charming, well-educated young man and a member of one of the country's wealthy families. When he became El Salvador's foreign minister, he was probably the youngest such in the country's history. By the time he was ruled out of the presidential race against Lemus, he had been beaten up by thugs and had nearly wrecked the family fortune in a very expensive campaign. He left the country disillusioned and appearing at least twenty years older than he actually was.

At about this time it became evident Colonel Rivera was laying the groundwork to become El Salvador's next constitutional president. No announcement had been made, but he had resigned from the directorate to organize the National Conciliation Party, a new political organization to replace the somewhat shopworn and discredited PRUD, which had crumpled under the weight of the Lemus overthrow. Five major parties immediately formed a coalition to stop Rivera before he got his political machine well in motion, but it was evident even then that there was no stopping him. It seemed certain he would have the weight of the armed forces behind him. It early appeared certain too that he was going after the support of the lower and middle classes. Several circumstances were conjoining to make him the most reform-minded chief of state in El Salvador's history.

In an interview with me in October 1961, the prospective candidate agreed he would be the presidential candidate if the party nominated him, a rather superfluous observation since he himself controlled the party. He denied that National Conciliation was to be an administration party as his opponents were claiming. He did agree, though, that he had the support of the directorate, or governing junta, from which he had just resigned. This made it plainer than ever he was going to base his campaign on the numerous reforms the directorate, under his supervision, had already put through and still more reforms he had insisted should be adopted.

To accomplish this he would first have to win a Constituent Assembly election to be held in December. This would be something of a test of his new party's strength. There seemed every likelihood his party would win easily since it had the full machinery of the government behind it. The military installations, from the smallest cantonal outposts to the largest battalion barracks, would provide support for his party in the first election and for him personally in the presidential elections to follow in 1962.

Colonel Rivera was forty years old when he formed the National Conciliation Party. He had been a relatively unknown officer when his junta overthrew the preceding one, but he developed remarkably between those first days I came into contact with him and the last time I interviewed him in the National Palace in 1965. He became considerably more assured and less brusque. Civilian life mellowed him. In fact it would have been difficult in that last interview I had with him to see at a glance that he had been a military careerist except for the neatness of his desk and the decisiveness of his commands to palace staff personnel.

Rivera is a well-proportioned man but leaves the impression he is always faced with a weight problem. His chief recreation until he had been in office a few years was motorcycling. He was persuaded to give that up after an accident which could have been very serious but ended with only a broken arm. His advisors convinced him that it was not only a bizarre pastime for a president of a republic but also rather nerve-jangling for his people as he tore along El Salvador's narrow, winding country roads.

The president was born in 1921 into a lower-middle-class family in a small village, his father a tailor and his mother a baker. He was graduated from the Santa Ana Military Academy in 1921 and from War College two years later. Shortly afterward he attended the Italian Military School and then studied briefly in Rome. He speaks Italian and, quite hesitatingly, English.

There is a diversity of opinion over President Rivera's interest in social and economic reform. His supporters maintain that he was always convinced that if such reforms were not made, there would be dangerous political consequences. His opponents are equally insistent that his various reforms have resulted from a combination of political exigency and prodding from the United States to contribute something substantial to the Alliance for Progress program.

The truth quite probably is considerably more involved. For example, there is some reason to believe that the oligarchic group, or at least the more progressive sector of the group, let their views on certain reforms be known to Colonel Rivera and to the directorate he headed. There were representatives of the oligarchy in the directorate's cabinet. As has been pointed out earlier, the more socially conscious of the ruling class felt the time was rapidly approaching when some reforms should be developed. With all of this granted, however, it became quite clear that even the most advanced were not prepared for the eventual developments.

Secondly, there undoubtedly was political motivation involved in the wave of reforms, particularly those affecting rural labor. Whether or not this was true in the beginning of the directorate's regime, it was certainly true toward the end when Colonel Rivera based his one-sided campaign largely on his record of reform. There was the further fact, too, that the junta headed by Colonel Rivera succeeded a junta which had itself developed some ambitious plans for reforms, plans which it was never able to put into action, of course. These had been given considerable publicity, and there was thus some pressure on the Rivera junta to do something about them.

Finally, and this probably was the most important of all, the United States did put considerable pressure on the Rivera directorate and, later, on the Rivera administration to demonstrate its ability to comply with the aims of the Alliance for Progress. In this sense it was fortunate for the United States and for Colonel Rivera and, depending on the viewpoint, for the nation as a whole that the sudden emergence of the Alliance came during the tour of duty of Ambassador Murat W. Williams.

Ambassador Williams, a young, strong-willed student of political affairs, was in an invidious position. He believed, or at least gave a first-rate imitation of believing in the Alliance for Progress as it affected El Salvador. Yet he was so directly challenged that he was faced with the alternatives of putting all of his efforts behind the Rivera reforms or requesting relief from his post.

If the Rivera administration was being placed under pressure from the embassy, Ambassador Williams was under twice the pressure. He had been widely known and something of a favorite among the aristocracy when he previously served his first tour of duty in San Salvador as a junior embassy officer. He had come into the diplomatic service in Central America as a young Oxford-trained intellectual and was eminently acceptable in the upper reaches of Salvadoran society. Thus with the embassy's support of the reforms, which the oligarchy termed "of a fundamentally punitive nature," both the United States and the Rivera junta, and later the Rivera government, were given the ice-water treatment by the oligarchy as a whole. One of the chief sources of difficulty for the embassy, incidentally, came from North Americans living in El Salvador. Some of these North Americans had married into oligarchic families and all of them were more or less influential in business affairs.

The oligarchic families, with the exception of some old friends, not only ceased inviting Ambassador and Mrs. Williams to their social functions but actually snubbed the ambassador in public. The opposition went to such ridiculous lengths that a team was sent to Washington to discover whether the ambassador was pushing the reforms as a matter of policy or out of some private vindictiveness. It was charged not only that the embassy was guiding the reforms into law but that the reforms were being written in the embassy and transmitted to Colonel Rivera.

In justice to the oligarchy and, for that matter, to the not-too-robust upper and middle classes just beneath the titans, the reforms, once they began, came too thick and fast to be assimilated without a certain amount of discomfort. In the first 270 days of the junta-directorate which took office in January 1961 there were 325 decrees signed into law and dozens more awaiting signature. A coffee planter related gloomily at that time, "I awake in the morning and immediately help myself to a couple of aspirins. When these begin working, I take a peek at the paper to see what new decrees have been issued and how much broker I am that morning than I was the night before."

During those days there was no let-up for the weary and discouraged oligarchy. Ambassador Williams did not endear himself further when he brought in a United States economist, Jay H. Cerf, assistant secretary of commerce, to address El Salvadoran businessmen, industrialists, and agriculturalists. Instead of giving them some consolation, he added another drop to their bitter cup by telling them in blunt and decidedly undiplomatic language that time was running out for their class unless they awoke to the dangers around them. He told them that Castro's revolution in Cuba was not a cause but a symptom of "legitimate demands for long overdue reforms which had been either ineptly met or ignored by many regimes in Latin America and have failed to evoke adequate support from United States policy makers."

The wave of reforms coupled with a drop in coffee prices and the consequent tightening of credit facilities had a traumatic effect in business and social circles in those days of 1961. This showed itself in a variety of ways, but, as usual, it was most obvious among the wealthier class where the reforms had hit hardest. Cadillac automobiles were in that period for some reason the prime success symbols, and some families had two or three of them. During the darkest times, I came onto the Cadillac dealer for El Salvador. He was whiling away his idle hours writing on the backs of invoices some aspects of his economic theories, quite bizarre theories they were too. The invoices he was using for his writing paper were for automobiles he had ordered for his clients but had had to cancel because of the depression. One cancellation was made, he explained, because a client had not been able to come up with $500 for a down payment.

Another class hard hit was the young sports car crowd. From San Salvador at that time I wrote, "Young members of the wealthy families have been hit by the economic transformation. Many of the sports car set who roared through the capital during vacations from United States Ivy League schools are not here in the capital now. Nor are they at the Ivy League colleges. They are disconsolately back on the 'fincas' or plantations.

"Under a type of absentee ownership most of the large planters left their fincas in relatively recent years and moved to the capital for the social life and to launch their young men and young women in school from there. Those who counted on an annual coffee income of $20,000 and up, virtually tax free, have suddenly seen their income reduced to $12,000 and less and even that taxable. Some have, temporarily at least, given up their homes in the wealthy residential districts and have moved back to the fincas until things blow over."

The year 1961 had been a hectic one and it ended on a properly hectic note. The first test of Rivera's new National Conciliation Party was a resounding success. The party candidates made a clean sweep, all fifty-four of the candidates for the Constitutent Assembly having been elected. The party was committed to the support of the directorate's reforms, and it was also committed to elect a provisional president, to be selected by Rivera himself, to hold office until the following year when Rivera would run for the constitutional presidency.

Thus El Salvador went into 1962 in a mildly schizophrenic state. On the one hand, it appeared to have taken a long step toward some kind of political stability. Colonel Rivera had successfully sidestepped the gathering suspicion he might be headed for a strong-man role. That there would be elections in 1962 was a virtual certainty. Thus there was an optimistic atmosphere on the basis of which the country could enjoy a reasonable assurance of future prosperity.

On the other hand, however, the year of factional strife had inevitably left its scars. There had been economic gloom and an intense feeling on the part of the middle and upper classes that they were being "taken" by an extraordinary series of coincidences. Fear was being expressed on all sides that the government, now flushed with its success, would likely push through more laws even more punishing to them than those of the past two years had been.

In January, in accordance with the December elections, the new Constituent Assembly, on the advice of Colonel Rivera, installed a mild-mannered, 62-year-old lawyer, Eusebio Rodolfo Cordón as provisional president until the forthcoming general elections.

Aside from this there were three relatively important occurrences in early 1962. The first was the naming of Colonel Rivera as National Conciliation's presidential candidate, as had been expected, and of a young attorney, Francisco Roberto Lima, as his vice-presidential running mate, which was something of a surprise. Thus, these two, barring a political upheaval, were assured of a five-year term in office. In choosing Sr. Lima as his running mate, Colonel Rivera had in mind economic planning with the help of the United States under the Alliance for Progress, for which he had given much and from which he was now expecting much. Sr. Lima, somewhat erratic in his personal habits, was a brilliant economist, well-educated, charming, and completely at home in Washington, where he had been El Salvador's ambassador.

The second occurrence of importance was the publication of an extensive letter in early February by the already-mentioned Major Oscar Rodríguez Simo, who had been national police director in the directorate's cabinet. There was some background to the publication of the letter. A short time before, there had been a conference of Central American ministers of defense, and rumors of another invasion of Cuba were floating all over Middle America. With that in mind I went to Managua, Nicaragua for an interview with General Anastasio (Tachito) Somoza, Jr., who was prominent in organizing the defense ministers' conference and certainly would play an important role in any Cuban invasion plan, should there be one. The Nicaraguan general denied emphatically that the object of the meeting was to plan such an invasion. The meeting, General Somoza said, was to arrange a pact to prevent Cuban penetration into Central America. He suggested with a grin that if that was all I came to Nicaragua for I could as well have written the story from Mexico.

Major Simo's letter, dated February 1, 1962, was published in San Salvador papers, covering two pages of tabloid-sized newspapers. It spoke of a leftist conspiracy against the directorate in which he had held the post of public security director. He then added,

At the same time, in the international field there was information that Guatemala and Nicaragua had prepared to participate in an invasion of Cuba.

Before initiating the operation both of the countries had to have their flanks covered as represented by El Salvador, Honduras, and Costa Rica. Trying to resolve this problem through diplomatic channels, Guatemala asked for a meeting of the chiefs of staff of the Central American Isthmus.

El Salvador was the first country to accept the invitation to the meeting, and it was verified in Guatemala City that the theme of the conference was to create a Central American Defense Council independent of ODECA.

El Salvador, the Simo letter noted, declined to enter any agreement outside ODECA, which she had helped create and the headquarters of which were located in San Salvador. Cuba, according to Major Simo, sensed the disunity of the nations and felt that its prolongation would be helpful in upsetting the invasion plans, and thus tried to instigate uprisings in San Salvador and Panama.

The revelation that El Salvador had even entered such talks was a shock to the country. The principal shock, however, was that the public security director hinted at wholesale corruption in the El Salvador armed forces, to which he belonged. He ended his letter with his resignation, explaining he would rather live on his officer's pension than continue in the prevailing atmosphere.

The letter quite naturally caused a sensation not only in El Salvador but throughout Central America. We received several copies of it from friends and contacts throughout the area, most of whom were living in exile from their respective countries. These exiles feared that, using Cuba as an excuse, the chiefs of staff of the various countries would agree to common action in opposition to any force threatening one or another of the governments. That, in fact, is precisely what eventually happened. A series of agreements were entered into through which the chief of state or the minister of defense of a country considered to be in danger of attack from without or within could call on one or another of the Isthmian republics to lend assistance. This, in effect, would "freeze" governments (most of them at the time composed of military men) in office and lessen the chances of overthrow by exile oppositionary forces.

Another preoccupation of the exiles at this point was that a Central American police-intelligence force was in the making. General Somoza denied there had been any talk of this, and I was unable subsequently to find any evidence of a formal force of this type although there were murmurings against the so-called Project Camelot. This plan called for a super intelligence network, composed largely of intellectuals, to report on factors disturbing stability in the various Latin American countries. It was eventually dropped in the face of widespread opposition, some of it coming from our own State Department.[4]

The asylum that such political exiles receive in one or another of the Middle American countries is a precious thing and something to be zealously guarded. I never ceased to be amazed at the numbers and types of exiles roaming over the area. The numbers are constantly fluctuating, of course, because some are granted reprieves and allowed to return to their countries while new groups are forced to leave. Some grow weary of the entire affair and if possible move to the United States or to Europe, usually to Spain if their political coloration permits. During revolutionary activities in the area, there would be literally hundreds of exiles from one country or another. Yet considering that with the discovery of a single

[4] Project Camelot, when it came into being in 1964 as an army undertaking supported by the Department of Defense, was described as a study whose objective was "to determine the feasibility of developing a general social systems model which would make it possible to predict and influence politically significant aspects of social change in the developing countries of the world." When the story broke in Chile, the project was categorized as an interventionist, continental spy plan. A week later the Defense Department cancelled Project Camelot less than a year after it had been initiated. While scholars were very dubious about the project's feasibility, most of the public opposition was to its advisability. The best account of the project and its unfortunate consequences for hemispheric intellectual relations is to be found in the volume edited by Professor Irving Louis Horowitz entitled *The Rise and Fall of Project Camelot* (Cambridge, Mass., M.I.T. Press, 1967). [Editor's Note]

plot in one or another of the countries as many as fifty persons could be formally expelled and perhaps as many more could flee to escape imprisonment or worse, the number of exiles was not surprising.

It is a routine part of the job of a correspondent assigned to the Middle American run to know where these exiles are and what they are up to. The amazing grapevines linking the exiles and connecting them with sympathizers within their own countries invariably provide tip-offs to political movements throughout the area. Actually it is not as difficult as might be thought to keep up with the movements of the exiles, inasmuch as from country to country they send along letters of introduction from one group to another.

In a majority of cases the life of an exile is a drab and joyless one. Some have ample funds, but most have just barely enough. They have been cut off, for the most part, from their livelihood and in a majority of instances the families they have left behind are just barely able to survive, much less send funds to the exiled head of the family.

The various exiles are forced to get along together through sheer circumstances, but they often have little in common except their mutually disliked position. Many of course belong to the same political party in their respective countries, but even this is not too much of a bond when they are far from their political roots. I recall visiting two political exiles once in a shabby rooming house. They were living in a small, badly furnished room and had little or nothing in common, either intellectually or socially. Their only bond was a political one for which they had been simultaneously exiled. They were a sad couple, but there was a happy ending. One of the exiles returned to his country and eventually became president. He appointed his roommate-in-exile to a cabinet post.

The exiles are rarely allowed to take jobs in the countries of asylum and, of course, are not supposed to enter into political activity of any sort. In spite of the latter restriction, they, with loads of time on their hands, are usually up and about early in the morning and by midday are in the favorite coffee shop of the exiles, sipping coffee and, without exception, plotting.

Returning to the three things of importance occuring early in 1962, we have seen that one was the nomination of Rivera and Lima and another was the publication of the Simo letter, with its attendant repercussions. The third was a sudden upturn in the economy, and this, in itself, had interesting repercussions. In mid-February 1962 I reported from San Salvador, "A combination of hard economic realities coupled with a greatly improved psychological atmosphere appears to be putting El Salvador back on the road to recovery after several months of gloom. There are several positive factors involved in the country's economic resurgence and these appear to be:

"The possibility of a seasonal marketing fund of $12,000,000 from the United States to stabilize coffee production for Central America on the international market;

"The early prospect of the beginning of an Alliance for Progress assistance program, especially an $11,000,000 low-cost housing advance;

"And finally the possibility of a rapprochement between the present reform administration and the capitalist class, which two have been at serious odds for several months."

The story, in reference to the rapprochement, noted, "Colonel Rivera has been in past weeks devoting considerable time to bringing about a reconciliation with the wealthy oligarchic families, which for years have been in effect running the country. The traditionally close ties between the government and the oligarchy were strained almost to the breaking point last year when a civil-military junta took over the government by coup and thenceforth directed the country along reform lines.

"The junta, of which Colonel Rivera was the directing member, initiated a series of tax and agrarian reforms. The oligarchy opposed in principle all of these reforms on three basic counts: The wealthy families maintained the reform decrees were 'soak-the-rich' in design and intent; that they were badly thought out; and, finally, that the people most affected were not consulted before the reforms were decreed."

The story continued, "In this reconciliation plan the vice-presidential nominee, Francisco Roberto Lima, will be one of the key figures. Sr. Lima has been an attorney for many of the wealthiest families in the country. Further he married into one of the oldest Salvadoran families, a wealthy one and a member of the oligarchic group."

Rivera and Lima were installed as president and vice-president respectively in July after a painfully one-sided election. The National Conciliation Party ran unopposed in spite of frantic efforts to pull together some opposition. But after the party's total victory the previous December there was no life left in the opposing forces, and Colonel Rivera, with all his persuasion, could not interest these forces in making a token race.

One of the first moves by the new president was to send Sr. Lima to Washington to work out an assistance plan, of which the mentioned $11,000,000 housing loan was a part. The president, as he had long before hinted he would do, brought a number of the oligarchic group into his government. The reconciliation, or, as it was sometimes termed, "the readjustment" between the warring parties was a matter of great significance in the political as well as the economic life of the republic.

Several months before, a member of the oligarchy prophetically remarked to me "They may not like us now but they are getting close to the bottom of the barrel for administrative personnel, and they will have to turn to us for help." The thaw even extended to the United States embassy, but to a lesser degree.

Aside from the government's urgent need for qualified personnel, there were other explanations for the thaw. One of the most direct of these came from a member of the oligarchy in reference to some of his fellow members. He observed, "Some of our people finally faced the fact that we ourselves might be responsible for a lot of what was going on." Still another explained, "Whether we like President Rivera and his government or not, we have found we will have to stick with him. If he goes down we all go down."

Ambassador Williams, a gregarious and sociable individual, had been personally hurt by the attitude of the oligarchy toward him personally and toward the embassy. His reaction to the reconciliation was, "They have finally seen the reason behind all of these things. That is why they are now beginning to see the whys and wherefores of the Alliance for Progress and what it can do when properly put into action." And another, non-committed observer said, "What really hurt the oligarchy was that for the first time the government acted without consulting them. This time they fought and lost, and so now they are regaining their lost ground through this readjustment."

There is one sector of the El Salvadoran upper class which suffers when all wealthy Salvadorans are lumped into one category, with the inevitable connotation of reckless wealth, obliviousness to social needs, and dedication to European vacations, fast cars, and strings of polo ponies. Some members of the oligarchy defend, with validity, their loyalty to the country and its citizens and their dedication to social betterment. There are a number of families in El Salvador which have distinguished themselves in this respect, amassing, along with fortunes, the goodwill of thousands of Salvadorans in all classes.

One of these is the DeSola family, which over the years, while pursuing its own fortunes, has been devoting time and money to bettering the economic and social conditions of all classes within the country. The late Herbert DeSola, head of the family, and his sons, have made invaluable contributions to the life of the nation. Their approach has been partially the pragmatic one that a better country socially and economically is a better area for DeSola business. Yet some aspects of their approach have been purely philanthropic.

The DeSola family, like most of the families of great wealth in El Salvador, is not an old one in the country. In fact few of the oligarchic families in El Salvador go back past relatively recent times, as compared to those in Panama, for example. Herbert DeSola and his wife came to the country in 1896. The family itself was an old Sephardic one driven from

Spain in the period of Jewish persecution. Its history had gone back to the tenth century in Spain. The family fled to Holland, as so many of the Sephardic families did during the persecutions, and from Holland it emigrated to Curacao in the Dutch West Indies.

Herbert was born there in 1865. After wanderings in many parts, he settled in San Salvador, establishing a small luxury shop. But the House of DeSola did not begin as an institution until Don Herbert took over directorship of a match company. This was followed by a sugar export operation and later by a soap and wax manufacturing works. Early in the twentieth century the House of DeSola was well on its way, with five sons to carry it on. Meanwhile the effort had turned to coffee, and the family became one of the largest processors and exporters of coffee in the nation, in one eleven-year period exporting 2,438,788 bags valued at several million dollars. The sons were growing, some attending universities in the United States or England, and one in France.

By the time the company had become DeSola and Sons it had added real estate, transportation, and other lines. Víctor, the eldest, became the first associate in the firm. After studying in the United States and serving a tour of duty with a Wall Street banking firm, he returned to El Salvador, where he eventually organized cotton cooperatives and took an active interest in the family enterprises. Ernesto, the second son, after studying at Stanford University and Oxford, finished in architecture at Massachusetts Institute of Technology. He returned home to become the outstanding architect in the country, with more than three hundred residential and commercial buildings to his credit.

Orlando began his studies at Oxford and transferred to medicine at the University of Paris, where he received his degree. He returned to his country and built up a large practice. He soon entered public medicine, however, becoming dean of the University Medical School, then minister of health, and finally rector of the Medical School. He was one of the country's most respected authorities on public health when he died prematurely.

Francisco, or "Chico," as he is known in his own country and throughout Central America, is the youngest son. He completed his undergraduate work at the School of Economic and Social Science at Oxford and returned to become a partner in the business. He has become one of Central America's best known authorities on land practices, on socio-agrarian reforms, and on industrial planning.

Don Herbert died in 1963 at the age of 98, but not before establishing the now-famous Foundation DeSola. Through it, with the three remaining sons as officers and administrators, the family has invested a fortune in health, education, and social projects in addition to distributing many university scholarships. Through the foundation thousands of dollars have been directed to Catholic charities, municipal libraries, schools for the blind, and health centers. The worth of the House of DeSola in the mid-sixties was somewhere between $25 and $50 million. Its combined enterprises employed 3,000 workers, and thus it was one of the largest single employers in the nation.

Returning for the moment to the reforms of the Rivera junta and of his administration, whatever the criticisms of them, they made the lives of the rural laborer more endurable, even if some of them proved impractical. One of the latter was the farm-labor diet decree, which particularly irritated the plantation-owners. The decree ordered that specified diets be set up for farm labor and even outlined the meals, indicating how many grams of each item should be served.

There was some validity in the argument that the decree had not been sufficiently thought-out, but there also was good reason for it. It had been repeatedly shown that the rural laborer was suffering from a dietary deficiency that practically amounted to malnutrition. An entire family, consisting on the average of father, mother and three children, would hire itself to a plantation primarily for the assurance of two meals daily. These meals generally consisted of coffee, beans, and tortillas, the latter being ground corn pancakes. A majority of rural families probably eat meat at only one meal a year.

There were a multitude of reasons why the diet decree could not be satisfactorily enforced. One planter complained he would have to have kitchen facilities on the scale of a hundred-room hotel to provide the specified meals. The scheme had to fail, but if there was any satisfaction on the part of the planters in seeing it fail, that satisfaction was dissipated in 1965 when, under Rivera's prodding, a minimum wage law was passed. Under the new law the laborer must be paid for a day's work without deduction for meals, and the laborer must pay for his meals himself.

Opposition to the new law was intense, as was to be expected, for it meant the end of an era in Salvadoran rural labor. The planters insisted the law would disrupt the entire farm labor structure. Briefly it meant the end of a family virtually having to consign its services in return for a guarantee against hunger. As stiff as the opposition was, however, there was considerable support for the reform, and much of this came, surprisingly enough from planters themselves. In fact, their support, prompted in part by social motives and in part by the desire to direct their fincas on a more businesslike basis, could be said to be the final factor in the government's determination to push the law through.

The future of the new decree was still in the balance when this was written. It appeared to have a good chance of survival, however, because the big planters could not only live with it but actually benefit to a degree, and the medium-sized operators could at least live with it. The marginal operators appeared to face a bleak future because the two-meals-a-day arrangement was a significant factor in operating at a profit.

Rivera's reforms were not, of course, confined to the rural areas. One causing much consternation even up to the time this was being written was the new income tax law which had been put together in 1963. It covered corporate and private income and in its day was considered a model of tax reform along the lines required by the Alliance for Progress. A representative of the private sector who helped draft the law observed, "We have given away too much in terms of the private sectors of other countries, but for us it will probably not be too bad." A great advantage, as it was viewed by the private sector, was that it clarified parts of old tax laws which had been the source of confusion for years in El Salvador.

The law primarily affected incomes between $8,000 and $40,000. In the highest brackets there was some relief, with maximum rates reduced to 60 per cent on income of more than $100,000, as compared with 76.5 per cent on income of more than $78,000 in the previous law. At the time the law was drawn up, in the last quarter of 1963, there were slightly over 9,000 persons and corporations on the income tax rolls. Under the new law the income tax population should eventually reach 27,000. In any case the treasury, announcing a surplus of $6,400,000, something unheard of in El Salvador or for that matter in most other Latin American countries, noted that tax receipts in the first half of 1965 were $13,000,000 over 1964 and attributed this to better income tax controls.

The new tax law was also something of an attack on interlocking corporations owned by various families of the oligarchy. As late as mid-1965 the financial sector demanded that this particular part of the law be rewritten wholly or in part. The latest line of attack was that the 38 per cent tax on profits was discouraging foreign investment.

El Salvador's reforms, despite all the flurries they have caused, have not made significant inroads into the growing rural problems. As early as 1932 attempts were made to bring about some sort of land distribution to the landless farm laborer, and toward this end the National Social Welfare Board was established. Later this agency became the Rural Colonization Institute. In its eighteen years of existence the Board acquired estates totalling slightly over 87,000 acres, which were distributed in small agricultural holdings and building lots.[5]

[5] Since 95 per cent of the national territory is under cultivation, it would appear that the Institute's major effort should be directed toward the dividing up of the 2,000 large estates, which, while constituting only 1 per cent of the total number of farms, control 46 per cent of the agricultural lands. Yet between 1962 and 1966 only 7,250 acres were distributed to 3,198 beneficiaries, while in 1966–67, 7,732 acres of public and private land were made available to 1,014 families. [Editor's Note]

In El Salvador, as throughout Latin America, there is a population drift from the rural to the urban areas, but it is not as pronounced as in most countries. For example, the United Nations percentage distribution in the urban areas for 1950 was 27.6 per cent; the estimated 1965 percentage in the urban areas was 30.6 per cent; and the projection for 1980 was 36.1 per cent.

Even without the influx of rural dwellers into the urban areas, however, the Urban Housing Institute of El Salvador found that the urban housing deficit in 1963 was 178,275, of which 162,575 units were carried over from previous years, 8,000 were due to population growth, and 7,000 were due to unfit units. The rural deficit of 186,800 units made the national deficit 362,000 units in 1963, meaning that somewhere in the neighborhood of seven-tenths of all the families in the nation were without adequate housing.

In 1964 the year's additional urban housing deficit was 26,724 units. It was estimated that 48 per cent of those in need of urban housing had incomes equivalent to less than $48 monthly. The rural deficit probably was comprised of a high percentage of families earning the equivalent of from $2 to $2.20 daily. Under the new rural minimum wage law the husband earns 2.25 colones ($.90) and women and children the equivalent of $.70 daily. The annual per capita income in El Salvador based on the gross national product in 1963 was $294, according to the Inter-American Development Bank. The true national per capita income, however, is estimated at between $150 and $200, with farm labor per capita income probably under $100 annually.

President Rivera was able to turn in a good year in 1962. In that year and the succeeding ones industrial growth was rapid and steady. In 1964 seventy-six new industries came into the country and 112 plant expansions were licensed. In the first four months of 1965 the Ministry of Economy granted Industrial Promotion Law benefits, that is tax and import privileges, to fifty-seven new companies.

In 1963 a prominent Salvadoran business man remarked in reference to the political situation that the crisis had passed, that the administration had learned to respect the ability of the oligarchy and wanted to be on good terms with it. He felt the military had been so discredited by the Simo letter that it was intent on repairing its image and he thus saw no possibility of a military dictatorship in the near future. There appeared to be a prevailing confidence that the country was good for at least five prosperous years. Our friend also remarked that with good economic years almost certainly ahead perhaps El Salvador could regain some of its lost ground in leadership of the Central American Common Market (CACM).

Actually by mid-1963 El Salvador was furnishing about one-half of all the goods traded between countries in the CACM. During her period of floundering, Guatemala and Costa Rica had made inroads into the Salvadoran position as leader of the market, but by the end of 1964 El Salvador had largely regained its position. It should be remembered that El Salvador has traditionally been a leader in Central American integration movements and has long been known in the region for its attempts to mediate conflicts between nations. Other republics have depended on El Salvador to take the initiative in integration schemes. It fought long and hard to keep ODECA well and vigorous, and even when that organization had become debilitated El Salvador remained loyal to it, as was seen in the Simo letter.

President Rivera was faced early in his term with widespread rumors that his government was in precarious shape. At that time in an interview he shrugged off the rumors. This was some months after the Guatemalan and Honduran overthrows. He said that there was no similarity in the conditions. In the other two countries, he explained, the armed forces had been under threats from the civilian governments and had reacted in order to preserve their identity. "There is no danger, no menace to the armed forces here," the former infantry colonel said. He explained that the armed forces were devoting much of their time to civilian projects, such as constructing drainage systems and clearing areas for government buildings. "That is why we are so tranquil," he said.

El Salvador, in recognizing the military government of Colonel Osvaldo López Arellano in Honduras, had resisted the arguments of the United States and of Costa Rica that such recognition should be withheld. Rivera had announced El Salvador's recognition simultaneously with Nicaragua's. Guatemala had already recognized. The reason for El Salvador's recognition, President Rivera noted in the interview, involved humane pragmatism and economy. There were at that time about 300,000 Salvadorans living and working in Honduras, he explained, and their welfare was on his mind. Repeated refusals to recognize the López regime could have meant hardship for these Salvadorans. The other factor was that the economic integration of Central America might be jeopardized by delay in coming to terms with the neighboring country. President López Arellano could not have advanced a better argument himself to get El Salvador's vote than that of jeopardy to a Central American integration scheme.

The last interview I had with President Rivera was in mid-1965 after he had gone through the harrowing experience of one of the most devastating earthquakes in recent years. The quake, in May, did millions of dollars worth of damage, took at least forty-three lives, and injured about three hundred. It was the sternest challenge to his administration thus far and required complete support from the entire nation, the wealthy class included. At the time of the interview the battle apparently had been won. The armed forces turned out for rescue and police work and to regulate the tent-housing of thousands of homeless. The leading citizens, financiers, architects, and engineers joined in a committee of rehabiliation. The country was together, fully so, for the first time in some years.

APPENDICES

Afterword

———

Suggestions for Additional Reading

———

The Base at Retalhuleu

———

by Stanley R. Ross

Afterword

In Paul Kennedy's account of his experiences along the "middle beat," his concern with the political, economic, and social development of these countries can be read between the lines. Although he was reasonably optimistic in his reporting in 1965, it is uncertain whether he would have assumed the same posture five years later. Changes in Mexico and Central America have been more rapid than the journalist anticipated, although it is quite clear that he recognized those indicators which were portents of the future. In parts of the area the early stages of economic and social growth have been overshadowed to some extent by increasing signs of tension and violence, the displacement of civilian by military rule, and a dangerously high birth rate. These developments have added urgency to the problem of achieving political stability, which Kennedy thought was in the process of solution.

He accurately recognized that Mexico and Costa Rica had acheived political stability to a far greater degree than the other countries of the region. As Kennedy noted, increased trade and communication in the area has tightened the interrelationship among these nations, and it is becoming increasingly difficult for one of these countries to experience an economic, social, or political crisis without repercussions throughout the region. The most obvious example was the 1969 border clash between Honduras and El Salvador, which affected and continues to affect all of the Central American countries.

Keeping in mind Kennedy's appraisal and sense of the direction in which the region is going, it seems appropriate to describe briefly the events in the respective countries since 1965, to bring up to date the material with

201

which Kennedy was so vitally concerned. Mexico in many ways represents at once the exception and the model. More independent and economically more oriented toward her northern neighbor despite increasing economic interests in Central America, Mexico was much less affected by the recent Honduran-El Salvadoran clash than were her neighbors to the south. Her unique political stability combined with exceptional economic progress has been justly described as the "Mexican miracle." An essential ingredient in all of this has been the role of the government party.

The "official party" structure has provided the mechanism for the maintenance of control over political and economic life, the means for reconciling internal strife, and the mechanism for responding to the needs of specific segments of society as well as society as a whole. While the present system allows considerable flexibility for the opportunistic maneuverings of aspiring politicians, once a decision has been made by the top of the "revolutionary family"—whether it concerns a presidential candidate or the orientation of a program—all further politicking must come to an end.

However, there have been signs in recent years of political tensions, both within and outside of the official party, erupting from below the surface into public view. New political and activist organized efforts have appeared on the left directed toward the less favored elements in the population. For the first time the recognized opposition on the right, the Partido de Acción Nacional (PAN), has made significant gains on the state and local level, making serious challenges in Sonora and Yucatán and winning control of 19 municipal governments, including two state capitals, since 1967.

There also have been evidences of tensions within the "family" of the official government party. In part this is a reflection of a worldwide phenomenon, as younger, more impatient party members have demanded more freedom and responsibility in the decision-making process. The resulting conflict became all the more obvious because of the conservative and forceful character of the Díaz Ordaz administration. Illustrative is the recent episode in which the former president of the party, Carlos Madrazo, with the support of some intellectual elements both within and outside the party, attempted to steer the organization toward more liberal policies, resulting in his forced resignation and expulsion from the party.

Perhaps the most dramatic development was the series of student disturbances beginning during the summer of 1968 and continuing into the fall of that year. The employment of excessive force to control internecine student disorders, the handling of these protest disturbances, and the occupation of university properties by the government, reversing a long-standing tradition of university autonomy, generated anti-government sentiment among students, intellectuals, and the general urban population beyond the wildest dreams of elements interested in agitation for its own sake. Those who were not interested in a constructive resolution moved quickly to take advantage of the unprecedented discontent, but the ardor of many cooled when they found themselves being exploited in this way.

These events occurred as Mexico approached the time when she would host the 1968 Olympics. Despite concern about possible disturbances, the games went off smoothly, favorably impressing untold millions around the world and providing a reinforcement for Mexican pride. While the immediate benefits in terms of the permanent facilities created and the long-range ones in terms of increased tourism are difficult to calculate, there is no question that the games were a costly venture for the developing Mexican economy. Add to this the construction of the Metro subway system in the capital, and the lack of resources for meeting basic social and economic needs becomes understandable.

Mexico also is approaching a presidential election year in 1970. Events of 1968–69 cannot be fully understood unless some consideration is given to the political maneuverings of presidential hopefuls and their supporting factions. The question of the country's leadership for the next six-year period was resolved with the selection of Luis Echeverría Álvarez as the presidential candidate of the PRI. Echeverría had been serving, until his nomination, as minister of the interior, the department responsible for the maintenance of internal order. The new administration must choose its policies carefully if the present uneasy calm of the student situation is not to erupt once again into agitation and if the political system is to demonstrate its responsiveness and the validity of the image of political stability.

Meanwhile the economic development of the country in the industrial sector has been progressing at a phenomenal rate, with an annual growth of the gross national product of 6 to 7 per cent. Because of limited investment resources, special pains have been taken to control economic policy through the banking system giving priorities to selected sectors of development. While economists may debate the appropriateness of these priorities, there is no question that agriculture has been placed in a disadvantageous position. The extensive use of foreign capital to finance many of the large-scale projects, including public works, is the source of considerable controversy. However, given the present rhythm of progress, it is hard to justify the termination or elimination of foreign investment.

In the realm of social progress, there has been the most criticism of the incompleteness of the accomplishments of the Revolution, particularly since some of the goals have been relegated to secondary importance. Education and social security have been the areas of greatest emphasis in terms of governmental expenditures, but the obstacles to be overcome are enormous. Schools get built in impressive numbers, but there never seem to be enough for the rapidly growing school-age population and there never are enough teachers to staff them. The task of bringing to the rural population, which still constitutes almost half of the total, sanitation, electricity, education, health services, and transportation is overwhelming. The implementation of legislation extending social security benefits to the rural population has been slow and halting.

At the same time, upper- and middle-class elements have benefited dramatically from the economic and social progress of the country. The disproportionate accumulation of capital resources, including new extensive landholdings, have widened the gap between the haves and have nots. Since 1964, Mexico's per capita income has risen nearly 50 per cent (from $394 in 1964 to $550 in 1968 and a reported $690 in 1969), but these figures are deceptive because of the uneven distribution of the additional wealth generated. It is principally these economic disparities and some resulting limitations on social mobility which help to explain recent evidences of discontent. Progress toward a more equitable sharing of the economic, social, and political gains of the Revolution is considered too slow in the light of rising expectations concerning the nation's potential.

In Guatemala, the second country treated by Kennedy, the Peralta administration attempted to clean up the graft and corruption which appeared to have run rampant under Ydígoras, to cooperate with the Central American Common Market, and to concentrate its efforts on public works. Despite the progress in these directions, it found itself unable to restrain press criticism, military intervention in politics, and the growth of guerrilla terrorism. However, Colonel Peralta did permit the promised elections to be held, and on July 1, 1966, turned over the reins of government to his civilian successor, Julio César Méndez Montenegro and his Revolutionary Party.

The new president, who had assumed the leadership of his party following the unexplained death of his brother, has tried to initiate moderate social and economic reforms which would antagonize neither the right nor the left, but he has met with frustration at almost every step of the way. His preoccupation with stability and his intense desire to survive politically through his designated term of office in order to be able to transfer power peacefully have motivated him to rescind certain tax measures and to limit land distribution to government-held properties in order to avoid alienating certain conservative interests. However, by rescinding of the tax of 5 per cent on most items and the 20 per cent levy on luxury items, the president eliminated a source of revenue much needed for development undertakings and social reforms.

It is not surprising that the Guatemalan economy continues to show only a 1 to 2 per cent advance annually in gross national product. If pressure from coffee and cotton growers leads to the removal of the revenue-producing export duty on those products, budget austerity will be even more necessary than at present.

Guerrilla activity, involving elements both of the left and of the right, has forced the government to convert the nation's cities into veritable armed camps. The situation improved somewhat when President Méndez removed from high governmental positions three military men who had been supporters of rightist activity. Leftists bands in the sierra continue to receive both moral and material support from Cuba and keep some areas in a state of constant commotion.

Several of the guerrilla leaders received their military training in the United States, experience which serves them well in outwitting the United

States-supported counter-insurgency forces of the government. The guerrillas seem to be able to keep the army off-balance by constant shifts in location and through the support they receive from discontented peasants discouraged by futile efforts to obtain either land or higher wages in the crowded sierra area. Attempts by labor unions and moderate social forces to organize the peasants have been handicapped by the reign of terror prevailing in the rural regions.

The persistence and spread of acts of terrorism, aided and abetted by both political extremes, has resulted in the military playing an ever increasing role in the maintenance of peace. The widely publicized kidnapping of Archbishop Casariego and the assassination of the United States Ambassador John G. Mein in 1968 were only two of many incidents of violence which have forced the government to decree a state of seige for extended periods. Thus far the counter-insurgency operations of the government have been effective enough, when added to the natural divisiveness of the guerrilla groups themselves, to prevent the formation of a well-organized force capable of overthrowing the national government. The prospect of presidential elections in March 1970 did not bring the anticipated increase in guerrilla action. However, on the eve of the election and immediately following it there were new incidents involving kidnappings of high Guatemalan and United States Embassy officials. The election returns revealed that the conservative opposition candidate, Colonel Carlos Arana Osorio had garnered a plurality of the votes in competition with candidates of the governing Revolutionary Party and of the Christian Democrats. Since no candidate received a majority of the votes, the president will be chosen by the legislature dominated by the Revolutionary Party. However, President Julio César Méndez Montenegro, leader of that party, had pledged before the election that the winning candidate's election would be confirmed. Nevertheless, it does not appear that the election has provided a solution to the polarization of political groups in the country.

Turning to El Salvador, recent years also saw a change of presidential leadership. In March 1967 elections were held in which the official candidate of the National Conciliation Party, Colonel Fidel Sánchez Hernández, won against two left-of-center candidates, Christian Democrat Abraham Rodríguez and Renovationist Fabio Castillo, both of whom had advocated sweeping changes in the small nation's social structure. President Sánchez has endeavored to continue Rivera's moderate liberal policies, but, like President Méndez in Guatemala, has considered it necessary to cater to conservative economic interests, proceeding very cautiously in regard to instituting reforms or encouraging public investment. His forward-looking economic minister, who had proposed a new banking law as well as new taxes to finance lagging development, resigned his post in 1968, attributing his action to the failure of the president to live up to his campaign promises.

El Salvador, which until 1967 could claim the most dynamic economy in the Central American Common Market, did not escape the slowdown which then affected the whole area. Through the early sixties the annual GNP growth was 6 per cent, but it declined to 5 per cent in 1967 and 1968. The shaky finances of the government, rising unemployment and population pressures contributed to a significant election victory for the opposition Christian Democratic Party in 1968. Matters took a critical turn during the summer of 1969 when Honduras objected to the increasing flow of migrant workers from El Salvador. President Sánchez Hernández, spurred on by conservative landowning and military interests, ordered an invasion of Honduras. The El Salvador government's action apparently was motivated in part by a desire to avoid having to come to grips with the question of land reform at home. However, the Salvadoran troops were subsequently forced to withdraw, taking with them all the migrants who had been working in Honduras. Tension and bitterness remain, handicapping Central American cooperation when it is most needed.

While Paul Kennedy regarded his book as a complete unit, the editor believes that had time permitted he would have written another volume with sections on Costa Rica, Nicaragua, Honduras, and Panama. Certainly this is suggested by his prefatory and introductory remarks on the region as a whole. While the editor would not presume to write the chapters of such a second volume, particularly since it would be impossible for him to do so on the basis of Kennedy's personal experience and observations in these countries, it does seem appropriate in the interest of completeness to add a few brief comments on each of these countries.

Costa Rica has the reputation of being the least militarist and most civilized of the Central American republics. Whether its relative political stability can be ascribed totally to the absence of a traditional military force is doubtful. The cultural homogeneity of the population, a larger proportional percentage of owner-operated small farms, and a higher literacy rate are other factors which have contributed to more stable social and political conditions. And it is clear that these environmental circumstances have been propitious for economic development.

Although Costa Rica has been freer of political upheavals, the country has suffered from unpredictable volcanic eruptions which periodically have brought disaster to particular regions. And the very stability which the country has enjoyed to a greater degree than its neighbors has not been an unmixed blessing. Some observers believe that it has contributed to the reluctance of the rural population to adopt new techniques and other measures to achieve higher production levels.

Certain economic problems persist, and some new clouds have appeared on the Costa Rican horizon. The nation continues to place major dependence on the international market for the sale of coffee and bananas, its two principal products. And the problems posed by a consistently high birth rate and rising unemployment figures have shaken the complacency of the contented population and enlightened leadership of Costa Rica. In recent years the country has benefited more than its neighbors from the Common Market in terms of the initiation of industrial enterprises associated with the processing of raw materials—an advance made possible by stable conditions, available investment funds, and the higher educational level of the population.

This small nation has an impressive record of peaceful transfers of power between the National Liberation Party and the conservative opposition following elections in 1958, 1962, and 1966. The National Liberation Party was the creation of José "Pepe" Figueres, the United States-educated (Massachusetts Institute of Technology) small *finca* coffee planter, who had led a successful civilian revolt against Otilio Ulate in 1948. Figueres, who has become one of the prominent democratic spokesman in the hemisphere, espouses socialist policies but without any tinge of authoritarianism. During his presidency, 1953–1958, he introduced a reformed constitution, dissolved the regular army and substituted a small national police force, improved schools, expanded government-sponsored social welfare, and negotiated beneficial contracts with the United Fruit Company. More specifically, he arranged for the powerful firm to pay 50 per cent of its profits to his government, while breaking its monopoly control of the cacao, hemp, and palm oil industries and forcing it out of its activities in the electrical utilities and railroad sectors of economy. In the process, he expanded state ownership in such fields as transportation, banking, communications, and public housing.

In the hard-fought 1966 election, occurring just as Costa Rica was recovering from the natural catastrophe resulting from the eruption of the volcano Irazú, which for more than two years had rained ashes on San José and the rich Central Valley, mathematics professor José Joaquín Trejos won the presidency, backed by a coalition of conservative forces. The margin of Trejos' victory was so small that a political stalemate was feared, particularly in light of the legislative majority won by the followers of Figueres.

Trejos endeavored to reverse the policies of his liberal predecessor, Francisco Orlich. The latter, applying the doctrines of his party's leader, Figueres, had tried to introduce costly socialist legislation with the approval and financial assistance of the United States. Trejos found it impossible to turn back the clock completely, as some conservatives had called for during the campaign, because of the National Liberation Party majority in the unicameral legislature. Nonetheless, economic progress has been slower in this administration, in part attributable to the president's unwillingness to commit such large amounts of the budget to public investment and public works projects. By the middle of Trejos' term, "Pepe" Figueres was giving serious consideration to once again standing for the presidency in view of the political situation of the nation and his party. Early in 1969 he announced his candidacy, and after overcoming opposition within his own party, won by a substantial majority over the government party's candidate in the election in February 1970.

Since the middle of the nineteenth century, Nicaragua has been plagued by a series of interventions in its affairs by foreign powers. The intervention of the United States in the early twentieth century was intended to reorganize the country's finances, but resulted in a deeper involvement in

Nicaragua's internal affairs than had been anticipated. The training and creation of a military force, which, it was hoped, would provide stability for the country, turned out to be the stepping stone to power for its leader, Anastasio Somoza.

For thirty years, "Tacho" Somoza was able to control Nicaragua both politically and economically, acquiring large land and commercial holdings for himself and his family. Despite his assassination in 1956, the Somoza dynasty continues to predominate not only politically but also in the economic sphere, where their interests penetrate to the remotest corners of the republic.

Luis Somoza Bayle, who had replaced his father after his death, served a full presidential term of his own ending in 1963. At that time he fulfilled his promise to step down, but he and his brother retained control of both the army and the congress. His successor, René Schick Gutiérrez, was an employee and personal friend of the Somoza clan. When Schick died in office, Luis' brother, Anastasio, Jr., took over. The presidential campaign of 1967 developed into a bitter political battle between Anastasio and his opponent, who enjoyed the support of one of the leading newspapers. However, the Somozas' virtual control of the nation's communications system, not to mention their resources for personal harassment, prevented the opponent from carrying out anything approaching an effective campaign.

Luis Somoza had realized the dangers inherent in the perpetuation of an unmodified family feudal control of the country. He had started a literacy campaign, placed a ceiling of 1,200 acres on agricultural holdings (other than those of the Somoza family), and sought Alliance for Progress development loans within the Common Market framework. Anastasio, educated in the United States, appears to be more cognizant of Nicaragua's problems than some of his predecessors. He has initiated additional reforms, including the institution of a federal income tax, with a view to providing development funds. Recently concern over economic problems and trade deficits have prompted him to increase the level of public investment.

Honduras has been described as still living in the "age of the caudillos." The dictatorial tradition which Honduras has endured most of its existence as an independent nation has not resulted in either a stable political system or a responsible military establishment. Juan Manuel Gálvez was an exception to the pattern when he refused to be a puppet of Tiburcio Carías, who finally stepped down in 1948 from the presidency which he had held since 1932. Gálvez not only attempted real constitutional government, but he moved toward the modernization of his country, sponsoring educational and public works programs which were directed toward improving the lot of the predominantly rural population. His anti-Communist posture, including his assistance in the ouster of Guatemalan President Arbenz, enabled him to obtain significant amounts of United States foreign aid funds.

The free elections which Gálvez insisted on in 1954 produced a three-cornered presidential race with inconclusive results, since no one received a majority. The resulting political uncertainty was taken advantage of by the incumbent vice-president to assume power and engineer his own election in 1956. However the army ousted him, and a constituent assembly chosen in the fall of 1957 elected Ramón Villeda Morales, leader of the Liberal Party.

Villeda Morales' six-year term was characterized by peace and progress almost to its very end. He established an impressive record, pushing through an agrarian reform law, labor legislation, the initiation of Alliance for Progress programs, and the appropriation of funds for an extensive highway construction effort. However, sixty days before the end of his term in October 1963, Villeda Morales was overthrown by the military in Honduras' 136th coup.

His military successor, Colonel Oswaldo López Arellano, seemed determined to re-establish a traditional military regime, but pressure from the United States led him to carry out the pledge to hold elections, which he did in January 1965. Under the resulting constitutional regime, López Arellano was promoted to the rank of general and elected president for a term scheduled to last until 1971.

The Gálvez reforms of the fifties have been largely forgotten. Bananas, constituting 46 per cent of Honduras' exports, remain an economic mainstay of the country, which has been regarded as the classic example of a "banana republic." The banana industry has continued to be plagued by difficulties with the influential United Fruit Company. In the fifties Gálvez not only achieved a new contract with United Fruit which included payment of 30 per cent of its profits to the government, but the company itself undertook to improve conditions of its workers in terms of sanitation, housing, and education. However, an unfortunate combination of strikes, floods, and leaf disease prompted the company to abandon Honduran plantings for greener fields elsewhere.

During 1968 the pressure of economic problems and mounting criticism forced López Arellano to reappraise his government's policies. As a result he has reshuffled the men in top government posts in an effort to revitalize the bureaucratic structure and appointed a United States-trained economist to concentrate on such vital issues as agrarian reform.

The administration has sought to encourage investment by private enterprise in order to reverse the trends toward capital flight, rising unemployment, and a slackening of trade which resulted from the policies pursued by Dr. Villeda Morales. López Arellano also has endeavored to heal past political wounds and quiet political rivalries by inviting his Liberal opponents to take posts within the government. However, these gestures have had only limited success, and internecine political battles are persisting. Honduras continues to be beset by enormous social and economic problems complicated by the nation's high illiteracy, the lack of an economic infrastructure, and the scarcity of trained technical and administrative personnel. These problems were not helped by the Salvadoran invasion of 1969 which disrupted trade patterns and diverted public investment, forcing Honduras to apply for substantial international financial assistance.

A small group of oligarchical families has dominated Panamanian affairs, controlling the purse strings. The fighting between political factions in this country has on a number of occasions prompted the United States to intervene and to bolster the National Guard in an effort to provide a stabilizing force. However, by the 1950's the head of the National Guard was powerful enough to install and unseat four presidents in the space of five years. Elections tend to be controlled by the clique in power and a coup or assassination of the incumbent is a not uncommon means to achieve transfers of power. In May 1960, for the first time in a quarter of a century, an elected president remained in office through the completion of his designated term and peacefully transferred power to his successor. That executive was moderate businessman Roberto Chiari, and his successor, chosen by a plurality in a field of seven candidates, was his cousin Marco Robles.

The Panamanian political maneuverings more recently have become entangled with foreign policy considerations involving control of the Canal Zone. This narrow strip containing the Panama Canal represents Panama's principal source of income, but perpetuation of foreign control of it has been a source of resentment and is viewed by many as a reflection on national honor. The revision of the 1903 agreement on the Canal Zone between Panama and the United States achieved by the Treaty of 1936 relaxed United States control of the strategic area. However, that instrument also included clauses granting the United States a ninety-nine-year lease on the Zone and providing for joint consultation and action in emergencies.

Angry and virtually continuous demonstrations by nationalists who demanded a share in the profits of the Canal and recognition of Panamanian sovereignty stimulated the renewal of negotiations between Presidents Chiari and Robles and Washington for a new treaty. The Panamanians tried to bargain during these negotiations from a position of strength or, at least, from one of dignity and equality. However, they found themselves continually at a disadvantage since the United States still had an option for building a more modern canal in another Central American country, and since new atomic blasting techniques suggested that a sea-level canal elsewhere had become feasible and it was known that the United States had sent representatives to sound out Colombia on the use of an alternative near-sea-level route.

Robles had been elected on a platform which included the pledge to negotiate a new treaty which would abolish the privileges of the Canal Zone and insure that any new canal would be in Panama. The new treaty as negotiated recognizes Panamanian sovereignty over the Zone and places the canal in the hands of a joint governing board through which both countries would share in the canal's operation and profits. No action has as yet been taken to obtain legislative ratification of the agreement. The Johnson administration did allocate funds for a study of two additional routes in Panama and for consideration of possible alternatives to widen and deepen the existing canal. There has been no public indication of any decision resulting from this study, if one has been reached.

Meanwhile, by 1968 the canal issue had been eclipsed by the impending presidential election, with the fiery, omnipresent opposition leader Arnulfo Arías posing a serious challenge to the government-backed Chamorro. When President Robles surreptitiously tried to advance the cause of the official candidate, the opposition launched a counter-campaign against the administration. Arías was able to engineer a vote in the National Assembly to impeach the president on the grounds of unconstitutional activities and seat the vice-president in his place. However, the Supreme Court declared the Assembly's action unconstitutional and received the backing of the National Guard, which was able to prevent a rump Assembly and its presidential choice from functioning.

Once order had been restored, President Robles fulfilled his promise to allow the elections to proceed peacefully and freely despite the politically charged atmosphere. Arnulfo Arías triumphed by a narrow margin, despite the apparent preference of the National Guard for the government's candidate. Arías was installed in October only to be ousted a few days later by the Guard, which charged that the new president was trying to manipulate its leadership in order to gain control of the military establishment as he had attempted to do in 1941. A military junta was formed under the direction of Colonel Pinilla with a mandate to rule until a civil government could be created.

The restlessness of certain business groups for a return to civilian rule manifested itself in an unsuccessful coup in December 1969 led by two colonels of the National Guard. General Torrijo, head of the National Guard, re-established control. However, by the end of the year he had installed a civilian president, giving at least the semblance of a return to constitutional rule. Meanwhile, the redefinition of Panamanian-United States relations relative to the Canal has been held in abeyance since the United States has refused to conclude an agreement with a military government.

While these oligarchical wranglings continue, basic economic and social problems have tended to be ignored or, at least, not given the attention they demand. Panamanians have devoted little effort to the development of any sizable industrial complex which could make them less dependent on the export of primary goods. And successive administrations have been unable to gather the necessary capital resources to develop the untapped natural wealth of Panama's forests, waters, and agricultural lands. Fundamental social measures to improve housing, sanitation, health, education, and labor conditions are needed, especially in the burgeoning cities, which have been growing at a phenomenal rate due to natural growth, internal migration, and the large influx of Caribbean immigrant labor.

Thus, with a few exceptions, unstable political conditions exist in the lands of the "middle beat." The peaceful transfer of power from one civilian regime to another without overt intervention by military forces has become more difficult as a result of economic and social pressures. This is understandable when it is recognized that the process of peaceful succession most often has developed and been maintained where certain economic and social groupings have had a vested interest in stability. What type of government will evolve in these countries, with increasing tensions, the winds of change current in the hemisphere, and the broadening of political participation to include lower-class groupings, both urban and rural? Will it be possible to create viable new institutions representative of and responsible to the needs of the population, or will the pressure of these be so diverse and uncontrollable as to encourage resort to strong man rule? These questions, which Kennedy thought he saw being answered five years ago, still appear unsolved today, as each country experiments with various partial solutions to these dilemmas.

Suggestions for Additional Reading

For the reader who wishes to delve further into the history and contemporary problems of the region discussed by Paul Kennedy, some suggestions for additional reading are offered below. The intent is neither to provide a definitive bibliography nor merely to duplicate the listings to be found in any one of the standard Latin American history texts. Rather what is provided is a selective list of standard works and recent pertinent publications about specific aspects of the recent history of the region as a whole or of a particular country. For the general reader's convenience, most of the titles listed are in English.

General

Alexander, Robert. *Organized Labor in Latin America.* New Brunswick, N. J., Rutgers University Press, 1965.

————. *Communism in Latin America.* New Brunswick, N. J., Rutgers University Press, 1957.

Castillo, Carlos. *Growth and Integration in Central America.* New York, Praeger, 1966.

Cochrane, J. D. "Central American Economic Integration; the Integrated Industries Scheme," *Inter-American Economic Affairs,* XIX:2 (Autumn 1965), 63–74.

Denton, C. F. "Interest Groups and the Central American Common Market," *Inter-American Economic Affairs,* XXI:1 (Summer 1967), 49–60.

Geisert, Harold L. *Population Problems in Mexico and Central America.* Washington, D.C., George Washington University Press, 1959.

Gigax, William R. "The Central American Common Market," *Inter-American Economic Affairs,* XVI:2 (Autumn 1962), 59–77.

Hansen, Roger D. *Central America: Regional Integration and Economic Development.* Studies in Development Progress, No. 1. Washington, D.C., National Planning Administration, 1967.

Hildebrand, J. R. "Central American Common Market," *Journal of Inter-American Studies*, IX:3 (July 1967), 383–395.

Lieuwen, Edwin. *Arms and Politics in Latin America.* New York, Praeger, 1961.

Martz, John D. *Central America, the Crisis and the Challenge.* Chapel Hill, N.C., University of North Carolina Press, 1959.

————. *Justo Rufino Barrios and Central American Union.* Gainesville, Fla., University of Florida Press, 1963.

Mecham, J. Lloyd. *A Survey of United States–Latin American Relations.* Boston, Houghton Mifflin, 1965.

————. *Church and State in Latin America,* rev. ed. Chapel Hill, N.C., University of North Carolina Press, 1966.

Nye, Joseph S. *Central American Regional Integration.* New York, Carnegie Endowment for International Peace, 1967.

Parker, Franklin Dallas. *The Central American Republics.* London and New York, Oxford University Press, 1964.

Parsons, James. "Cotton and Cattle in the Pacific Lowlands of Central America," *Journal of Inter-American Studies,* VII:2 (April 1962), 149–159.

Rodríguez, Mario. *Central America.* Englewood Cliffs, N.J., Prentice-Hall, 1965.

Stuart, Graham H. *Latin America and the United States,* 5th ed. New York, Appleton-Century-Crofts, 1955.

Tamagna, Frank M. and Gregory B. Wolfe. "A Financial System for Economic Development: Problems and Prospects in Central America," *Journal of Inter-American Studies,* VI:4 (October 1964), 436–87.

Waggoner, Barbara, George Waggoner, and Gregory B. Wolfe. "Higher Education in Contemporary Central America," *Journal of Inter-American Studies,* VI:4 (October 1964), 445–62.

Waggoner, George R. "Problems of the Professionalization of the University Teaching Career in Central America," *Journal of Inter-American Studies,* VIII:2 (April 1966), 192–212.

Mexico

Ashby, Joe E. *Organized Labor and the Mexican Revolution under Lázaro Cárdenas.* Chapel Hill, N.C., University of North Carolina Press, 1968.

Astiz, Carlos A., ed. *Latin American International Politics: Ambitions, Capabilities and the National Interest of Mexico, Brazil and Argentina.* Notre Dame, Ind., University of Notre Dame Press, 1969.

Brandenburg, Frank. *The Making of Modern Mexico.* Englewood Cliffs, N.J., Prentice-Hall, 1964.

Castañeda, Jorge. "Revolution and Foreign Policy: Mexico's Experience," *American Political Science Quarterly,* LXXVIII:3 (September 1963), 391–417.

Cline, Howard F. *Mexico: Revolution to Evolution, 1940–1960,* London, Oxford University Press, 1962.

————. *The United States and Mexico.* Cambridge, Mass., Harvard University Press, 1953.

Corwin, A. F. *Contemporary Mexican Attitudes Towards Population, Poverty and Public Opinion.* Gainesville, Fla., University of Florida Press, 1963.

Cuevas Cancino, Francisco. "The Foreign Policy of Mexico," in J. E. Black and K. W. Thompson, *Foreign Policies in a World of Change.* New York, Harper and Row, 1963, pp. 643–71.

Cumberland, Charles C. *Mexico: The Struggle for Modernity.* New York, Oxford University Press, 1968.

Edwards, Emily. *Painted Walls of Mexico.* Austin, Tex., University of Texas Press, 1966.

Galarza, Ernesto. *Merchants of Labor: The Mexican Bracero Story. An Account of the Managed Migration of Mexican Farm Workers in California, 1942–1960.* San José, Calif., Rosicrucian Press, 1964.

Glade, William P. and C. W. Anderson. *The Political Economy of Mexico.* Madison, Wis., University of Wisconsin Press, 1963.

Hancock, R. H. *Role of the Bracero in the Economic and Culture Dynamics of Mexico: A Case Study of Chihuahua.* Stanford, Calif., Hispanic American Society, 1959.

Hilton, Stanley R. "The Church-State Dispute over Education in Mexico from Carranza to Cárdenas," *Americas,* XXI:2 (October 1964), 163–83.

Lewis, Oscar. *Five Families: Mexican Case Studies in the Culture of Poverty.* New York, Basic Books, 1959.

Millon, Robert Paul. *Mexican Marxist Vicente Lombardo Toledano.* Chapel Hill, N.C., University of North Carolina Press, 1966.

Murillo, Gerardo (pseud. Dr. Atl). *Como nace y crece un volcán, el Paricutín.* México, Editorial Style, 1950.

Myers, Bernard S. *Mexican Painting in Our Time.* New York, Oxford University Press, 1956.

Orozco, José Clemente. *An Autobiography.* Tr. by Robert C. Stephenson. Austin, Tex., University of Texas Press, 1962.

Padgett, Vincent L. *The Mexican Political System.* Boston, Houghton Mifflin, 1966.

Rivera, Diego, with Gladys March. *My Art, My Life: An Autobiography.* New York, Citadel Press, 1960.

Ross, Stanley Robert. "Mexico: Cool Revolution and Cold War," *Current History*, XLIV:258 (February 1963), 89–94.

————(ed.). *Is the Mexican Revolution Dead?* New York, Alfred A. Knopf, 1966.

Ruiz, Ramón E. *Mexico: The Challenge of Poverty and Illiteracy.* San Marino, Calif., Huntington Library, 1963.

Schmitt, Karl M. "Congressional Campaigning in Mexico: A View from the Provinces," *Journal of Inter-American Studies*, XI:1 (January 1969), 93–110.

————. *Communism in Mexico: A Study in Political Frustration.* Austin, Tex., University of Texas Press, 1965.

Scott, Robert E. *Mexican Government in Transition.* Urbana, Ill., Illinois University Press, 1959.

Senior, Clarence. *Land Reform and Democracy.* Gainesville, Fla., Florida University Press, 1958.

Simpson, Eyler N. *The Ejido: Mexico's Way Out.* Chapel Hill, N.C., University of North Carolina Press, 1937.

Simpson, Lesley Byrd. *Many Mexicos,* 3rd ed. Berkeley and Los Angeles, Calif., University of California Press, 1952.

Tannenbaum, Frank. *Mexico: The Struggle for Peace and Bread.* New York, Alfred A. Knopf, 1950.

Turner, Frederick C. *The Dynamic of Mexican Nationalism.* Chapel Hill, N.C., University of North Carolina Press, 1968.

Vernon, Raymond. *The Dilemma of Mexico's Development: The Roles of the Private and Public Sectors.* Cambridge, Mass., Harvard University Press, 1963.

Wilkie, James. *The Mexican Revolution: Federal Expenditure and Social Change Since 1910.* Berkeley, Calif., University of California Press, 1967.

———— and Albert Michaels, eds. *The Revolution in Mexico, 1920–1940: Years of Upheaval.* New York, Alfred A. Knopf, 1969.

Wolf, Eric Robert. *Sons of the Shaking Earth.* Chicago, University of Chicago Press, 1959.

Wolfe, Bertram David. *The Fabulous Life of Diego Rivera.* New York, Stein and Day, 1963.

Guatemala

Adams, Richard N. "El problema del desarrollo político a la luz de la reciente historia de Guatemala," *Revista Latinoamericana de Sociología,* 2(1968), 174–98.

Arévalo, Jaun José. *Anti-Kommunism in Latin America: An X-ray of the Process Leading to a New Colonialism.* Tr. by Carleton Beals. New York, L. Stuart, 1963.

————. *The Shark and the Sardines.* Tr. by June Cobb and Raúl Osegueda. New York, L. Stuart, 1961.

Bush, Archer C. *Organized Labor in Guatemala, 1944–49.* Hamilton, N.Y., Colgate University Press, 1950.

Comité Interamericano de Desarrollo Agrícola. *Guatemala, tenencia de la tierra y desarrollo socio-económico del sector agrícola.* Washington, D.C., Unión Panamericana, 1965.

Galeano Eduardo. "With the Guerrillas in Guatemala," in James Petras and Maurice Zeitlin (eds.), *Latin America: Reform or Revolution? A Reader.* Greenwich, Conn., Fawcett Publications, 1968, pp. 370–80.

Hildebrand, J. R. "Guatemalan Colonization Projects: Institution Building and Resource Allocation," *Inter-American Economic Affairs,* XIX:4 (Spring 1966), 41–51.

————. "Farm Size and Agrarian Reform in Guatemala," *Inter-American Economic Affairs,* XVI:2 (Autumn 1962), 51–57.

Holleran, M. P. *Church and State in Guatemala.* New York, Columbia University Press, 1949.

James, Daniel. *Red Design for the Americas: Guatemalan Prelude.* New York, John Day, 1954.

Kelsey, Vera and Lilly de J. Osborne. *Four Keys to Guatemala,* rev. ed. New York, Funk and Wagnalls, 1961.

LaBarge, R. A. *Impact of the United Fruit Company on the Economic Development of Guatemala, 1946–1954.* New Orleans, 1960.

Martz, John D. *Communist Infiltration in Guatemala.* New York, Vintage Books, 1956.

Pearson, R. "Land Reform Guatemalan Style," *American Journal of Economics and Sociology,* XXII:2 (April 1963), 225–34.

Rodríguez, Mario. "Guatemala in Perspective," *Current History,* LI:304 (December 1966), 388–43.

Rosenthal, Mario. *Guatemala: The Story of an Emergent Latin American Democracy.* New York, Twayne, 1962.

Schneider, Ronald M. *Communism in Guatemala, 1944–1954.* New York, Praeger, 1958.

Silvert, Kalman H. *Study of Government: Guatemala.* New Orleans, La., Middle American Research Institute, Tulane University, 1954.

Sloan, J. W. "1966 Presidential Election in Guatemala: Can a Radical Party Desiring Fundamental Social Change Win an Election in Guatemala?," *Inter-American Economic Affairs,* XXII:2 (Autumn 1968), 15–32.

Taylor, Philip B. "Guatemalan Affair: A Critique of United States Foreign Policy," *American Political Science Review,* L:3 (Summer 1956), 787–806.

U.S. Department of State. *A Case History of Communist Penetration: Guatemala.* Publication 6465, Inter-American Series 52. Washington D.C., Government Printing Office, 1957.

Vielman, Julio. "Stabilization of the Post-revolutionary Government in Guatemala," *Journal of International Affairs,* IX:1 (1955), 73–81.

Woodward, Ralph Lee, Jr. "Octubre: Communist Appeal to the Urban Force of Guatemala, 1950–1953," *Journal of Inter-American Studies,* IV:3 (July 1962), 363–74.

Ydígoras Fuentes, Miguel. *My War with Communism* as told by Mario Rosenthal. Englewood Cliffs, N.J., Prentice-Hall, 1963.

El Salvador

Osborne, Lilly de Jongh. *Four Keys to El Salvador.* New York, Funk and Wagnalls, 1956.

Raynolds, David R. *Rapid Development in Small Economies: The Example of El Salvador.* New York, Praeger, 1967.

Turner, George P. *An Analysis of the Economy of El Salvador, April 1961.* Los Angeles, Calif., University of California Press, 1961.

Williamson, R. C. "Some Factors in Urbanism in a Quasi-Rural Setting: San Salvador and San José," *Sociology and Social Research,* XLVII:2 (January 1963), 187–200.

The Base at Retalhuleu

It was in Guatemala that Paul Kennedy made one of his striking efforts to remove the blanket of official secrecy from noteworthy and newsworthy developments. His involvement was not an unmixed blessing since it earned for him the denunciation of the official Guatemalan newspaper, critical singling out by the president of the United States, and a rather jaundiced view of his journalistic efforts by two recent writers on the affair. Involved was the guerrilla training base at Retalhuleu, which proved to be the staging location for the disastrous "Bay of Pigs" invasion of Cuba in April 1961.

On November 19, 1960, *The Nation* carried a report of·the existence of the base and its alleged purpose. Noting that the affair had been "aired" in the Guatemalan newspaper *La Hora, The Nation* editorially called for checking of the reports by news media with correspondents in Guatemala. Victor Bernstein and Jesse Gordon, authors of a critical study of the role played by the press in the Bay of Pigs episode, viewed quite negatively the timing and efficacy of the low-keyed responses of the Associated Press and *The New York Times* to this suggestion, insinuating that there might be sinister explanations for the handling of the story.[1]

Regarding the *Times,* the authors note that it took the newspaper nine days to react and that then it printed on page 32 of its November 20 issue an unsigned dispatch from Guatemala based on its correspondent's interview with President Miguel Ydígoras Fuentes. The president was asked about "repeated reports" of "a base established with U.S. assistance as a training ground for military assistance against Cuba."[2] Bern-

[1] V. Bernstein and J. Gordon, "The Press and the Bay of Pigs," *The Columbia University Forum,* X:3 (Fall, 1967), pp. 5–13.
[2] *Ibid.,* p. 6.

stein and Gordon limited their coverage of the *Times* article to a single additional paragraph:

> The president branded the reports as a "lot of lies." He said the base . . . was one of several on which Guatemalan army personnel was being trained in guerilla warfare. The object of the training, he said, was to combat invasions of the type that have occurred recently in Honduras, Nicaragua, and Panama.[3]

While recognizing that President Ydígoras was consistent in lying to both the Associated Press and *Times* correspondents, the writers fault the reporters for failing to interview anyone connected with *La Hora* and for choosing to go to the one man who would be sure to deny the story. In response to a query from Victor Bernstein, Mr. Clifton Daniel of the *Times* noted that the newspaper had been able to turn up nothing but hearsay and rumors. He identified Paul Kennedy as the author of the unsigned Ydígoras interview:

> The Ydígoras interview was written by Paul Kennedy. He was in Nicaragua at the time that *The Nation* article reached us, and we asked him to go to Guatemala to look into the situation. He met a blank wall *in his inquiries* and on the 19th sent the Ydígoras interview. Mr. Kennedy left Guatemala on the 21st.[4]

We know nothing of Kennedy's instructions, or even whether he was aware of the reports that *La Hora* had aired the problem. It is clear that he had been in Guatemala a week or less when he filed the interview story and that he had made other inquiries, unfortunately without results, in an effort to go beyond the presidential statement. It should be noted that the day after the appearance of the Ydígoras story, Kennedy left Guatemala.

However, the dispatch itself gives a much better insight to Kennedy the reporter. Its full text reveals that President Ydígoras admitted that United States weapons were being used and United States military personnel being consulted, while he emphatically denied that the operation was being subsidized by the United States. Kennedy also reported that opposition deputies in the Guatemalan Congress had demanded an investigation, which government supporters had voted down on the grounds of national security, and that Ydígoras had offered to have a congressional

---

[3] *Ibid.*
[4] Letter, Mr. Daniel to V. Bernstein, April 27, 1967, as quoted in Bernstein and Gordon, *op. cit.*, p. 7.

commission designated to investigate the matter—an offer which Kennedy later characterized as an enormous bluff.[5]

During the succeeding weeks, rumors and more solid pieces of information—including stories in the *Los Angeles Mirror* and the *St. Louis Post-Dispatch*—continued to accumulate, and the *Times* decided to send Kennedy back to Guatemala with instructions to get out of the capital and find out what was going on. Kennedy's second report, lengthier than his first, appeared on the first and eleventh pages of the January 10 issue of the newspaper.[6] While Bernstein and Gordon contend that the article "was written with the utmost circumspection," they concede this second Kennedy piece "broke the log-jam on the story. . . ."[7]

Despite its pivotal importance, Bernstein and Gordon label the Kennedy article not only "circumspect" but also "somewhat equivocal." Kennedy is criticized for balancing the sinister with the innocent; for identifying as "opponents of the Ydígoras Administration" the source of allegations that an offensive against Castro was being prepared; for quoting an American official as saying that the United States was supplying only such matériel as would be needed for defensive action (when actually Kennedy identified the source as "an authority who has negotiated with the United States"); and for failing to identify the nationality of the guerrillas. They even accuse him of "laughingly" observing that the base seemed to be on the wrong side of Guatemala if it was indeed intended for defensive purposes against an assault on the Caribbean coast.

In their impassioned eagerness to indict the American press for its handling of the Cuban affair, the critics appear to forget the canons of good journalism. The canons of good journalism are not, or should not be, far from the canons of good scholarship. Polemicism is another matter. The Kennedy reportage did seek to provide his readers with a rounded account, and the identification of sources suggests a strong sense of journalistic integrity. If Paul Kennedy was laughing in his final paragraphs on the inappropriateness of the location of the base, a reasonable reader might conclude that it was because he was dubious of the validity of the official explanation. As in the earlier article, he identified accusing elements as belonging to the opposition. It could not have been otherwise, and this hardly constitutes evidence that Kennedy was trying to discredit such sources.

[5] *The New York Times,* Nov. 20, 1960.

[6] Letter, Mr. Daniel to V. Bernstein as cited in Bernstein and Gordon, *loc. cit.,* p. 8.

[7] Bernstein and Gordon, *op. cit.,* p. 8.

Even the authors of this sharply critical evaluation observe "that Mr. Kennedy knew [the true purpose of the base] . . . , or at least strongly suspected it, *was apparent in his text. . . .*"[8] The *Diario de Centro América,* newspaper voice of the Guatemalan government, printed an article by its editor denying the report on the base printed in the *Times* and calling Kennedy an inaccurate reporter, a "liar," and an imposter.[9] Since the Kennedy article proved to be of such importance and provides a singular example of his journalism, it seems justifiable to supplement the brief paragraph quoted in the text and the even briefer selections employed in the Bernstein-Gordon analysis. The dispatch, dated January 9 at Retalhuleu, was headlined "U.S. Helps Train an Anti-Castro Force at Secret Guatemalan Air-Ground Base." The subheads read "Clash With Cuba Feared—Installations Built with American Aid."

The story begins with the paragraphs quoted by Kennedy, describing the area as the focal point of Guatemalan preparations for an anticipated clash with Cuba, noting the intensive air and guerrilla training, and identifying United States' assistance in personnel, matériel, and construction of facilities. From this point the report continues, stating that

Guatemalan authorities from President Miguel Ydígoras Fuentes down insist that the military effort is designed to meet an assault, expected almost any day, from Cuba.

Opponents of the Ydígoras Administration have insisted that the preparations are for an offensive against the Cuban regime of Premier Fidel Castro and that they are being planned and directed, and to a great extent being paid for, by the United States.

The United States Embassy is maintaining complete silence on the subject. Guatemalan authorities will speak only guardedly about it.

One authority who has negotiated with the United States for assistance in the Retalhuleu land and air operations said that application for certain amounts of war materials over the amount already received had been turned down by the United States.

The reason, he said, was that Washington considered that the amount and type of materials applied for were beyond the needs of defensive operations.

After explaining this official's reasons for concern over this denial, Kennedy continued his report on the Retalhuleu base:

President Ydígoras agreed in an interview that training in guerrilla warfare tactics was being carried on in the foothills of the large plantation named Helvetia. This plantation is situated a few miles from the provincial capital.

---

[8] *Ibid.*
[9] Kennedy Obituary, *The New York Times,* Feb. 3, 1967.

The president also said that the air base about three miles west of the capital toward the Pacific was being used for military purposes. However, he added that he hoped that it would be transformed to a commercial base in the foreseeable future.

The airfield is partly fenced in by a corrugated metal wall. The present airstrip was constructed last summer over an already established base that had been used in the 1954 revolution by fighter planes with American pilots who attacked military objectives in Guatemala, the country's capital.

The present installation was constructed in an around-the-clock operation by a North American construction company. The name given here was Cornwall-Thompson.

After a *Times* bracketed insert explained that efforts to contact officials of the concern had been unsuccessful, Kennedy's report gave more information on the construction according to a Guatemalan authority who had helped to arrange the details of the construction. His informant stated that

it was paid for partly by subscriptions from landowners in the Fourth Military Zone, in which the State of Retalhuleu is situated, and partly by the United States. The latter was by far the heavier contributor.

The concrete strip, more than 5,000 feet long, is used by two B–26 planes and two DC–4's or 6's. A third B–26 on the field is inoperable because of some damage apparently caused in landing. None of the craft have any identification letters or numbers.

Besides a large civilian-like terminal building, the field has several buildings that look like barracks as well as a radio shack and other minor installations.

The field is not a military installation in the true sense. It could not possibly serve in its present state as a large-scale offensive base. It has no dispersal areas, hardstands for plane parking or lateral exiting and entering runways.

According to persons assisting in directing the construction of the base, the strip will take four-engine planes up to the C–54 type. It was agreed that in an emergency the present strip could handle jet fighters, but only in limited operational scope and with an element of danger.

Kennedy next described how the air-operation and commando-training areas were geared for quick cooperative action, as had been demonstrated during a revolt in early November. Then he resumed his description of the Helvetia estate:

The Helvetia finca, or plantation, lies high in the foothills about five miles east of the road to the port of Champerico on the Pacific coast.

Its nearly 3,000 acres are operated and largely owned by Roberto Alejo Arzu, president of the National Association of Coffee Planters and probably the largest independent coffee producer in the country. He is a close friend and adviser of President Ydígoras, who spent last weekend at the Alejo Helvetia home.

At the entrance of the Helvetia estate the visitor is challenged by armed guards. He is challenged again five miles beyond the entrance by many more guards. Here, and in the plantation village, there is a relatively heavy detachment of troops and stored munitions.

This writer, because of a momentary lapse in security proceeded nearly two miles farther up into the mountains before being stopped and sent back down to the plantation village.

Only plantation workers with special passes were supposed to reach that point. Except for a few lounging troops in green commando garb, there was nothing at that point to suggest any unusual activity.

A Guatemalan authority at the Helvetia plantation village said the secret activities were taking place considerably above that point. He added that guerrilla operations, which he repeatedly referred to as "anti-guerrilla" tactics, had been hindered by "snoopers" and that several nights the guards had used rifle fire to repel intruders.

The authority said the guerrilla training originally had been assigned to Guatemalans who themselves had been thoroughly trained, presumably in the United States or by United States personnel.

However, he said, the project had grown so rapidly that foreign trainers had been brought in. Most of these, he said, were North American guerrilla-tactic experts. Experts from several other nations also were brought in, he said.

He indicated that the latter group included Cubans, but he denied that Cubans were being trained now in Helvetia. He said that among the trainers were two Russian-speaking persons who were used primarily for shouting orders in Russian so that the trainers could become acquainted with the language.

Residents of the quiet, tree-shaded city of Retalhuleu appeared to be increasingly restive over the mystery surrounding the air base and the Helvetia installation.

There appears to be a stepping up of formation training flight activity from the air base. The planes, usually four in formation, sweep over the plantations daily.

An informant said there were a number of United States military personnel and other foreigners at the air base for training purposes.

Officers appearing to wear United States Air Force uniforms have been seen in downtown Retalhuleu driving automobiles, but none thus dressed have been seen walking on the streets.

The Kennedy dispatch concluded with two paragraphs treating the seeming inappropriateness of the location of the base and the officially proclaimed purpose for which it was intended:

Some speculation has arisen over the feasibility of the air base, whose site near the Pacific coast is across the country from the scene of any possible Caribbean invasion.

However, it has been explained in Retalhuleu that the field's inland site affords it greater defensive preparation and that it is the best site available in mountainous Guatemala for obstructionless take-offs and approaches.[10]

The *Times* appended a brief article, captioned "Cuban Charges Recalled," in which reference was made to speeches by Cuban Foreign Minister Raúl Roa at the United Nations accusing the United States of aggressive intentions and charging that camps for the training of "mercenaries" were active in Guatemala, Honduras, and Florida. The reconditioning of Retalhuleu was specifically mentioned in a speech before the Security Council on the preceding Wednesday (January 4).

The events of April 17, 1961, brought belated substantiation of the persistent rumors, reports, and allegations of the real purpose of the Retalhuleu operation. It should be noted that Paul Kennedy states that "for security reasons I did not use sizable portions of the material gathered." The discretion did not save him from having his story cited by President John F. Kennedy as an example of premature disclosure of classified information.

This occurred at a meeting of a group of press executives with President Kennedy at the White House some two weeks after the Bay of Pigs disaster, according to an account by Clifton Daniel before the World Press Institute: "President Kennedy ran down a list of what he called premature disclosures of security information. His examples were drawn mainly from *The New York Times*. He mentioned, for example, Paul Kennedy's story. . . ."[11] When Turner Catledge, managing editor of the *Times*, protested that the information had appeared in *La Hora* and *The Nation* before its publication in the *Times,* the president replied, "but it wasn't news until it appeared in the *Times*." In an aside to Mr. Catledge, the president revealed his own view, in retrospect, of what he had come to regard as a mistaken undertaking: "If you had printed more about the operation, you would have saved us from a colossal mistake."[12]

[10] *The New York Times,* Jan. 10, 1961.
[11] Bernstein and Gordon, *op. cit.,* p. 10.
[12] *Ibid.*

Index*

Acción Mundial, 125
Acebal, Víctor Mirabel, 155
Action d'Art, 125
American Federation of Labor–Congress of Industrial Organizations (AFL-CIO), 114n
Agency for International Development (AID), 13
Agrarian reform, 22; in El Salvador, 173–174, 194; in Guatemala, 135, 146; in Mexico, 67, 69
Agriculture, 23; in Guatemala, 133, 147; in Mexico, 79
Aguascalientes (state), 68n
Air power, 6
Alejo Arzu, Roberto, 223–224
Alejos, Roberto, 166
Alemán, Miguel, 61n, 66n, 67, 85n, 86
Alliance for Progress, 13; in El Salvador, 183–184, 186, 190–191; in Mexico, 70; in Nicaragua, 208
Alvarado, Pedro de, 3
Álvarez, Luis H., 57
Álvarez, Manuel, 54–55
American Chamber of Commerce, in Mexico, 102n
American International Association for Economic and Social Development, 21
Anaya y Diez de Bonilla, José G., 88
Andino Carías, Tiburcio, 10
"El Angelito," 44
Anti-Americanism, 8
Antillean Islands, 2
Apostolic Congress, in Mexico City (1961), 74
Arana Osorio, Carlos, 205
Árbenz Guzmán, Jacobo, 131, 135–138, 139–141, 154, 161, 208
Arce, Manuel José, 5
Archbishop of Mexico, 85n

Arévalo, Juan José, 135, 160–162, 166–167; The Shark and the Sardines, 162
Arías, Arnulfo, 211
Atl, Dr. (Gerardo Murillo), 124–126
Atisbos, 90–91
Atole, 23
Ávila Camacho, Manuel, 61n, 66–67, 85–86
Ayuntamiento (City Hall), of Mexico City, 41
Aztecs, 36, 47, 50–52

Baja California: businessmen of, 29; reaction to import decrees, 29–30
Banco de Guatemala, 160
Bank of Mexico, 78
Barrios, Roberto, 71
Barrios, Rufino, 171
Batista, Fulgencio, 98n
Bay of Pigs invasion, 159, 219, 225
Belize, 4n
Bernardino, Juan, 92
Bernstein, Victor, 219–221
Betancourt, Rómulo, 11
Beteta, Mario Ramón, 78
Blanco, Ramón, 153
Blas Roca, see Francisco Calderío
Bolivia, 104n, 106–107
Bosch, Juan, 10–11
Braceros, 110–113, 114n
British Honduras, 1, 4n, 20, 93
Bolsón de Mapimí, 30–32
Brownsville-Tampico Canal, 35

Cabildo, 2
Caciquismo, 51
Calderío, Francisco (Blas Roca), 105
Calderón de la Barca, Marquesa Frances, 40
Calles, Plutarco Elías, 45, 45n, 52, 66, 82, 84, 88

* This index was prepared by Evelyn and Dean DeHart and Honor Griffin, under the direction of Wilber Chaffee.

227

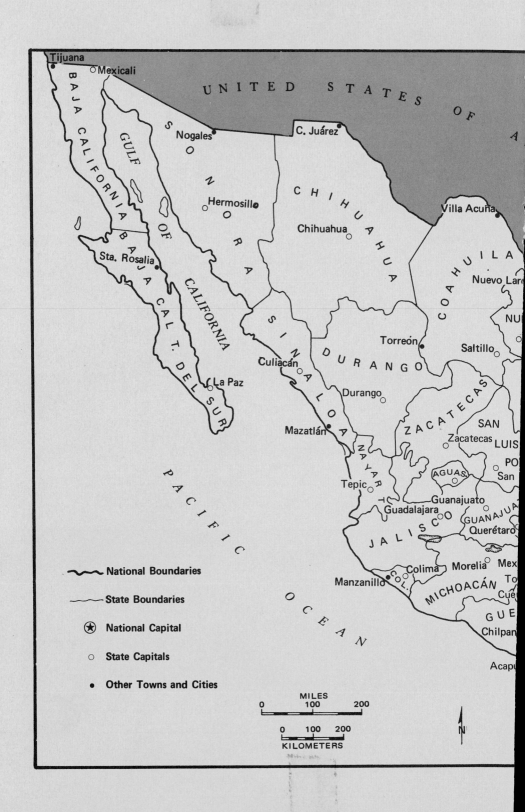